Through These Eyes

A World War II Eighth Air Force Combat Diary

by

James Lee Hutchinson, EdS
WWII Eighth Air Force Combat Veteran
Tech Sergeant/Radio Operator

Edited by Susan E. Hutchinson, Ph.D.
Associate Professor
University of Memphis

authorHOUSE

AuthorHouse™
1663 Liberty Drive
Bloomington, IN 47403
www.authorhouse.com
Phone: 833-262-8899

© 2005 T/Sgt. James Lee Hutchinson, Ed.S. All rights reserved.

No part of this book may be reproduced, stored in a retrieval system, or transmitted by any means without the written permission of the author.

Published by AuthorHouse 08/17/2020

ISBN: 978-1-4208-6644-5 (sc)
ISBN: 978-1-4520-5202-1 (e)

Library of Congress Control Number: 2005905841

Print information available on the last page.

Any people depicted in stock imagery provided by Getty Images are models, and such images are being used for illustrative purposes only.
Certain stock imagery © Getty Images.

This book is printed on acid-free paper.

Because of the dynamic nature of the Internet, any web addresses or links contained in this book may have changed since publication and may no longer be valid. The views expressed in this work are solely those of the author and do not necessarily reflect the views of the publisher, and the publisher hereby disclaims any responsibility for them.

Table of Contents

Introduction

    My World War II Story xi

Chapter One

    The Early Years 1

        Limestone Quarries 2

        Our Depression Home 3

        Depression Christmas in the Thirties 10

        The Pre-Teen Years 12

        Hey, What's an Allowance? 15

        The Ice Man Cometh 18

        Dad and the Baby Buggy 19

        They Rode Off in All Directions and Went That-a-Way! 21

        Our Leisurely World 24

        Medicine Shows, Carnivals and the Circus 25

        Churches and Revivals 27

        Hobos and Veterans 30

Chapter Two

    Calm Before the Storm 35

        "Dutchtown" and the "Huckster Wagon" 39

        The Teen Years 41

        Otis Park----I Discover Golf 43

        Happy Days – High School 47

Pearl Harbor---December 7, 1941 52

War Time for Civilians on the Homefront 54

Chapter Three

You're In the Army Now! 58

    Basic Training in Texas 61

    Kilroy Was There, Too 69

    Radio Operator Training 71

    Gunnery School, Yuma, Arizona 75

    Combat Crew Training 79

    Off to Camp Kilmer and Overseas 84

Chapter Four

Early Air War---The Eagles Gather 95

    The Early Eighth Air Force Bombing Missions 101

    The Box Formation 103

    Early Bomber Losses 104

    Target--- Berlin! 107

    The Memphis Belle 110

    Air Force Ground Crews 114

Chapter Five

England—The Combat Zone 124

    Eye, Our 490th Airbase 125

    Home Sweet Home---Hut 29 126

    German Buzz Bombs 132

    A War-Time English Newspaper 133

    The B-24 Liberator 134

    Nose Art and Plane Markings 136

    Moment of Truth 137

    First Mission   Berlin   December 5th, 1944 140

    Lutzkendorf (Aborted)   December 6, 1944 146

    Practice Flight   December 7, 1944 147

    London Pass   December 10, 1944 148

    London Passes 151

    Letters From Home 156

Chapter Six

    The Wild Blue Yonder 166

        Mission Two   Hanover   December 15, 1944 166

        Hazards of Flying 171

        Mission Interrogation 174

        Mission 3   Stuttgart   December 16, 1944 175

        Battle of the Bulge   December 16, 1944 177

        Mission 4   Frankfort   December 24, 1944 178

        Germany's Fighters 182

        Special Targets and the German Anti-Aircraft 183

Chapter Seven

    Lead Crew – Taking the Point 194

        Mission 5   Bad-Kreuznach   January 2, 1945 194

        Training Flights 197

        A Bed-Time Story 199

The Norden Bombsight 202

Air War Success 203

Mission 6   Aschaffenburg   January 3, 1945 205

Mid-Air Collision   January 5, 1945 207

Airmen Downed in Combat 209

Closer to Heaven   January 10, 1944 214

The Life of Riley 216

Mission 7   Derben   January 14, 1945 218

U.S. Air Force Fighters – Our "Little Friends" 220

British Fighters 223

Building the Arsenal of Defense 224

Tactical Bombers and Fighters 229

German Aces 230

Mission 8   Augsburg   January 15, 1945 232

RAF Augsburg Raid 234

Mission 9   Sterkade-Rheine   January 20, 1945 234

Chapter Eight

Our Crew's "May Day" 242

Mission 10   Hohenbudburg   January 28, 1945 242

Flak Casualty --- "May Day!" 244

Mission 11   Frankfort   February 17, 1945 246

Combat Fatigue 249

Mission 12   Ansbach   February 22, 1945 252

Mission 12-B   Ulm   March 1, 1945 254

Mission 14   Plauen   March 21, 1945 255

viii

    A Freakish Mid-Air Collision 258

    Mission 15   Hanover   March 28, 1945 259

    The Fifteenth Air Force 260

    The Tuskegee Airmen 263

    Mission 17   Roudnice   April 17, 1945 268

    Our Crew's Black Thursday 269

    Mission 18   Nauen   April 20, 1945 272

Chapter Nine

    A Truce and Peace 280

        Mercy Missions 280

        Mission 19   Rotterdam Food Drop   May 1, 1945 282

        Mission 20   Schipol Food Drop   May 2, 1945 283

        The Axis Reign of Terror 285

        Hitler's Terrible Legacy 286

        International War Crimes Trials 293

Chapter Ten

    Operation Home Run 300

        End of the War in Europe – VE Day   May 8, 1945 300

        The Grand Tour 301

        No Foxholes in the Sky 302

        Home from the War 308

Chapter Eleven

    Victory's Price 312

        Realities of War 312

Medals and Honors for the Mighty Eighth 315

Britain Says "Thanks Yanks" 316

The Mighty Eighth Museum 318

U.S. World War II Memorial 319

United States Air Force Museum, Dayton, Ohio 319

The Mighty Eighth 320

Taps 321

The G.I. Bill 329

B-17G Specifications 330

Eighth Air Force Bomb Groups in England 331

Summary of "Hutch's" Missions 333

Bibliography 334

Introduction
My World War II Story

Sixty years have passed since thousands of Eighth Air Force bombers and fighters filled the skies over England. Frozen white contrails of their engine exhausts followed the planes as they flew out to bomb Adolph Hitler's Third Reich. They had been flying these missions for three years. John Palmer, narrating an NBC documentary, "All the Fine Young Men", said: "The skies over Europe became a field of honor for the Eighth Air Force…like knights of old, the young men of the Eighth flew out to do battle".

Today, World War II veterans are passing away at a rapid pace. Libraries and other agencies urge veterans to record their combat experiences. I participated in such a project conducted by Indiana Senator Richard Lugar. At the age of 77, with most of my senses and lots of time, I began a three-year effort to tell my story. As a retired school principal I remember the old adage, "Old principals never die, they just lose their faculties!" My story is based on my combat diary and memories of eighteen combat missions as a teenage radio-gunner on a B-17 Flying Fortress in the Eighth Air Force.

I first describe my life growing up in the Great Depression to illustrate the background of many of the young men who served in World War II. My childhood was typical of many of the youngsters who fought and won gigantic air battles over Europe. Each bombing mission recorded in the diary is in italics. Content following the diary entry includes comments based on memories, research and statistical information that provides a historical context. Each bombing mission was a crap game; you just prayed that when the Fates rolled the dice, the flak would spare your plane. An airman's life depended on Lady Luck and the grace of God!

Today when I travel, I proudly wear my "hero cap", a cap with "World War II Veteran" and the Eighth Air Force emblem inscribed on it. I've met veterans in restaurants, malls, airports and other places. Young men often thank me for my service, and I've even received a few salutes! I am always happy to meet WWII vets, but there aren't too many eighty to ninety year-olds on the road these days. I encourage all veterans to wear "hero caps" to show pride in their military service.

My writing project led me to attempt to locate former B-17 Flying Fortress crewmembers. I learned that most of the crew are incapacitated or have passed away. However, after 57 years, I located Bert Allinder, armorer and waist-gunner, and Ewing Roddy, engineer and top turret-gunner. We have had several phone conversations, and Bert and I met at a 490th Bomb Group reunion September, 2002. This is an amazing coincidence because I have a snapshot of the three of us in front of our Nissen hut in May, 1945. After all these years, we are the survivors! I have also located and corresponded with our former tail gunner, Ralph E. Moore's widow, Doris, and their son, Chip. Ralph completed over thirty combat missions. He remained in the USAF, and served in Korea and Vietnam. He retired after thirty years as a Chief Master Sergeant, and was one of the last enlisted combat air crewmen from WWII to retire from active duty.

I wish to thank my wife, daughters, and son-in-law for their help and encouragement during this project. My younger daughter, an Associate Professor of Social Work at the University of Memphis, volunteered as editor. She has spent many hours of typing and computer work to transform my handwritten text into a finished product. My other daughter, a Research Librarian, provided resource books and materials. Writing one's military history is a very satisfying activity which I heartily recommend. I close with one of my favorite stories that summarizes my military career.

During my tenure as an Administrative Assistant to the Superintendent of our school system, I had several secretaries. One day during a break, one of them asked me how I got my education. I told them that shortly before my senior year of high school, my rich uncle took me out of school and sent me on a tour of the United States. He then sent me on an ocean liner to England where I flew all over Europe for six months. This uncle then flew me home and paid for five years of college. The secretaries were awed and one said, "I wish I had an uncle like that!" They all laughed when I pointed out that they all had an Uncle Sam.

We owe our country's freedom to the veterans of all wars and the members of today's Armed Forces. Freedom is not free----it must be earned and protected. We should honor those who have fought for our country and those protecting us today.

Dedicated To My Family

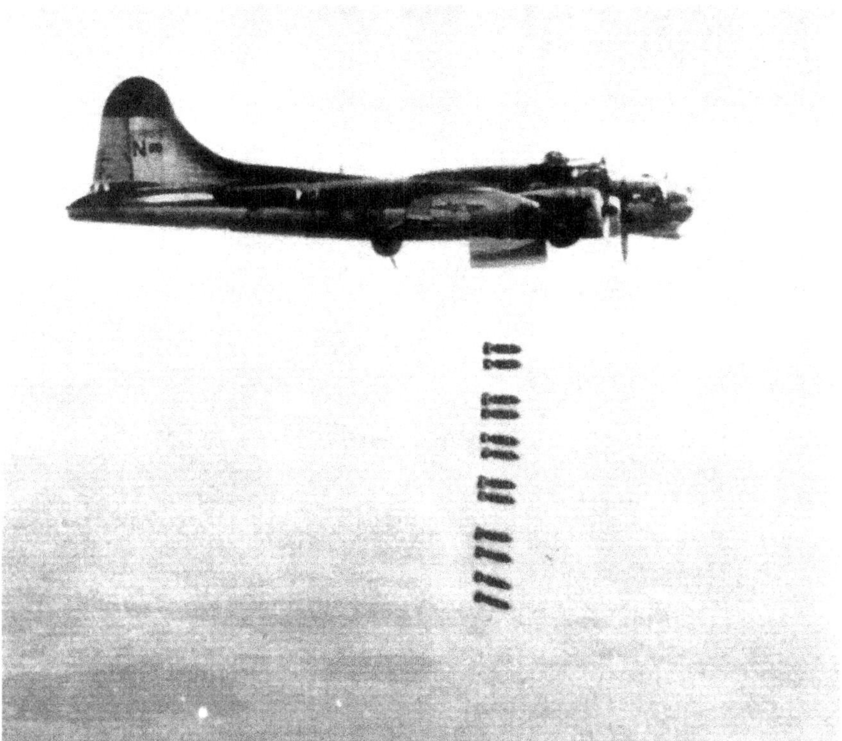

Chapter One
The Early Years

Growing up during the Depression was a full-time job. The economy was going well when I was born in 1925 in a farmhouse near Leesville, Indiana. Dad was a tenant farmer on a large farm owned by his uncle Emory who was also a schoolteacher. In those days, most births took place in the home. The doctor, when summoned, cranked up his Model "T" Ford and came to the house where he was assisted by female relatives or friends. I guess the menfolk "boiled lots of water" or just sat around and whittled. I don't remember the details!

When I was three, Dad went to work in a Bedford limestone quarry and we moved to a new house on Grandad Hutchinson's farm where my sister was born. I remember that hot August day when a lot of relatives came to our house and my aunt took me down over the hill to get a bucket of water. We got our household water from a hillside spring near the creek that ran through the valley behind our house. My aunt let me play in the cool creek water a long time that hot August afternoon. Well, when we got back to the house I heard a baby crying inside the house. Baby sister Jean had arrived, and I was no longer an only child. I later decided I wasn't going back to the spring again!

We later moved to a house on a dairy farm on Bedford's outskirts. Just before the "great depression" Dad bought a four-room in the southeast edge of town. The house had no utilities, so we carried water from a neighbor, used kerosene lamps, and heated with wood or coal stoves. My brother, Kenny joined the family and we settled down just in time for the stock market crash and recession.

Limestone Quarries

Indiana limestone was quarried from large deposits left by the skeletons of sea creatures left millions of years ago when the Great Lakes area was a large inland sea. Hundreds of limestone workers migrated from Italy to Lawrence county for employment. The quarried stone was removed from the ground and hauled to one of the many area stone mills to be sawed into blocks or veneer stone for beautiful limestone buildings. Many of the most famous buildings such as the Empire State building, state capitols across the U.S. and the Washington Cathedral were built with Indiana limestone. Stone carving was also important on these buildings, and we had many talented stone carvers in southern Indiana. George Vanderbilt had a special railroad siding built to his property to haul in the limestone from southern Indiana to build his mansion. The Biltmore House in Asheville, North Carolina is visited by thousands each year. Our stone mills were kept busy supplying the draftsmen, stone carvers and masons he hired to come over and build his magnificent Biltmore House. This structure is a perfect example of the merits and durability of limestone. A stone carving shop is included in our local high school art department even today.

In the 1920's the local economy was built on the limestone industry and many men were employed in the quarries and stone mills. My future father-in-law lost his left arm in a quarry accident. After the Depression the idle stone quarry holes filled with water and made excellent swimming holes. The lime in the stone helped turn the water blue and we had several "blue holes" for summertime recreation. There were often stacks of huge blocks of limestone in the water on which we could climb and sun in our birthday suits or use as diving platforms. There were underwater tunnels to swim through if you dared. Diving from the high ledges was a daredevil stunt. Our favorite swimming holes were Blue Hole, Big Brown and Swinging Bridge. Many boys used these swimming holes, and I remember that there were several drownings over the years. One of my classmates drowned in the spring of our junior year. The limestone industry recovered after the war and quarry swimming became a thing of the past.

Our Depression Home

The stock market had failed, and the limestone industry had no customers. Jobs were nonexistent and poverty became the order of the day. Keeping food on the table, coal for the heating stove and kitchen range, and clothing on our backs was always a problem. We now had a four-room house for a family of five. The unpainted house was of board and batten construction and had a tar paper roof that leaked. During rainstorms we used lots of pots and buckets to catch the leaking water. Dad mopped the roof each summer with melted tar. The house had no electricity or plumbing. There was a two-hole outhouse back on the alley. The "outhouse" or "privy" was a basic necessity in town neighborhoods which didn't have access to city sewers. They were usually built on the alley away from the house. Pushing outhouses over was an activity enjoyed by neighborhood teenagers on Halloween. Local citizens were enraged at this prank, especially if they were sitting in the outhouse at the time it happened!

In winter, we huddled around the pot-bellied stove and went to bed in an unheated room with hot sad-irons wrapped in towels. Sometimes we used hot bricks to keep our feet warm until body heat could warm the bed. The bedroom was off the heated living room and very cold in the winter. We didn't have enough blankets, so Mom would spread overcoats and extra clothing on top our bed.

Food was another problem. Occasionally we received a grocery order from the Township Trustee. People called it a "bean order" because beans and dry food were cheaper and the money would go farther. The federal government set up a program to provide surplus foods to needy families. Every week families stood in long lines to receive food such as beans, flour, canned beef, rice, peanut butter, and grapefruit. The program really helped our family survive. However, I remember that the flour sometimes had weevils in it, so I would feed it to the chickens. They loved the extra meat and the eggs never had weevils.

There was also a program that allowed the local dairy to distribute free milk. One summer, while in grade school, I stood in the "free milk" line every week to get my Karo syrup bucket full of a gallon of milk. When we ran out of free milk we had water gravy with our meal. Dad planted and tended gardens all over the neighborhood on shares with the landowner. I always got in on the hoeing, weeding and harvesting. We raised lot of potatoes, yams and black-eyed peas to keep as dry vegetables for the winter months. Mother canned tomatoes and green beans. Dried beans were a main part of our diet. Beans grown in gardens were easy to store, and were also distributed by various agencies which helped feed the poor. A large pot of Great Northern beans flavored with a chunk of pork (sow belly) could feed a family of five for lunch and supper. Beans were delicious with cornbread and buttermilk, and provided a good source of protein. It is still one of my favorite meals. Most families kept a pot of beans warming on the back of the cookstove all day. Beans played a big part in our vocabulary. We said a fibber was "full of beans", a tattler "spilled the beans", and a food order from the trustees was a "bean order". If you had a good idea, they said "that's using the old bean". We even had a poem for beans.

"Beans, beans the musical fruit,
The more you eat the more you poop!
The more you poop the better you feel,
So let's have beans for every meal!"

I imagine the "pull my finger" joke originated sometime during the Depression. Food was scarce for city families, but farm families fared much better as they could raise and store food. They often "shared" with relatives in town. Farmers with milk cows, pigs, chickens, orchards and large gardens weren't nearly as hungry as their city cousins. Our family received help from Grandad Hutchinson and several uncles. However, I remember one Aunt who didn't follow that pattern. If we were at their house during mealtime, family members took turns slipping out to the kitchen to eat while others visited with us in the living room. My pesky cousin always gave it away with a wink and a belly rub when he came back to join us. There was a standard rule parents gave their children: "If you are at a friend's house at mealtime, don't beg; but if they ask you to eat----you eat!" Clothing was for warmth—not style. My first year of school I had no coat, so I wore my two sweaters, jeans and my aviator cap. Shoes wore out quickly and Mom often cut out cardboard insoles to line the old brogans (high top shoes). The school nurse decided I needed a coat and pair of shoes. She took me to a private home on the other side of town and outfitted me with used clothing. When I was warmly dressed we went to J.C. Penney and bought new brogans made from roughed-out leather with steel heel caps. Those used clothes and shoes that didn't leak kept me warm all winter.

Teachers and the PTA (Parent-Teachers Association) established a "clothing bank". Families in the school district cooperated by donating used clothing, coats and shoes which were distributed to children in need. Most parents cooperated in this recycling project and the kid appreciated the "hand-me-downs".

The kitchen was the heart of my early childhood home. We had no electricity, plumbing or central heat. We carried our household water from a faucet in our neighbor's basement, and later from a town pump, and we ate and read by coal oil kerosene lamps. Cold and rainy days would find Mom and we three kids enjoying the warmth of the big black kitchen cookstove. The stove was so old that the side of the firebox had burned out and we'd sit by the side of the stove and enjoy the heat of the cheery flames nibbling at the oak wood. It was like having a fireplace in the kitchen. The flames and the steaming teakettle filled the room with warmth and humidity. We had a humidifier and didn't realize it.

The stove top had four removable lids on the cooking surface which could be lifted with a special handle. Mom used a short poker to rearrange the burning coals or shove in more firewood through the door on the front of the firebox. There was a large oven for baking, a reservoir (water tank) on the side for warming water and a warming oven above the cooking surface which was also heated by the black stove pipe connecting the stove to the brick chimney behind the stove. Keeping the wood box and the coal bucket behind the stove well-stocked was one of my daily chores.

I remember the day Dad bought Mom a new green and cream-colored Kalamazoo cookstove for $36.00. We were happy to say goodbye to the old stove with the burned-out firebox before it burned down the house. (I have two granddaughters who are graduates of Western Michigan University in Kalamazoo). Now, if we wanted to watch dancing flames, we went into the living room to the pot-bellied WarmMorning heating stove. We could see the flames through the glass windows in the door. The cookstove was one of our most versatile pieces of equipment. Cooking and baking was our first priority, but it was also used to heat water on bath and wash days, heating "sad irons" on ironing day, and keeping that pot of beans warm on the back of the stove. I did a lot of homework by those cookstoves. Recently, I saw an old cookstove in an antique shop—the price was $1800! Today a Kalamazoo Stove Works cookstove and a pot-belly coal stove are part of the décor of the Bob Evans Restaurant across from the Opryland Hotel in Nashville, Tennessee.

Monday was wash day. Laundry was done in a large galvanized tub with lots of hot water, a big bar of yellow O.K. soap and a washboard. Mom had a second tub to rinse clothes, and she had to wring them out by hand before hanging them on the clothesline. We didn't have lots of clothing so laundry was light, but done often. Later, we used a neighbor's electric washer in turn for doing his laundry. Baths were taken in the same tubs in the kitchen behind the warm stove and a sheet hanging on a rope line. Winter wash days were exciting because Mom put up temporary clotheslines in the two heated rooms of our four room house. We kids romped and played in a maze of hanging sheets, towels and clothing dangling from the makeshift clotheslines. The wet washing put plenty of moisture into the air.

Ironing day was Tuesday, and the sad irons were heated on the kitchen stove. The heavy irons had removable handles so she could keep two or three heating on the stove to replace an iron after it cooled. Mom set up an ironing pad on the kitchen table and ironed away. We didn't have a lot of clothing, but we went to school in clean duds.

Baking day was usually Wednesday when Mom baked yeast buns for the week. All the kids in the neighborhood wanted to play at our house on baking day. Mom would bring out those tasty buns and let us share. They were delicious, steaming hot, with butter and mustard! She baked several pans, wrapped them in linen and stored them in a five gallon tin lard can. This supply would last several days. The kitchen table was a multiple- use piece of furniture. The big old round oak table served as an eating surface, ironing board, kitchen counter for preparing food and a game board. We often used it for table-top games with marbles, cards and coloring books. It became a desk in the evening, as we sat around the kerosene lamp to do our homework.

The living room and pot-bellied Warm Morning coal stove were the center of our winter evenings. We played and studied on the floor around the stove and the stand-table which held the lamp. I still have that table that we sat around over seventy years ago. Singing was a great family winter activity, and we three kids would gather around the pump organ and sing hymns and favorite songs as Mom pumped away and led the singing. The pump organ was fascinating with all its keys and knobs (stops). The three-legged stool with its spiral adjustable seat was great fun.

I attempted to take free piano lessons in the sixth grade and went home to practice on the pump organ. After a few weeks, the music teacher decided I needed a piano to take lessons. I was crushed because I loved music, but to this day I play only the CD and TV! An ironic twist is that my son-in-law has played the huge Holloway pipe organ in our Presbyterian church for the past thirty years. So I still get to sing hymns with an organ!

Depression Christmas in the Thirties

Believe it or not, Christmas was a happy time at our house. We would cut a cedar tree in the red clay fields behind our house and decorate it with ornaments, tin foil icicles and colored paper chains made in art class at school. Mom would cook a big boiling hen with dumplings, sweet potatoes and all the trimmings. Dad always brought in five or six sacks of peanuts and various kinds of candy, and there was usually a coconut to crack open for the "milk" and white meat . There was always plenty of popcorn.

Presents were simple and few, mainly a toy or two and some clothing. One Christmas I received three iron World War I toy soldiers. I still have two of them. Gift exchange at school was limited to a ten cent gift, but a dime bought a lot in those days. I usually got a Big Little book about Dick Tracy, The Phantom or Tom Mix. The teachers and P.T.A also provided treats of a sack of candy and an apple or orange. During the Christmas season we often walked to town to see the Christmas lights and store window displays around the town square. We had no electricity but we enjoyed seeing the glowing Christmas trees in the windows of houses we passed. Our favorite Christmas Toyland was upstairs at the Fair Store on the square. This family-owned store created a toy department only at Christmas. I believe the owners really enjoyed watching the children parade through the store and up the winding stairs to "window shop". They knew most of us didn't have a dime to our name. Maybe they were after the ten cent gift exchange money. The Fair Store went out of business years ago, but not before I bought my wife June a set of Rogers silverware for our first anniversary!

We kids always visited two or three churches to see the Christmas plays and get the sack of treats they gave out. Various churches would host Christmas suppers for needy children selected by the schoolteachers. A teacher friend's Depression story concerned "Christmas tree lights". Her farm family purchased a gasoline powered electrical generator, but regulated its use to keep the cost down. The daughters were allowed to decorate their first "electric light" Christmas tree, but could only turn on the lights when a car passed the house. Years later at family Christmas gatherings they would remember those days when they yelled, "Here comes a car—turn on the tree lights!"

The Pre-Teen Years

My boyhood from ages five to twelve was spent in the south-end neighborhood of Bedford. We had moved to town from a dairy farm tenant house. So during my early school years, we lived on the edge of town in the south end, and there were fields and woods across the alley that ran over a half mile to Leatherwood creek. People in our area used this land as a park, and the family who owned it was very understanding. We picked mushrooms and dandelion greens in the early spring, berries in the summer and persimmons and nuts in the fall. Men and older boys would set rabbit snares during the winter months when the dead catch wouldn't spoil. The woods behind our house was a favorite trapping area. A big fat rabbit would add needed meat to the family meal. Occasionally, a snare would get robbed. We always said that anyone low enough to steal a dead rabbit was worse than a horse thief.

It seems that Leatherwood creek south of town has always flowed through my life. My mother loved picking wildflowers along the creek, and she would take the neighborhood kids along. My buddies and I also enjoyed playing in the creek. It provided fishing spots and swimming holes during my boyhood. Most of us learned to swim in potholes in Leatherwood. Three of our favorite "swimmin' holes" were "Nine-Foot", "Sycamore" and "Clay Banks". We all thought

"Sow Belly" was too shallow, although it was waist deep and well shaded, and was a wonderful ice rink in the winter. We would hike a half mile over the hill to the creek, and swim and cool off for awhile. We often had a grapevine or strong rope we could use to swing out over a swimming hole and drop in like Tarzan. There were a lot of squeaky Tarzan yells along the creek in those days. Of course, by the time we hiked back up the hill and home, we were hotter than we were before we swam! "Nine-foot" was also used by several local churches for baptismal ceremonies. We always enjoyed watching the preacher "dunk" those new church members. Leatherwood also flows through our city golf course. I've put more than a few golf balls in that creek through the past sixty-five years!

Spring meant "barefoot days", and every kid in the neighborhood welcomed the warm weather. Parents were happy because it saved shoe leather and kids could hardly wait to shed their socks and shoes after school. Summer vacation was our time to run barefoot. Stone bruises and cut toes were a small price to pay for freedom to run through grass, dirt and mud puddles. The soles of our feet were as tough as leather by the end of summer. Summertime and hot weather saw a great decline in the use of the cookstove except for baking and canning times. We had an outdoor campfire for heating wash water, and we generally only cooked supper in the kitchen. Garden vegetables and fruits were canned when available. Every family canned all the food they could gather in preparation for the coming winter. The women would fill tin cans with cooked tomatoes, tap on lids and seal them with red sealing wax. Glass jars with zinc lids and rubber sealing rings were used for green beans, preserves and fruits. The successful housewife would end the summer with several dozen jars and cans of food in her pantry. Dried beans, potatoes and fruits were stored in cellars or cool rooms in wooden bushel baskets. We could wrap apples or pears in newspapers and keep them for several months. Turnips were buried in a straw-lined pit in the garden. We dug them up as they were needed during the winter, and sorted the good from the rotten. There's nothing slimier or stinkier than a rotten turnip!

During the "dog days" of summer when stifling heat became a problem, my mother would grab a book and take me, my sister and baby brother across the alley back to the shade of a giant oak in the pasture. We didn't have electric fans or air conditioning, so we were happy playing in the dirt under that big oak tree. I think it's very appropriate that a group home for troubled children stands on that site today. Our playmates often went along for the shade and summer breezes. Our house was unbearably hot, so we threw open all windows with screens, patched the holes in the screen doors and endured the heat as best we could. At night we made "pallets" (spread a blanket) and slept on the floor near the door or camped out on the roofless front porch. Sleeping on a blanket in the yard was also fun, but the "chiggers" would get us and we would itch for a week. The best treatment for chigger bites was to rub a mixture of lard and salt on the spot where the mite burrowed into your skin.

Chigger prevention while picking berries was accomplished by tying kerosene-soaked rags around our wrists and ankles.

Years ago, an entomologist, H.B. Hungerford, wrote a limerick to honor the lowly chigger.

> The thing called a chigger
> Is really no bigger
> Than the smaller end of a pin,
> But the bump that it raises
> Just itches like blazes
> And that's where the rub sets in!

Hey, What's an Allowance?

As a skinny elementary school kid, I managed to earn a little spending money collecting junk. The local junkyard would buy paper, rags, brass and zinc, so my buddies Chad and Jimmy and I went into business. We used my red coaster wagon, Dan Patch, to haul our loot and we ran the local alleys every Saturday morning to raise enough money to go to the movies. Rags and paper were easy to find, but old light bulbs had brass bases and glass jar canning lids were zinc, so we spent time crushing those objects to get the metal. On a good Saturday morning we could earn enough for the matinee and maybe even some jelly beans. We had plenty of competition from other "collectors", and there were also several pushcart men who cleaned stores and shops for the paper and cardboard boxes.

I retired from the junk business at the age of twelve, and became a paper boy for awhile. Bedford had two daily newspapers and the subscription was ten cents per week. Few people could afford a paper and some subscribers were hard to find on Friday when I stopped to collect for the week.

I was the oldest child, so I got assigned a lot of the chores as I grew older. Dad would split the firewood or kindling and I would carry in a supply each day around suppertime for the kitchen cookstove. My job was to keep the wood box behind the cookstove full. Winter was harder because I also carried coal for the potbellied stove in the living room. We had a garage and coal shed down on the alley where Dad stocked up wood and coal piles. Fuel wasn't easy to come by. Dad usually found someone with a Model A truck and they would go out to Grandpa's farm and cut wood by hand. Their tools were an axe, a two man crosscut saw, and lots of muscle. Coal was about $5.00 a ton, if you had the $5.00! Grandad Hutchinson's farm was the source of our hard-earned firewood. Dad and a neighbor with a truck cut many cords of wood during those Depression years. Chainsaws had not been invented, so all wood was cut with an axe or a six-foot crosscut saw. A man on each end whipped the saw back and forth to cut the wood into stove-length chunks. The beech, oak or ash wood was then split into small pieces with an axe. Woodcutters said their sweat would help keep their families warm all winter. A large woodpile was a necessity for the long winter months. Men could also earn extra income selling wood. Some weekends I got to go along and help load the truck. The teamwork of the two men on the crosscut saw could make the sawdust fly.

Grandpa Hutchinson's farm was my favorite place to visit. He farmed over 150 acres with horse drawn equipment. Dad was the oldest of eight boys, so Grandad had plenty of farm hands but I was his first grandson! It was a storybook farm with chickens, pigs, milk cows, horses and mules. My uncles often let me ride Old Ned, the white saddle horse. Another of my favorite steeds was the old mule Grandad used to till the corn. There were dozens of trips up and down the cornfield. I sat on the harnessed mule while Grandpa trudged behind, long reins around his neck and guiding the plow. I developed my love for horses early in life.

Sometimes we had to ask the township trustee for a free coal order. The county welfare office would help out occasionally, especially when children were involved. If all else failed, some men would hop a night freight train when it slowed down on the river hill upgrade coming into town and throw lumps of coal from the coal cars. Then it was a matter of hopping off and filling their "gunny sacks" (burlap bags) and hiking two or three miles back home. Cars and trucks were seldom used because gas was 13 cents per gallon and people could not afford a car. The streets were our playground, and we used them for stick-ball, roller skating, kick the can games and any other games that called for a firm, smooth surface. Children and adults would go to the door when a car passed. It was usually a truant officer, police car or welfare worker on official business, or the sheriff looking for someone suspected of stealing chickens. The ice man used a horse and wagon, but everyone else used "shanks mare", which meant they walked. I thought teachers were rich because they had cars. Traffic was practically nonexistent and the city officials often blocked off areas for street dances or roller-skating. Hilly city streets were great for sledding.

The Ice Man Cometh

Refrigerators were unheard of in those days because most families couldn't afford electricity. Of course our house wasn't even wired for it. The icebox was a necessity for even the poorest family. Ours was an oak cabinet about four feet tall with a hinged lid on top and two doors on the front. It also had a drip pan underneath to catch water as the ice melted. We had to empty it everyday. A twenty-five pound block of ice in the top compartments kept the lower compartments cool. If you kept the icebox in an unheated room, the ice lasted much longer in the winter. Kids loved the ice man in the summer time because of the free samples. " Butch" Jones was our ice man, one of our favorite guys all summer long. I can still see him driving his old white horse hitched to his green ice wagon with the orange wheels. The wagon was loaded with blocks of ice covered with a heavy black tarp. Every customer had an ice card to place in his screen door so the iceman would know what block of ice to deliver. It was usually a ten cent order for twelve and a half pounds. Upon seeing the sign, Butch would stop the horse, chip off the correct size block, pick it up with his ice tongs and tote it to the icebox in the house. When the coast was clear, we would rush to the back of the wagon, lift the tarp and pass out the ice chips. It was a glorious summer treat, and free!

We were especially blessed at our house when Butch stopped at one neighbor's house he would carry the ice into the basement and stay a little longer. So, we had extra time to lift the tarp and chip off ice in case there wasn't enough to go around. Many years later I learned that our neighbor usually had a bottle of home brew in the ice box for Butch's lunch break.

Dad and the Baby Buggy

Many men made illegal beer (homebrew) wine and whiskey (moonshine) during the Depression. Prohibition had banned alcohol so money could be made from making and peddling (boot-legging) these "spirits". I heard this story a few years after my father passed away, but it was from a reliable source and I have no reason to doubt it.

Our family owned a large high-wheeled rattan baby buggy which my mother had used for both me and my sister. Dad, being unemployed, took a sudden interest in taking my baby brother for buggy rides to town and around the neighborhood. My mother learned that he was stashing several bottles of homebrew under the buggy's mattress, and was making deliveries for a friend who was a "moonshiner". She soon put a stop to this fund-raising venture. I think my baby brother missed those buggy rides.

My grandfather Hutchinson had once assisted "revenoors" in locating and smashing "moonshine stills" in the hills of Jackson county. My grandfather Hoar, a very religious man, was visiting at the time. Both would have been livid if they had learned of Dad's brief venture into bootlegging! The word "bootlegging", which means transporting alcoholic beverages illegally, comes from the practice of smuggling liquor by hiding bottles in your boots.

A bright red wagon named after Dan Patch, a famous race horse on the Indiana county fair and harness race circuit, was Mom's answer to the transportation problem. She would load us three children and off we would go up the sidewalk to town or to the grocery store. As I grew, I was glad to give up my seat and walk up hill and down the eight blocks to town. I later used the red wagon in my "junking" venture.

There were "mom and pop" groceries in nearly every block of our neighborhood but our meager amount of money would go farther at the big Jay C store. Whether it was $5.00 in cash or a "bean order" from the welfare department, it would buy enough groceries to feed our family of five for a week! Of course, this was supplemented by our store of garden supplies and Mom's home canning. The local groceries were popular places to buy penny candy and bottles of Nehi pop for a nickel. Storekeepers usually allowed customers to buy on credit, or run a "bill" until payday. There was a sack of candy as a treat for the kids when the bill was paid.

Most men and school boys carried a pocket knife in their jeans or overalls. A knife was a necessity for whittling, cutting a chew of tobacco off a plug of Red Mule, cleaning fingernails, carving your initials on a tree or playing mumble peg. Knife trading was always a possibility for the older men when they were loafing under a shade tree or in the barber shop. A Barlow knife was a cherished possession. Mumble peg was played with an open knife, which was dropped, handle down, from the eye, nose, chin, elbow etc. The object was to flip the knife so it would stick in the dirt. The player who had the most "sticks" was the winner.

A big game for us was playing marbles. Everyone had a bag of marbles with favorite shooters or "aggies". A circle was drawn and each boy placed some marbles in the center and the players took turns shooting to knock marbles out of the circle. Each shooter kept the marbles he knocked out, so this was a form of gambling and the older boys and best players usually had large jars of marbles to sell or trade. Losers were said to have "lost their marbles". Later, in education circles, there was a story that when you became a teacher the superintendent gave you a bag of marbles. When you had "lost all your marbles" he made you a principal.

They Rode Off in All Directions and Went That-a-Way!

Saturday matinees were a real bargain in those days before television. A dime bought a ticket for a Western, a "B" movie (a low cost production non-western), and best of all---another episode of an adventure serial! Serials were usually produced with twelve chapters of thrilling action. One fifteen-minute chapter was shown each week and always ended with the hero facing death in a hopeless situation. Of course, we all wanted to go back next Saturday to see if and how he escaped (he always did). Movie cowboys were our heroes and we all had our favorites to imitate with our "cap" guns and stick horses. A box of caps (five rolls) was only a nickel, so we had lots of noise to make our cowboy battles more realistic. It never mattered that our heroes never reloaded their guns and had horses that could run forever. Westerns had plenty of "chase scenes", only they were horseback, stagecoach and covered wagons. The majority of the low budget films were made on the studio "back lots". During those years we watched our heroes race past the same scenery in film after film! We were fascinated by the six-shooter action and the cowboy who saved the pretty girl's ranch and rode off into the sunset. Westerns promoted the Tom Mix cowboy club's motto: "Straight-shooters always win—lawbreakers always lose."

My favorite matinee idols were Tim McCoy, Buck Jones, and Ken Maynard (I saw him and his horse Tarzan when he came to Bedford in 1935). Hopalong Cassidy, Gene Autry and Roy Rogers came along later. Tim McCoy was awarded the Bronze Star in World War II. Recently on cable television I saw a 1936 "oater" starring Ken Maynard in *Lawless Rider*. The film just didn't have quite the same allure as when I was eleven at the Saturday matinee. Buck Jones starred in many movies and serials and I tried to see all of them. There was one minor problem---the ten-cent ticket. I think Ken and Buck were my favorites because they were Hoosiers. Buck's hometown was Columbus and Ken was from the Ft. Wayne area. Bob Steele was another Saturday matinee hero. He was very athletic and rode like the wind on his horse, Pal. Once his "hero" days were over, he became a character actor and appeared in "big name" westerns for many years.

The Daisy BB gun was a highly desired possession for older boys. It was great for shooting at homemade targets, bottles and frogs. The Red Ryder carbine BB gun was a really hot item. The BBs (shot) were only five cents for a large packet. It was great to be "armed" when we went to the woods or down to swim in the creek. Another weapon was the "bean flipper", a homemade slingshot. The bean flipper was very effective and would fit in the hip pocket. Making this economical "weapon" was fairly easy. We cut a forked limb from a tree, preferably hickory, to get a "Y" and then tied a strip of rubber on the top of each "Y". The next step was to find a piece of leather and attach it to each strip of rubber to make a pouch to hold the object to be shot, usually a rock or marble. The flipper let you do a lot of target shooting. Usually you didn't feel "dressed" unless you had a few pebbles and a bean flipper in your hip pocket.

During the depression years of the thirties, a small amount of money would buy many of life's pleasures for a small boy. The grocery stores sold penny candy and nickel RC Colas, Eskimo Pies and Twinkies. We could also go to the movies for a dime and see a Western, a B-movie, and a serial. A kind cashier at the Von Ritz movie theater would take my dime and let my little sister and brother in free. I remember a Jack Holt western was playing one Sunday afternoon and the three of us had the magic dime. We walked the eight blocks to the theater but the cashier had to turn us down. We were all getting too old. It was a long walk home. I never did get to see that Western!

Nicknames were very common and were often carried to the grave. Area obituaries usually included the life-long nicknames of the deceased. Otherwise, many might not recognize the proper names. I remember monikers of many of my boyhood buddies. Some referred to their character or physique. Others made no sense at all. Shanks, Snake, Stretch and Shorty were all tall, talented basketball players. Butch and Tuffy would fight any kid in the neighborhood. Ham, Dopey, Ducky, Dutch and Doc were also in our gang. I was Hutch.

Our Leisurely World

Imagine a world without electricity, cell phones, computers, radios or televisions and you get an idea of life in the 1930's. Also, there were very few cars and therefore no traffic problems. Life in our neighborhood was slow and easy. Kids had plenty of free time as did most adults. Winter evenings found us gathered around the stove to keep warm or doing homework by the kerosene lamp.

Summer evenings were hot and muggy, and most families sat on the front porch or in the yard under a tree to cool off in the evening breezes. That was also a good place to visit with neighbors or passers-by. "Come on up and sit a spell" was a common invitation. There was plenty of time for small talk, gossip, politics, the weather or just tall tales. Maybe a neighbor lady would come over to borrow a cup of sugar, or better yet, come over to pay back something borrowed. The neighborhood kids could play "hide and seek", and "run sheep run" in the yard or "stick-ball" and "kick the can" in the street. Listening to the adults or the older folks was always interesting, especially when old Granny Sheeks would tell tales about her childhood when panthers screamed in the forest and wolves howled around her family's log cabin! Tales of the gypsies coming through town and kidnapping children always sent shivers up and down our spines!

Medicine Shows, Carnivals and the Circus

The medicine shows, like tent revivals, traveled from town to town providing entertainment, and "snake oil" salesmen peddled bottles of their own "miracle" medicines guaranteed to cure everything from warts to rheumatism. There were dozens of "quacks" with the title of "Doctor" or "Professor" touring the country. Their wonder cures could be purchased for a quarter a bottle. The medicine usually contained a high percentage of alcohol with vanilla and few herbs for flavor. Prohibition being in effect, the medicine man usually had a brisk business. Customers bought the bottles for "medicinal purposes". The Medicine Show people could move into town and be open for business in a very short time. The fake doctor always had assistants to provide entertainment and help with chores and sales. I remember one show featured a "mad man" in a cage, biting the heads of live white rats. These types of "geeks" were usually depraved men needing drinking money. The show could pack up and move out of town even faster, especially if the police insisted. Everyone knew the true character of the Medicine Show, but heck, they enjoyed the free entertainment!

Carnivals were a bigger attraction with all the rides and tents set up at the fairgrounds. They usually traveled by trucks and there were always a few jobs for local men and older boys who wanted to earn a few extra dollars setting up and taking down tents. The rides and sideshows were always intriguing and available for five or ten cents. Everyone knew the "games of chance" were rigged but kept trying to win one of the tempting prizes. Games like the "ring toss", "shooting gallery", etc. just looked so easy! I enjoyed the fast-talking sideshow "barkers" and their invitations to buy a ticket to see the "wonders" inside their tents. The Sultan's Harem and the exotic dancing girls seemed especially interesting to the high school boys, however, at age ten, I wasn't sure why. Parents got lots of begging for extra coins with promises of "I'll be good" or "I'll do all my chores" during the time the carnival was in town. Like the Medicine Shows, carnivals could pack up and move on quickly if the "law" made that suggestion.

A traveling circus was the biggest event of our summer. Bedford was located at the intersection of the Monon and Milwaukee railroads, and easily accessible from all directions. The large circus traveled by train with specially constructed railroad cars for wild animals, circus wagons and personnel. Our fairgrounds were more than a mile from the train depot. Therefore, every circus coming to town by train would put on a grand parade down main street. The steam calliope usually led, with its shrill music, followed by many brightly painted circus wagons with their cages of wild animals. The crazy clowns and scantily clad circus girls riding elephants or horses were followed by the Wild West riders which made for a long and wonderful parade. It was great advertising for the circus and the crowds loved it! One of my biggest thrills was the Tom Mix Circus and seeing the famous movie cowboy relaxing behind the Wild West tent between shows. Today, they call it a "circus" when five people come to town with an elephant and a dog and pony show.

Churches and Revivals

Religion played an important role in our lives during the Depression. Churches held many special programs to encourage attendance. There were also "missionary" churches that were set up in neighborhood vacant stores or houses. Children could earn prizes by attending Sunday school for so many weeks. One winter I earned a New Testament by attending for ten weeks. Bible School was big during summer vacation. Established churches sponsored "revivals" and special programs to encourage religion and save souls. Religion also came to our neighborhood with the traveling preachers and their "tent revivals". These were often sponsored by local denominations, but more than likely they were "itinerant evangelists" spreading their message of "fire and brimstone" or claims of "faith healing".

James Lee Hutchinson, EdS

The large brown tarpaulin tent was usually set up on a vacant lot for a week, depending on the attendance and money collected. The sides of the tent were rolled up for ventilation and paper fans were usually provided for the audience. The "faith healers" sometimes decorated the altar platform with "no longer needed" canes or crutches. Bystanders outside had a good view of the services and freedom of movement which I didn't enjoy. Once Mom got me seated in that rickety folding chair, I was there for the duration. The preaching was loud and long until finally the "collection plates" were passed and we could walk home in the cool, quiet summer night.

There was also an old wooden Pentecostal church about eight blocks up the street that my mother liked to attend. This church had more than its share of emotionally religious members. Many caught the "spirit" early in the services and there was a lot of arm waving, dancing and talking in "tongues". The rest of the people in the congregation clapped their hands, stomped their feet and sang hymns, and the wooden floor of the old building took a beating. The windows and doors were open on hot summer evenings and the church services could be heard all over the neighborhood. Admittedly, some went for the show rather than for religious reasons. There were the usual number of men and boys hanging in the windows or waiting outside to walk wives or sweethearts home after the services. I remember one time when my buddy Charlie and I decided we would dress up. Our shoes were worn out so we painted them with black enamel, made insoles of cardboard to cover the holes in the bottom, and set them out to dry. That night we put on our "new shoes" and walked to church. By the time we arrived, the paint had cracked and we were wearing "alligator" shoes! The community's established churches carried out many projects to aid the poor. Members contributed money, clothing and food to local agencies. Church doors were open to everyone, but Mom always felt that our family lacked "proper clothing" to attend. However, we kids attended Sunday school and Bible schools in the summer.

Mom's foot-pedaled Singer sewing machine was an important item in our house. She could make clothing for my little sister and herself. That sewing machine and Mom's skill with needle and thread extended the life of our "everyday clothes". Rips and tears required lots of sewing time. Most of the boys in the neighborhood wore jeans or knickers with patches on the knees or seats. Kids in large families wore hand-me-downs from their older brothers and sisters. I'm glad I didn't have an older sister! There were lots of kids running around in ill-fitting clothing. We saved our "good clothes" for special occasions. Feed sacks were a great source of material for the Depression seamstress. Women used the cloth for curtains, pillowcases, aprons and dresses. Grandad Hutchinson had plenty of feed sacks to share. The feed companies knew their empty cotton sacks were being used for curtains, pillow cases, aprons and dish towels as well as clothing. So, they began printing the white sacks with colorful patterns of flowers, stripes and plaids. There were also light tan sacks that could be bleached to take off the manufacturer's name. One of the standard jokes was about the farmer's daughter and her "feedsack bloomers". Every time she bent over, she advertised the local feed store!

Hobos and Veterans

The Depression, fueled by the stock market crash of 1929, was very serious. Banks closed and some 32,000 businesses had failed by 1932, and there was a twenty-five percent unemployment rate. Three of every four families were without jobs. Two million men roamed the country seeking work. In the words of old-timers, "Jobs were as scarce as hen's teeth"! Men were forced to travel to find ways to earn money to send home to their families. They weren't the usual "tramps" who traveled the country. These were men from all walks of life who simply couldn't find jobs in their home communities. They became migratory workers or "hobos". Railroads provided the transportation for the travelers, although railroad detectives did their best to prevent the "free" rides. Hobos waited until the last minute to "hop" a freight train as it pulled out of the railyard. They would ride on top or inside empty boxcars.

While hunting employment, hobos existed by doing chores for families or farmers in exchange for food or money. People usually shared what they had with these unfortunate men. Riding the "rails" was a dangerous way to travel and hobos carried very little baggage. Their bedroll or "bindle" consisted of a blanket and meager supplies. The "bindle" was usually wrapped with a waterproof material. A rope tied to each end allowed them to throw it over their shoulder before they "hopped" a moving boxcar. There were "hobo jungles" or camps along the railroads near each town. These were often on a long grade so the men could hop on or off as the train slowed down for the hill. The jungles provided a camping spot where the hobos might rest in tents, shacks or abandoned buildings, and perhaps share a pot of "Mulligan Stew". Our town's hobo jungle was rumored to be in the woods east of town along the Milwaukee tracks.

This hobo pattern continued until the government established programs for employment. Hoosier Theodore Dreiser memorialized the hobo in the chorus of this song "The Wabash Cannonball":

> "Oh listen to the jungle,
> The rumble and the roar,
> As she glides along the woodlands
> Through the hills and by the shores.
> Hear the mighty rush of engines,
> Hear the lonesome hobo's call,
> We're traveling through the jungles
> On the Wabash Cannonball".

World War I veterans had been promised economic aid. In 1924 Congress approved a bonus payable in 1945. Veterans called this a "Tombstone Bonus" because many would be dead before receiving payment. A march on Washington was organized in May 1932, and thousands of destitute veterans, some with families, converged on our nation's capital. This "Bonus Army" of an estimated 25,000 people demanded that Congress pay the bonus promised in 1924. These men camped in shanty-towns called "Hoovervilles", named after the President. There were 27 of these camps, and the largest held 15,000 inhabitants.

One veteran said, "War is hell, but loafing is worse". The "Bonus Army" encampment lasted over two months. Fearing riots, President Hoover ordered the army to evict the veterans and destroy the camps. They were literally escorted out of Washington by U.S. troops, tanks and tear gas. The "Bonus Army" was eventually successful, and paved the way for benefits for future veterans. Congress approved an average $600 bonus in 1936. The government had learned its lesson, and in June 1944 while WWII armed forces were still liberating Europe. Congress approved a year's unemployment payment plan and the G.I. Bill of Rights for returning servicemen (5). The G.I. Bill was a stroke of genius on the part of the government. G.I. (government issue) was the term for all service men in World War II. The American Legion originated and sponsored passage of the G.I. Bill of Rights through Congress in 1944. The bill provided tuition and stipend benefits for millions of veterans returning to civilian life. President Theodore Roosevelt said in 1903, "A man who is good enough to shed his blood for his country is good enough to be given a square deal afterwards". This landmark legislation enabled some 7.8 million veterans to secure advanced training or take advantage of loan guarantees to purchase homes. I was lucky enough to benefit from both programs.

The W.P.A. (Work Projects Administration) was a revolutionary program to provide work for unemployed Americans. My current address include the words "W.P.A. Road" because this county road was built by W.P.A. workers 66 years ago. When President Franklin D. Roosevelt started the NRA (National Recovery Act) Dad got a laborer's job on the WPA and earned $48.00 a month. Old FDR really pulled us out of a hole, as our family was getting bigger, appetites were growing and there was not always enough food. I remember that I was a 150 pound six-footer when I was drafted at age eighteen.

Most jobs were manual labor, so the men with jobs were glad to lay back and rest in the cool of the evening. The women who had cooked, washed, and ironed in the hot house all day were also ready for rest. The WPA program was just getting off the ground and employment was picking up in 1934. Building roads, digging ditches or mowing parks for $48 a month, or $1.60 a day, beat loafing on the "Liar's Bench" in the front yard of the courthouse.

There was a running joke about how slowly the WPA gangs worked (or rather how they avoided it) in the poem about eight guys mowing:

"Two a comin'

"Two a goin'

"Two in the outhouse

"Two a mowin'

There were also stories of men being injured by falls from leaning on their shovels until the handle broke. Life was slow and loafing became an art. This all changed after December 7th, 1941 when America had to rev up its industrial machine and go to war! Despite these shortcomings, the WPA gave employment to those who needed a job. Men found work and self-respect, and families were grateful for the $48 monthly salary. The WPA accomplished all sorts of needed projects, issued contracts for the construction of many useful parks and public buildings, and financed recreational and arts programs. I sometimes took Dad's lunchbox to him when his crew was working in our end of town. It usually contained a couple of biscuits, a five-cent can of pork and beans, a spoon and a can opener.

The government in 1933 established a program to provide employment and training for young men or those with families. The Civilian Conservation Corps (CCC) helped nearly three million men find meaningful work and helped keep their families off welfare programs. The CCC camps of up to 300 men were run as a military type operation with men living in barracks away from home. Each man was paid thirty dollars monthly, a dollar a day, twenty-nine of which was sent to his family. Salaries were later raised so the young workers would have more pocket money. The free housing, nutritional meals and meaningful work were appreciated by these workers. The program was very successful and some men stayed with it for several years. CCC men built roads in state and national parks, fought forest fires, constructed buildings and dams, and planted thousands of trees in government forestlands. A majority of the young men later enlisted or were drafted into service during World War II. The CCC conservation projects greatly benefited our southern Indiana hill country and thousands of young people familiar with military life provided a base for enlarging our armed forces after Pearl Harbor.

Chapter Two
Calm Before the Storm

School was a great place for a poor kid during the Depression. Our parents wanted us to learn, our teachers wanted to help us, and we appreciated their concern. Lincoln School (southside) and Stalker School (northside) were big, two-story limestone buildings built in 1899. Little did I realize that later in life, I would be the last school principal of each of these buildings. There were wide wooden stairways at the front and back doors of Lincoln, and every time a class moved for recess or dismissal we marched in columns of twos very quietly. Woe to any child who whispered or made unwarranted noise. One day our fourth grade class was going downstairs when the teacher jerked me out of line and slapped my face for making too much noise. I explained that my brand new clodhopper shoes were squeaking. She gave me a big hug, apologized profusely and I was "teacher's pet" after that incident! There was a line for the boys and one for the girls. Every boy hoped to get a pretty girl or his buddy for a partner. I seldom succeeded in that department. I usually ended up with someone who wouldn't talk to me. I guess that was the teacher's plan. Quiet and orderly behavior was expected of every child, and there was swift punishment for the unbelievers! Discipline made school days easier for us because the classes were very large. I still have my class photos with 40-50 children in a class. Parents were very cooperative with teachers and gave their children a warning seldom heard today "If you get in trouble at school, you'll be in trouble when you get home!"

Spanking was used as needed in those days, and every teacher had a wooden paddle. Children behaved and studied their lessons and were seldom discipline problems because they knew the consequences. The teachers and principal were in charge, and the parents and community expected and received good results from the primary grades through high school. This was mainly true because of one important factor: DISCIPLINE. Those children of 1931 through 1945 were the men and women who worked in the factories and fought and won World War II. The children educated during my career (1950-1987) are now running the nation. Public schools lost ground when they lost classroom discipline!

Schools provided nutrition for impoverished children by serving free milk at morning recess and free lunches. The lunches consisted of a half pint of milk and a bowl of hot soup or sandwich served from a "make-shift" kitchen in the basement. Our kitchen was a gas stove, sink and serving counter in a small space under our giant wooden stairs. Today's fire marshall would have a field day writing all the safety violations in that kitchen which served so much food to so many hungry children. Tables and chairs were set up in the central basement. Parents often volunteered to help serve the children. Of course, they also got a hot lunch. Due to lack of space, children who brought lunchboxes or sack lunches ate at desks upstairs in the "lunch duty" teacher's classroom. However, they could buy a half pint of milk for three cents.

The Lincoln elementary school was a formidable two-story limestone building built in 1899 with nine classrooms for grades 1-6, and an assembly hall on each floor. Kindergarten was unheard of in the 1930's. A large percentage of the children came from impoverished homes. Looking at my old classroom group pictures, it's easy to pick us out. The free recess milk and free lunch of milk with a bowl of soup were a treat. In the winter we walked to school and really appreciated the warmth of the classroom and the chance to get a free lunch and stay in at noon. Rainy or snowy days would find several children in each room drying their coats or shoes on or around the warm steam radiators. Warm fall and spring days were another story. We hated the hot classrooms and used every excuse to stay home, and the truant officer was very busy. Those of us who trudged to school on those hot days usually soaked our heads at the town pump down the street before entering the building. However, it was never too hot for the fifteen-minute outdoor recess on the playground each morning and afternoon. The dusty playground was covered with cinders from the school's coal-fired furnace. Running and falling resulted in skinned knees and elbows. Cleaning the wound usually involved picking out cinder particles. Playground games were tag, dodgeball, kickball and horseshoes. My elementary teachers were wonderful women who taught the three R's to classes of 35-40 children year end and year out. Unemployed parents were especially grateful for the education, food and clothing provided for their children. This dedication to the education of their pupils helped me decide to become a teacher many years later.

In elementary school we sat in wood desks with iron frames which were bolted to the floor in rows of eight seats to a row. The inkwells in the desks weren't used, but each student had a bottle of ink to use with the penholders and steel pen points (no ballpoints until much later). Periodically the teacher would gather all the ink bottles to be refilled by the janitor. The teacher's desk was in the center of the room in front of the blackboard. Good eyesight was a distinct advantage to the children in the back rows. The movie "A Christmas Story" presents a good example of a Depression era elementary classroom. The furniture and kids' clothing are especially accurate. I too, wore an imitation leather aviator cap with snap-on goggles. There was always a neighborhood bully to keep us in good running condition. The classroom teacher taught all subjects, but we had traveling teachers for art, music and penmanship supervision. They served four elementary schools, all grades, one day per week.

Supplies from the Central Office included writing and art paper and a gallon of ink. Parents purchased crayons, paints, pencils, pens, textbooks and workbooks. Each September there was a huge used book sale by the P.T.A. The Parent-Teacher Association was very large in those days. Some parents had a sincere desire to help less fortunate families and children, and many parents joined to be helped. The P.T.A. benefited schools in many ways through volunteer work in lunch kitchens and clothing drives.

After graduating from Indiana University in 1950, I returned to Lincoln school as a teacher, replacing one of my former teachers who was retiring. I had twenty-five fifth graders and fourteen sixth graders assigned to my room. My first teaching contract was for $2,256 for nine months! Five years later I replaced my former principal, a wonderful woman who had held the position for 40 years.

"Dutchtown" and the "Huckster Wagon"

We moved to "Dutchtown" when I was twelve and I had to go to Junior High school across town. In Bedford's earlier years, Dutchtown was a neighborhood of many German families. There was even a German Methodist church, a small building with a tall steeple and a long bell rope in the entryway. I attended Sunday school there for several years there, but never got to ring that bell.

Our Dutchtown house was roomier and much better constructed than our last house. No more leaky roof or crowded bedrooms. We also had electricity but no water, and we still had the "two-holer" outhouse down on the alley. We had a corner lot with a town pump across the street. The water was very good and many neighbors used the well. Some carried buckets of water for more than a city block. I carried thousands of buckets of water from that town pump in the six years we lived in Duchtown. Dad always said it would build muscles and improve my golf game. Our family never lived in a house with indoor plumbing until after I was drafted. Although we had lived inside the city limits for thirteen years, an outhouse on the alley was standard for most houses in our neighborhood.

A busy family-owned neighborhood grocery store was just across the street on the other corner. The owner had two sons and so the business grew. The store allowed "credit" to its customers so families could "run the bill" for groceries as long as they paid up every week or two according to agreement. Another way to buy groceries was the country "huckster wagon". This was a long-established business in the horse and buggy days. Peddlers would outfit a wagon with goods and groceries, hitch up the horse and peddle their wares to families in rural areas. Most farm families only came to town to "trade" on Saturday.

In the mid-1930's our neighborhood grocery owners decided to revive this business so they purchased three old school buses, tore out the seats and installed bins and shelves to hold groceries. These "Huckster Wagons" were literally stores on wheels and they covered different rural routes five days a week selling groceries, kerosene and sacks of feed. The huckster wagon's driver could also accept eggs, chickens or produce for payment, so each bus had a rear platform for a kerosene barrel and one or two wooden chicken coops. Most of the county roads were paved with creek gravel or crushed stone. The huckster wagons came back to town covered with dust or mud, depending on the weather. We neighborhood boys could earn money hosing them down and re-stocking for the next morning's route.

The store also bought large flocks of chickens or bushels of produce for resale. Teenage boys were often hired to help deliver sacks of feed to a rural customer. We were also hired to go out at night with a truckload of chicken coops to catch half-asleep roosting chickens in some farmer's henhouse. Saturday was often "chicken-picking"day at the store, and jobs were available to kill, scald, pick feathers and "dress" the chicken for sale at the meat counter. That's one job I never applied for, but I loved to re-stock the buses each evening before they hit the road again the next day.

The Depression continued and we survived until the 1940's. Life was difficult, but our family and all the neighbors were in the same boat. We were a close family and had lots of fun doing simple activities in spite of financial hardships. Perhaps it made our generation stronger and more willing to learn, follow orders and succeed in school.

The Teen Years

Leaving for grades seven and eight in the Bedford Junior High school was a real psychological jolt for the sixth graders completing elementary school. We had to leave our neighborhood school and walk an additional seven blocks across town to an ancient three-story brick junior high school. We also faced a new daily class schedule of home rooms, study halls, and changing rooms and teachers for each subject. Gone was our classroom with one teacher all day. Gone was the security of belonging to one small group all day. Sixth graders from four city schools were grouped according to ability for junior high classes, so I lost old classmates and had to make new friends and adjust to new teachers, new subjects and moving from class to class in the big, old junior high school building. The gym classes and physical education were really great, and study hall required self-discipline to complete my lessons at school and avoid homework. Our health and science classes met in a lab room up narrow, winding stairs to the third floor. We always wished for a fire drill in this class. The rickety iron fire escape on the north side of the building was an adventure to scramble down on "Fire Drill Day". There was always a lot of talking and nervous giggling and the teacher yelling, "Boys, stop looking up!" Of course, teenage boys often didn't hear him!

Two years in junior high prepared us for the routine of high school. We had used the high school gym, cafeteria and auditorium so we were acquainted with the senior high school building, and the ritual of moving into the ninth grade was fairly easy. Most of my teachers in grades one through eight were older women. One of the most exciting events in the eighth grade was the "new teacher" hired in the elementary school next door on the campus. She was a buxom young blonde and a classy dresser. Most of us didn't know that there were young lady teachers! She later married our junior high coach.

My eighth grade English teacher, a customer on my paper route, organized debating teams as a class project. My team was paired against two top students. My buddy and I debated the question, "Is it better to live in the country or the city?." We argued for the country life and were soundly defeated. One of my opponents, Claude Akins, went on after WWII to become a movie and television star and character actor. His best-known television series of three was "Sheriff Lobo". I didn't feel too badly losing to Claude because he was a regular guy. I used to be embarrassed by the W.P.A. sewing shop clothes I wore, but he said they looked fine. However, my English teacher's paper missed her porch several times in the next week. Claude attended our high school class 50th reunion in 1994, and we played a round of golf.

Otis Park----I Discover Golf

After we moved to Dutchtown, the golf course became my source of income when my Dad arranged for me to caddy for the County Clerk. I carried that golf bag eighteen holes and earned the regular caddy fee of 50 cents plus a tip. I had discovered a grand new source of funds just as I was entering junior high school! Now I could buy a bicycle and clothes, so I caddied all summer at Otis Park golf course. Dad took me to the Goodyear store and made the down payment on a bike. It was up to me to earn the $1.25 weekly payments. I rode that bike for six years and handed it down to my brother. I was mobile; no more "shanks mare" for me. I rode to the golf course, school and on errands for Mom. I even taught my dog Zero to ride in the basket on the handlebars.

Caddying allowed me to earn money all summer. Being the youngest put me at the bottom of the "pecking order" at the caddyshack as several young men and adults were also caddies. Golfers had favorite caddies as regulars and we smaller boys got the duffers and low tippers. Occasionally when things got dull around the caddy shack, the big boys would grab us, march us down to the creek and throw us in, clothes and all. I got "cooled off" often but I enjoyed earning money and also Caddy Day when we got to play golf free! I started playing golf 65 years ago, and I'm still trying to learn the game! However, I have shot my age several times the past three years. It gets easier as you get older!

Caddies were treated as "minorities" in those days. We were required to stay down in the caddy shack beyond the parking lot. We were not allowed to hang around the clubhouse unless we wanted to buy something. This was especially hard because my classmates who weren't caddies could use the swimming pool and hang around the juke box in the clubhouse. I usually got an RC Cola and a small box of "Cheez-Its" for my fifteen cent lunch. We were the "untouchables" and stayed in our place until we were called up to caddy. I guess I learned something about intolerance and discrimination in the six years I caddied. I got better jobs as I got older, and by the age of sixteen I would often carry two bags and double my income. Hot summer days would find caddies "skinny dipping" in the Big Bend swimming hole in Leatherwood creek where it crossed the 15th fairway.

One summer the new golf pro hired me to work at the concession counter with his nephew. He only paid us a dollar a day for about five hours work. However, he said we could have free hamburgers and cokes. After about a month he fired us because we were eating up the profits! I really enjoyed that month out of the caddy shack because I got to sell food and cokes to all my classmates using the swimming pool, and listen to the Wurlitzer juke box records. I can still hear Tommy Dorsey's band with "I'm Getting Sentimental Over You".

Winter put an end to caddying, so I would get a paper route. The routes were long with subscribers spread over a large area. Many households could not afford the ten cents a week subscription. Others found it hard to pay up on Friday when I stopped to collect. I remember one instance when a customer owed me for four weeks and I decided I was going to get my money. A loud knock on the door brought no response so I stepped over to a window and I could see a movement in the house. I knocked again. Sure enough, there was movement in that room. I reached over to the door to knock again and saw the shadowy figure move more clearly. It was me! There was no one home, I had been seeing my own reflection in a mirror on the living room wall.

At age sixteen I went to work in a shoe repair shop. Shoe repair was a good business because people couldn't afford new shoes so they would have the cobbler replace their soles and heels. Many parents repaired the family shoes at home with a twenty-five cent shoe repair kit containing a pair of "stick-on" soles and a tube of glue. There were also iron "shoe lasts" with different sizes to nail on the "Cat's Paw" brand heels. My job as a cobbler's helper was to grind the edges of the new leather soles and heels and polish the newly repaired shoes. This was only a Saturday job unless we were on vacation from school. There was also a National Youth Corps program in high school where needy students could work 24 hours a month and earn $6.00. I thought 25 cents an hour was okay for staying after school and helping a history teacher I really liked.

I hit the big money at age 17 when I got a job at Bill's Auto store on the town square. I worked two hours after school and all day Saturday (8:00am to 9:00pm) for $6.00 per week. I kept this job until I went into the Air Corps. I worked at Bill's Auto store summers and weekends while I was in college and several years after I began teaching. When I needed a job, Bill's Auto would hire me at $1.25 per hour! I continued working part-time at Bill's for sixteen years.

Setting pins at the bowling alley became a source of income during my senior year. There were no automatic pin-setting machines in those days. The bowler would roll the ball and we would reset the pins by jumping into the pit and grabbing pins and putting them into the rack. We would put the ball up into the return gutter to send it back to the bowler, pull down the pin rack and hop up out of the pit while he rolled the ball again. We would hop back down, load the rest of the pins, send the ball back and draw down the pin rack to set the pins up for the next bowler. It was really a fast operation. We usually set two alleys at a time, and received the magnificent sum of 10 cents a game for each bowler. On League nights, with five men on a team, you could make good money if you set double. Leagues usually bowled three games so I could have a six dollar night! My senior year I was working at Bill's Auto store from 4:00pm to 6:00pm, would eat a snack, walk across the square and set pins from 7:00pm until 10:00pm. So, it's understandable why I weighed only 150 pounds when I was drafted.

Happy Days – High School

The Junior High School and High School were located in the same block with the basketball gym. The gym was the hub of athletic activity for sports fans. Basketball was king, and Bedford is still often regarded as the basketball capital of Indiana. In those days we had ten high schools in our county and we held our own sectional tournament each March. There was intense rivalry among the schools and basketball stars and coaches were local heroes. Many boys went on to play college basketball. The towns of Mitchell and Bedford both reached the state finals by 1943.

Many years later, the state encouraged school reorganization because of inflation and the need for more modern school buildings. Eventually eight high schools under the township trustee system were closed. A large school corporation was created on each side of White

James Lee Hutchinson, EdS

River which bisects the county. In 1965, Bedford North Lawrence Community Schools and Mitchell Community Schools emerged from reorganization. Both new corporations remain strong in all sports. Three state championships were won in the last decade of the century by Bedford-North Lawrence by girls and boys teams. New buildings and facilities have greatly improved educational opportunities for children. I was an administrative assistant to the superintendent at the time and am glad I had a small part in the process.

Hoover's Confectionary was our malt shop in the town square and was a popular hang-out for teenagers. Parking was scarce, but few of us had cars anyway. Shanks mare (walking) was the order of the day and if you did pick up a girl, you could enjoy walking her home. Parents in those days were very wary of a boy with a car! I first met my wife, June, at Hoover's. The confectionary featured Coneys, hamburgers, sodas, shakes and cokes---all at reasonable prices, and every booth had a juke box selection unit with six records for a quarter. Hoover's prices were very reasonable in 1941-42. Fountain cokes were five cents, sodas or shakes were fifteen cents, and Coneys were two for a quarter.

A former Bedford High basketball team member from those days recently told me this story. "We got meal money after each home game---50 cents if we won and 35 cents if we lost. We always went to Hoover's and ate well." The crowd was really big on Friday nights after the basketball games and on Saturday nights before the midnight movies, which started at 11:00pm. Standing on the sidewalk on the square in front of Hoover's was a good place to hang out----to see and be seen. Also, it cost nothing and all the girls passed by to enter the place! "Hubba-hubbas" and wolf whistles were usually appreciated! Firpo's was the other big teenage watering hole only a block from the high school. Firpo's was a rustic drive-in for those with cars. It was our Arnold's from the television show "Happy Days". Those without cars could always ride bikes or walk with the their dates.

The public square was the commercial center of our town (as in every county seat). Shopping malls hadn't been invented yet. There were many independently owned shops and stores along with Montgomery Ward and J.C. Penney stores. Saturday night saw every store open, and in warm weather people loved to walk around the square greeting friends and neighbors. Parking spaces were at a premium as families would park and watch the pedestrian paraders. All car windows were rolled down. Remember, there were no automobile air conditioners or televisions in those days. Our three movie theaters operated two movies and a serial all day starting early in the afternoon through midnight. Our little town of Bedford, with a population of 12,000, was an active community and county seat. The many small shops and businesses around the courthouse square had not yet faced the giant superstores of today. Sometimes we old-timers reminisce about all those many small businesses where we used to shop. We all remember high school days when the town square was full of stores and businesses and money was scarce. Today, the supermarkets and retail giants have closed the family-owned groceries and the small specialty stores. Business has moved out to the four-lane highway that bypasses our town square.

Money was still tight in 1940 and I was still wearing blue jeans and flannel shirts although I earned caddy money in the summer and bowling alley money in addition to my job at Bill's Auto store. I still have my $11 gold 1944 class ring. I wear it when I attend our monthly class get-together at Hobby's Inn, a local restaurant. That's one of the benefits of spending your life in a small hometown. Two dozen or so of the local high school class of 1944 survivors enjoy visiting and exchanging news of others who live out of town. We recently met for our 58th class reunion.

High school was loaded with older teachers intent on making scholars of all of us I enjoyed the freshman year with all the new teachers and classes. Lunch in high school, like my prior schools, was soup, Sloppy Joes and milk. I could have chili, a Sloppy Joe and a pint of milk for 25 cents. Later, I learned from my buddies that the grocery across the street also had a lunch. Jones' Grocery, a "Mom and Pop" enterprise, had a back room with benches around a pot-bellied stove. We could get two doughnuts and a pint of chocolate milk for twelve cents. For entertainment, boys could go down to the alley and smoke, or feed the Jones' milk goats in his barn. So guess where I ate lunch most of the time?

I joined the Bedford High Pioneer staff (the school yearbook) in 1941 and worked at the concession stands at all basketball games. It was great because I became concession stand manager my junior year and was in charge of buying supplies. I could get out of study hall and bicycle downtown to the two candy wholesale warehouses to buy gum, candy, and popcorn for the four stands the Pioneer staff operated at each home game. Things fell apart after Pearl Harbor. Each month it became harder to find anything to sell. Rationing had set in and sugar was at the top of the list making candy bars extinct. We ended the year selling dill pickles and popcorn! I inaugurated the Sadie Hawkins Day dance to raise funds for the yearbook. Sadie Hawkins was a character in "Li'l Abner" comic strip who was an old maid at eighteen. Her Pa, the mayor of Dogpatch, proclaimed a Sadie Hawkins race for the girls to chase the boys and drag them to the dance. We arranged to have boys buy votes for their girl friends to be elected "Daisy Mae", the prettiest girl in Dogpatch. It was a very successful fund-raiser and continued for several years.

Regular high school classes of math, English, Latin, and science were offered, but we also had a woodwork shop, limestone carving shop, art and a radio class. I took every art class because I loved to draw and paint. I always planned on attending the John Herron Art School in Indianapolis. I knew it was a long way from home (seventy-five miles), but that was my goal. I took the radio class my junior year as an elective course to learn Morse code. That class may have saved my life because in Air Corps basic training, I passed the aptitude test for radio operator school which allowed me another five months of training before leaving for Europe.

Pearl Harbor---December 7, 1941

I well remember the family sitting around the old Atwater-Kent radio to hear President Roosevelt's war speech to Congress after Pearl Harbor.

> "Yesterday, December 7, 1941---a date which will live in infamy---the United States of America was suddenly and deliberately attacked by naval and air forces of the Empire of Japan...."

The attack on Pearl Harbor destroyed our peaceful high school days. Nine days after the sneak attack by Japan, the Selective Service Act became law providing for the "common defense by increasing the armed forces of the United States and providing for its training". I was midway through my junior year, and was in the Army my senior year. The war gained momentum and more and more classmates prepared to enter the service. Few of us realized the danger we would face in the next four years, and the large number of friends and acquaintances who would be wounded or lose their lives. The families in these homes lived in constant fear of receiving that dreaded telegram: "The war department regrets to inform you......". Blue star banners decorated front doors of more and more houses. This emblem indicated the family had a son or daughter in the armed forces. As the war gained momentum and the draft board flew into action, larger numbers of boys entered the service, and several teachers went along. The draft age was lowered from age

20 to 18 in October, 1942. Most of those graduating went directly into the armed forces. Later, those blue star banners began to be replaced by gold star banners which indicated the family had lost a son who paid the ultimate price in the fight for freedom. There were eventually 126 gold star families in Lawrence county. Today, there is a limestone monument on the courthouse lawn to honor those who lost their lives fighting to defend our country. The 126 names are there, carved in limestone. There also more than 150 wounded and 36 prisoners of war in Lawrence county. Seventeen of those heroes who lost their lives were my former childhood playmates, neighbors or Bedford High class members. The Selective Service Act, or draft, was in full effect for all able-bodied men over the age of eighteen. We couldn't vote, but we could fight for our country. America was "on the ropes" and needed men in all branches of the service. Women were encouraged to join the services for non-combatant duty to free many servicemen for duty overseas. More than 200,000 women serviced in uniform between 1942 and 1945. Military duty was available in the following services:

    WAVES – Women's Reserve of the U.S. Navy

    WAC - Women's Army Corps

    WAF – Women in the Air Force

    WASP – Women's Air Force Service Pilots

    SPARS – U.S. Cost Guard Women's Reserves

    Women Marines – Marine Reservists

All males were required to register for the draft. Draft cards from 1A to 4F were issued to all men. The 1A card meant you would soon be called to service. A 4F card meant "unfit for service", usually for medical reasons. Deferments were allowed for men needed in defense plants, agriculture or other skills critical to the defense effort. Most students were classified as 1-A, ready to go!

President Roosevelt made a speech in June, 1941, part of which should be etched in every American's mind:

> "We too, born to freedom, and believing in freedom, are willing to fight to maintain freedom. We and all others who believe as deeply as we do, would rather die on our feet than live on our knees" (25).

Earlier, the President had warned that the United States must become "the arsenal of democracy".

War Time for Civilians on the Homefront

The attack on Pearl Harbor destroyed most of our Pacific Navy fleet except for the aircraft carriers. Our country was near panic and our sense of security shaken. The government forced the Japanese families living in California into several internment camps as a precaution against sabotage. A Civilian Observation Corps was organized nationwide. This air-raid watch and warning system used volunteers as Air-raid Wardens to search the skies for enemy bombers. Black-out drills and air-raid drills were practiced in schools. One of the nation's first air observation towers was erected in Cairo, Indiana. I remember one summer night in 1943 when I sat on a hill at the golf course and watched the entire town go dark as the air-raid siren screamed for a practice blackout. I didn't realize that before long, I would hear the real air raid warnings in England.

Life changed drastically after the U.S. entered the war. There were many shortages of food and materials. Gasoline and tire rationing began in late 1942. Rationing coupons were issued to conserve supplies. Rationing gasoline, tires, sugar, meat and coffee became a fact of life. Gas ration cards in class "A" allowed the driver only three gallons per week. There was a "B" card for workers driving to defense plants. The shortage of tires and innertubes was a huge problem. Hoarding was illegal, and motorists could only own five tires per car. Priorities were given to doctors and essential workers. A permit from the County Ration Board was needed to purchase a new tire. I was working at Bill's Auto Store, and we sold hundreds of innertube repair kits containing glue and rubber patches. There were also heavy patches (boots) to glue inside worn out tires to cover holes. Car repair parts were in great demand because no new cars were manufactured in 1942 through 1944. "Shade tree mechanics" did their best to keep people's cars on the road. Our auto industry concentrated on jeeps, trucks and tanks! Speed limits were lowered to 34 mph and carpools were encouraged to save gas and tires. This wasn't a drastic change, as many cars in those days couldn't go much faster. Locally, a railroad hauled defense workers twenty-five miles to the assembly lines at the new Crane Naval Ammunition Depot. This large Naval Depot was constructed in the county west of Bedford for the production and storage of shells and bombs. Crane is still an important facility for our national defense. A large Army munitions plant was constructed at Charlestown and many men and women from Lawrence county made the 120 mile round trip daily to work at the "powder plant". Special gas ration cards were available for defense workers in carpools. It was easy to identify these workers. They all had stained, yellow hands from working with the powder on the assembly line preparing powder charges for artillery shells.

Several of our idle stone mill buildings were converted for defense work making tanks and aircraft engine parts. A number of boys in my class became welders and worked nights until they too entered the armed services. Millions of women went to work in factories for $1.35 per hour and helped produce the planes, tanks, and ships needed for victory. "Rosie the Riveter" was one of the popular songs as workers built the "Arsenal of Democracy". Aircraft workers built approximately 230,000 airplanes for the war effort. The U.S. Army Air Corps became a force of over two million men and women before war's end. A large percentage of the aircraft workers were women who did the riveting in airplane construction. Norman Rockwell's famous painting of "Rosie the Riveter", a red-headed beauty with her riveting gun, appeared on the cover of The Saturday Evening Post. The original painting sold for 4.9 million dollars at an auction in May, 2002. Nationwide, thousands were employed in munitions plants. "Praise the Lord and Pass the Ammunition" became a popular war-time song. There were War Bond drives, and schools encouraged children to bring in loose change to purchase War Stamps. Defense plants in my home state of Indiana produced B-17 engines at the Studebaker factory in South Bend. The Allison Division of General Motors in Indianapolis made several thousand fighter engines. Evansville's Chrysler facility produced millions of .45 caliber bullets. Aircraft wings for the P-47 Thunderbolts were also made in Evansville by an appliance factory. Most importantly, an Indianapolis plant secretly produced 14,000 of the top-secret Norden bombsights. One of those famous bombsights is now on display in the Air History museum at Grissom Air Base in Peru, Indiana. A B-17 Flying Fortress and fourteen other World War II planes are also on display.

I had experienced the hardships of civilian life for about eighteen months. The armed forces needed more young men. Deferments to finish school were a thing of the past. The Selective Service called more and more young men and my turn came in August, 1943. They were "scraping the bottom of the barrel", and now I would experience the war!

Chapter Three
You're In the Army Now!

Well, there I was!!! Sitting in the radio room of a B-17 Flying Fortress with my electric suit plugged in, helmet, headsets, an insulated suit, parachute harness over that, a flak jacket, steel helmet, oxygen mask, and electric gloves and boots. My crew and I were flying over Berlin, with flak (anti-aircraft shells) bursting all over the sky around us. We were five miles high, on oxygen and it was 60 below zero! The bomb bay doors open, I could feel the flak bursts shaking the plane, and felt the sudden lurch of the plane upward when we released our bombs. How did I get here?

Oh, yes. It was June 12, 1943, my eighteenth birthday. I was a high school junior on summer break, needing only six credit hours to graduate. On June 13, 1943, I received my notice to register for Selective Service and was classified 1A. The " Order to Report for Induction" came on July 22nd. It read,

> "Greetings: Having submitted yourself to a local board composed of your neighbors for the purpose of determining your availability for training and service in the land or naval forces of the United States, you are hereby notified that you have now been selected for training and service therein. Your friends and neighbors ask you to serve your country. Report for examination August 4, 1943."

Sure, I was drafted, but when did I have time to enlist? They were taking everyone who was warm. If you didn't have a deferment, you were in uniform. I never made it back to Bedford High. There were a few deferments for workers needed in agriculture or critical skills in the defense industry. Then there were some medical deferments that were "suspect". They claimed "heart trouble". We always thought they didn't have the "heart" to go into service. One guy in our neighborhood went AWOL (absent without leave) and came home. The M.P.s (military police) found him hiding under his front porch and took him back to a guard house (jail). It was a stern lesson for all teenagers in the neighborhood.

I was inducted into the Army in Louisville, Kentucky on August 4, 1943. I had selected the Army over the Navy or Marines because I got to stay home another three weeks. So, on August 25th, a week before my fall semester of high school started, I was on a Greyhound bus headed for Fort Benjamin Harrison in Indianapolis. There were about 15 of us from Lawrence County. A ramrod straight corporal who immediately informed us that we were in the Army now and we had better "shape up" met our bus. He guided us to the supply room and we began the process of changing from draftees to Privates. We were issued tan summer uniforms and army boots. Everything else was "olive drab"; dress uniform, work clothes (fatigues), underwear and socks. Our "civies" were shipped home. Each man was issued his aluminum identification tags. These "dog tags" contained name, serial number and blood type and were to be worn on a chain around our necks as long as we were in the Army. I am still identified by my serial number when I visit a Veterans' Administration Clinic. They assigned us to our bunks in a large two-story barracks. We were scheduled for medical exams and shots the next day. The "Old Timers" who had shots the day before were quite willing to tell us about the shots, especially that six-inch square needle in the left testicle! We all hoped they were were lying---and they were!

I was in the infantry waiting for assignment. Duties for the guys in my barracks included mopping floors, cleaning the latrine and laying sod around the parade ground. One hot August day on the "sod detail" I guess I didn't move fast enough. They said I was "gold bricking" (loafing) so the next day the Corporal made me scrub the barracks stairs to the second floor with a bucket of soapy water and a toothbrush! I didn't mind it too much; at least I was not out in the hot sun all day, or on K.P. in the mess hall. Irving Berlin expressed it in his 1942 song:

"This is the Army Mr. Jones,
No private baths or telephones.

You've had your breakfast in bed before,

But you won't have it there anymore."

Basic Training in Texas

The Air Corps was a division of the U.S. Army during World War II and was seeking recruits. I immediately signed up and tested out of the infantry into the Air Cadet program. Two weeks in the infantry was enough for me! I was now a Volunteer Flight Trainee (VFT) and carried that designation throughout my Air Corps service. A few days later, several hundred VFT's boarded a troop train for basic training in Amarillo, Texas. I later learned that the Air Corps had recruited VFT's from all branches of the Army. Troop trains were our main means of transportation in the states. It was a three-day trip with no bunks, so we slept in our seats or on our pile of duffel bags in the back of the car. When we reached the camp in Amarillo, we were assigned barracks and issued bedding. Everyone had a burr haircut before leaving Fort Benjamin Harrison, but our new Corporal said we all needed a GI haircut. He marched us down to another barracks where the "non-coms" (non-commissioned officers) had set up a "barber shop". We were all clipped again for a 50-cent haircut. Most of us only had a few dollars but we contributed to the "fundraiser". We figured we had been "clipped" twice. One guy was so broke he wrote a letter home on toilet paper to ask for money.

We settled into our barracks designated as Training Group 904, Tech School 409. I was an Air Cadet ready for training as a pilot, navigator or bombardier, and I wasted no time purchasing a sterling silver Air Cadet ring which I still have. As enlisted men, we were earning $21 a month, so I bought the ring for thirteen dollars, sent money home, and was broke the rest of the month. I was a thousand miles from home, tired and lonesome.

Thomas Paine had it right in 1777 when he wrote,

> "Those who expect to reap the blessings of freedom must, like men, undergo the fatigue of supporting it."

Non-commissioned officers had almost as much authority as officers, and in basic training the Corporals and Sergeants laid down the law. As the saying goes, when Sarge said, "Jump" we yelled, "How high?" The guardhouse was full of "goldbricks" (slackers) who thought they could outwit the military system and "goof off" from their duties. It was understood that men in every fighting unit were expected to follow orders of their officers and "non-coms" without question; this was necessary for success in combat. Aircrews were especially dependent on every man doing his assigned job to the best of his ability. Basic training was an intensive program to make sure we all understood what the Army expected!

Army life was geared for the good of the group and there were some guys who felt they were treated unfairly. These whiners and complainers were usually told, "tough s--t". In other words, "Shut up and get with the program". This common expression was often the only sympathy given. Any G.I. griping around the barracks might be advised to go see the Chaplain and get his T.S. (tough s--t) card punched! Goals had been set for us and most of the boys expected to do their best to help win the war!

Our basic training group was mostly a group of high school kids. We were really "raw recruits", mostly from Indiana and Ohio. Most of us were farther away from home than we had ever been. I was amazed that my first train ride had ended 1,000 miles from home in a hot and dusty Army camp. Our basic training schedule kept us from being homesick. Our daily drill ran from the 6:00 am roll call and march to the mess hall, until suppertime dismissal and mail call. We were generally too fatigued to worry about anything other than mail, food and rest. If misery loves company, we had it in spades! Mail call was a high point in our day. Everyone looked forward to letters from family and friends. Mail was a great morale builder. Letters were our connection to our homes in the Midwest. My mother kept the postal service busy and I got more than my share of letters. I answered all my mail and encouraged friends to keep me posted on all the news at Bedford High. I still have some of those letters with the three-cent stamp.

We were up and in formation for roll call each morning at 6:00 am. It was cold enough for a field jacket over our fatigues until the sun rose. After inspection our drill sergeant had our formation double-time it to the mess hall for breakfast. Often it was scrambled eggs and French toast but there was also the dreaded chipped beef and gravy on toast. Some called it beef stroganoff we called it s--t on a shingle!

Sergeant Sakakini loved to yell the order "double time", and our formation often ran to build our lungs. Singing while marching was also a "lung builder!" I remember many of those patriotic songs like "You're a Grand Old Flag" and "I've Got Sixpence". Singing also lifted our spirits while undergoing the rigors of basic training. Marching, close order drill and being processed through the training made up those rugged days.

We stood in line quite often in the Army. We moved as a barracks group, so there was always a line. Extra long lines were caused when there was a SNAFU (situation normal all fouled up) by some drill sergeant who didn't get the word. At least, that's what we buck privates said. "Hurry up and wait", was our comment for this phase of our training. Our favorite line was the "chow line" at the Mess Hall.

The drilling and marching in the Texas heat took a lot of energy. It was cool at night and blistering hot by noon. By afternoon dismissal we were all so dusty and sweaty that we usually went into the showers fully dressed. We washed fatigues and shoes and wore them back to the barracks to dry out. Everybody had two sets of fatigues and shoes, so it was a neat deal and we had clean clothes every morning for inspection. We polished those shoes until you could see your face in them. We could buy a special cloth at the PX (Post Exchange) for polishing our brass belt buckles and uniform insignia. Our barracks had to pass Friday inspections to get those Saturday passes to go into Amarillo. We loved those short passes and time away from the base. We liked to spend time at the Amarillo USO Club. It was a great place to relax and forget barracks life for a few hours. The hostesses welcomed us with coffee, cokes and snacks. The USO with its overstuffed furniture, music and reading materials was a comfortable place to hang out and regroup before returning to reality. The USO Clubs were very important to servicemen wherever we were stationed.

Saluting was a part of our military training and enlisted men understood the need for respect of officers in leadership and command positions. Failure to salute on base could result in a good "chewing out" or other punishment. However, it seemed to be a different situation when we were in town on a pass. We soon learned that some officers were impressed with their rank and importance and demanded that snappy salute while on the streets of Amarillo. When our group saw one of these officers, we formed a single line as we passed and forced him to return every salute he was given! Saluting was seldom required once we entered the combat zone. Every man was expected to do the best job for the war effort and all were respected for their skills.

The Post Exchange, or "PX," was an Army-operated store on the base which carried souvenirs, stationary and personal items. It also served ice cream soft, drinks and sandwiches. Supper was usually okay at the Mess Hall but just in case, we always had the soda fountain at the PX. Temperatures fell rapidly after sunset and we had a few hours to enjoy the cool evening and relax.

The word "police" was used by the Army for duty involving keeping the camp clean. K.P. (kitchen police) was one of the most dreaded. It meant a busy day in the hot, steamy mess hall preparing and serving meals. Cleaning up was even worse. Scrubbing pots and pans and the large cookers was rough duty. However, the dreaded "China Clipper" (dishwasher) was the wettest and hottest duty. Operators loaded the metal serving trays and kitchen utensils into wooden trays and shoved them down a conveyor belt and into the steaming dishwasher. The worst job was unloading the hot trays. K.P. was a tough day's work, but it was a duty that every G.I. pulled. Actually, I thought the mess hall a pretty good place to spend a day off from drill. I also loved having access to all that good food. It was just the thing for a skinny teenager and I really enjoyed the extra goodies to boost my energy. One day the cook got after me for eating too much of the sliced pineapple.

Latrine orderly was another duty that required a day of mopping floors and cleaning. The large company area restroom building served several hundred men. A soldier was assigned daily to clean showers, sinks, urinals and stools. He was to keep the latrine clean all day. It was a real "Mr. Clean" experience, and your work was always subjected to a surprise inspection by the Officer of the Day. I remember one instance of using a razor blade to clean the stains off the inside of the stools. Unlike Private Will Stockdale in "No Time for Sergeants", we VFT trainees never drew permanent latrine duty, we were needed elsewhere!

Yardbird duty was a walk in the sun, assigned to two or three guys at a time. We had to "police our camp area", in other words, pick up all paper, cigarette butts and trash that had been blown or thrown on the ground. Our equipment included a large sack with a shoulder strap and a broomstick with a sharp nail in the end. Of course, our barracks leader, Corporal Gannon, checked our work before we could quit. It helped a great deal that camp rules required soldiers on break to "field strip" (tear apart) their cigarette butts. Candy wrappers, coke cups, and such were to be carried in their pockets until a trash can became available. This rule was not debatable.

Basic training was the start of the Army's favorite routine---inspection. I stood inspections wherever I was stationed until I went overseas. Inspections by sergeants and officers covered parades, full dress uniform and barracks. Our drill sergeant "toured" our barracks weekly and our corporal constantly urged us to keep our small bunk area clean. Each man had a bunk-bed, clothing rack and foot locker and was responsible for his side of the bunk. Everyone in the barracks wanted the floor clean, so we all chipped in and bought a bag of sweeping compound to keep our concrete floor shining. One day Sarge said the floor was clean enough to eat from.

We usually stood "barracks inspection" in clean work fatigues. Our dress uniform and extra clothes were hung properly, our footlocker lid open and our bunk made so tightly you could bounce a dime on the blanket! It was a "spit and polish" affair. We polished our boots and brass belt buckles for extra effect. Our footlocker was a wooden box about the size of a small trunk. It contained personal items such as socks and underwear, all clean and neatly arranged. We all stood at attention as the "brass" passed down the aisle. Occasionally the inspecting officer wore white gloves to search for dust! Failing inspection had dire consequences, such as KP duty or loss of a 12-hour pass.

We all had the standard basic training activities to prepare us to be fighting men. I drew guard duty twice. The first time I was assigned to guard a gate at the airfield. I was dressed in full summer uniform and they gave me an unloaded rifle and told me to challenge all who passed. So, I challenged a General who had just gotten off a plane. I said, "Halt, who goes there?" He responded, "Get out of my way soldier!" Well, that wasn't the right answer but I let him pass. Legally, I guess I could have shot him—but I had no bullets. I was a lot like Barney Fife in those days. They trusted me with the gun, but not the bullets! My next guard duty was at night. They put three of us inside the camp prison with no guns! There were four or five barracks and a latrine surrounded by a ten-foot fence topped with barbed wire. Guard duty consisted of walking up and down the boardwalks in front of the barracks and latrine. We were to sound the alarm if any of those deserters, rapists or murderers came out of the barracks before dawn, or caused any problems. I don't know what possible good we could have done in case of trouble. Maybe the Officer of the Guard thought our screams, while the prisoners were beating up on us, would sound the alarm and give him time to call for re-enforcements!

Kilroy Was There, Too

"Kilroy" was one of the first guys recognized by all servicemen in World War II. He appeared everywhere on every military base. This fictional character was a cartoon figure with a long nose, peeking over a board fence. Servicemen secretly drew him on walls, restroom doors and equipment. The appeal of "Kilroy" was wartime graffiti! The Kilroy drawing was reportedly copied from an Army sergeant named Kilroy. He would inspect and inventory equipment and write "Kilroy was here" on it (19).

Our class spent September, October and November in basic training, marching, marching, and marching. Summer was extremely hot, dry and dusty in Amarillo. Actually, the dust is sand and blows into the barracks through cracks around doors and windows. The heat of the day was lost as soon as the sun went down. We had summer barracks but no fans. The wind was so strong that the barracks were anchored with steel cables at each corner. Group latrines were located in a separate building in the center of several barracks. One night, about 3:00 am, I ran to the latrine in my shorts and hit a cable about chest high. I did a complete flip and landed on my back. I got up and limped the rest of the way to answer Mother Nature's untimely call.

The rifle range was a fun experience. We trained with rifles, carbines and a tommy-gun (machine gun). We would line up on the firing line with loaded rifles (only one shell). The Sergeant would give the command, "Ready on the firing line." The targets would go up and he would yell, "Fire at will." Invariably, some guy would yell,

"Which one is Will?" The tommy-gun was fun because when firing, the gun barrel would climb, which was a good reason to fire short bursts. We also spent our time pulling targets in the pits. After each group fired we would pull down the target, patch it with a square of paper, raise the target back up and use a long pole with a red disk to mark where the shooter hit the target. We waved "Maggies' Drawers" for those guys who completely missed the target. Maggies's Drawers was a red flag in the shape of a large pair of drawers. Apparently Maggie was a big girl! Everyone in our barracks eventually won the coveted "marksmanship medal" which was our first decoration!

There was a full dress parade (summer uniforms) every Saturday afternoon in the full heat of the day. Each barracks would march to the parade ground and into their proper place. We would stand at attention until ordered to "march in review" past the dignitaries in the reviewing stand. If the base commander didn't like our marching, he would order every formation off the field and we would do it again! Each barracks formation (40 men) had a soldier who marched in the front line carrying our "guidon", (a small red and white pennant on a long pole). The Sergeant picked Oscar, a six-foot, five-inch big man to be our guidon. Oscar was very military and enjoyed the honor. One blazing hot parade day we had spent a long time in formation at attention when guys began fainting. They were falling like bowling pins. Drill Sergeant Sakakini and his helpers were creeping in from the back and dragging guys to the rear. He was yelling, "Stand at attention—eyes straight ahead, dammit!" We were doing our best until up front Oscar and his guidon fell like a redwood tree. I think he was still at attention after he fainted!

There were forty of us in the barracks, but most of us "washed out" of the cadet program. Only three continued as Air Cadets. The rest of us were suddenly aerial gunnery volunteers! Aerial gunners received a few months of gunnery and air crew training and then sent overseas. Fortunately, I had completed a radio class in high school, so I passed a radio-aptitude test for radio operator training school which delayed my arrival in Europe by about five months. I would later realize that this was a fortuitous delay.

Radio Operator Training

Although I had "washed out" as an Air Cadet, I was ready for radio school. We completed basic training and a group boarded a troop train on Thanksgiving Day, 1943. Our destination was Sioux Falls, South Dakota, otherwise known as the "frozen north". Several of the southern boys had never seen snow. They were really excited but their enthusiasm faded after a few days in ankle-deep snow and zero weather. There was also a housing problem; we still had "warm climate" barracks with three pot-bellied stoves for heat. Our new address was squadron 809, barracks 421. The latrine to serve several barracks was 100 yards out the back door, a real problem when it was minus zero!

There was a great bunch of guys in our barracks and also a few characters. One guy "Joe" was a pest. Several times he came in late from a pass in town and woke everyone in the barracks. He was drunk and loud and usually came running through the barracks and dived into his bed. We got tired of his antics after a few weeks. One Saturday night after he left for town, we put his steel cot up in the rafters. About midnight he came in yelling and running as usual and dived for his bed. He landed spread-eagled on the concrete floor. Of course we were all awake to see the show! Then we helped him get his bunk out of the rafters. He got the message! He was the same guy who boasted that he was going to flunk out so he wouldn't have to go overseas. He achieved his goal. A year and a half later I was at Baer Field, Ft. Wayne, Indiana, awaiting my honorable discharge. One day I was going through the chow-line at the mess hall and there was "Joe" serving food. He had pulled every trick in the book to avoid going overseas and had earned very few "points" towards early discharge. He was on permanent K.P. duty! I don't know if he ever got out of service. Tom was another memorable character in our barracks. He was a "gold brick,"a slob, his bunk area was always a mess and his personal hygiene left a lot to be desired. He usually had a certain "air" about him and his top bunk was empty because his buddy had moved to another bunk. One week our barracks nearly failed inspection and our weekend passes could have been lost! The next week a "committee" ushered Tom to the showers and made him scrub up with a bar of laundry soap. He was warned to clean up his bunk and footlocker before the next inspection. Tom got the message! Those Saturday passes were important to our morale.

Through These Eyes

It was so cold that we had to leave one man out of the class everyday to be barracks guard. His job was to keep the pot-bellied stoves fired up. There was also the duty of keeping the gallon can of water on each stove filled---they were our humidifiers. Temperatures were below zero most of the winter. We wore lots of clothing to march to the classrooms in the middle of the camp and often wore gas masks to protect our faces against the severe winter temperatures. Those southern boys really missed home! Saturday passes were available, but before we were allowed to leave the base we had to pass clothing inspection. Every soldier had to be wearing the required winter uniform or be sent back to the barracks. The guards at the gate made us get off the bus and checked for knit caps, long johns, boots, gloves and overcoats. In spite of wearing everything I had, I still got pneumonia and spent a week in the base hospital. I always blamed my illness on the poor food at the mess hall. They had a rule that you had to eat all the food they plopped on your tray. Often, it was so bad that I wrapped it in my napkin and carried it out in my pocket. I guess I skipped too many meals in favor of milkshakes and candy bars at the PX. However, I managed to catch up with my classes and my barracks buddies.

Radio school consisted of six hours of classes Monday through Friday with time equally divided between Morse code and radio mechanics. The classroom had mock-ups with all radio equipment arranged in the same space it would be on a plane. We had to become proficient on the Morse code sending key, at least 20 words per minute. Code was the long distance communication link for bombers. We also had to be competent in radio repair. One of my instructors was Jim Guthrie from my hometown. After the war, he became a banker, local historian and fellow Rotarian. He married a girl from my high school class and later served two years as chairman of the Indiana Sesquicentennial Commission. Several of us became close pals while suffering the rigors of five months of radio school. One pal, Keen Umbehr, and I exchanged visits while in England. He was with the 486th Bomb Group near the down of Sudbury. We have recently exchanged letters and photos.

Sioux Falls was an interesting town. The Chamber of Commerce called it, "The Meeting Place of the Northwest". We saw the frozen falls on the Big Sioux river and much of the city. We would often board a city bus for a dime and ride around town. We were really wild and crazy guys! We also loved the USO club and the Nickel Diner. There was also a music hall that featured big bands and dancing on the weekends. It was a great break from Army training routine, and several big name bands performed that winter. The city had a large meatpacking industry. The war had created a need for part-time workers. Some soldiers would work there during weekends for the extra money. I never gave up my free time; all I needed was a few dollars for passes and milkshakes, cokes and Hershey bars at the PX!

The city had its own ace fighter pilot, Col. Joe Foss, a Marine pilot in the South Pacific. Foss shot down 26 Japanese planes over Guadacanal in 1942. He was awarded the Congressional Medal of

Honor and was named America's number one ace when pictured on the cover of LIFE magazine. There was a story of how he had buzzed the airbase in his F-4 Wildcat fighter. Joe Foss later served as Governor of South Dakota and commissioner of the American Football League. He passed away recently in December, 2002 at the age of eighty-seven.

Gunnery School, Yuma, Arizona

Spring finally came to South Dakota and we were graduated from radio school. We had completed six months of training in electronics and Morse code. Many "washed out", but we graduates passed equipment operation and repair tests and could send and receive over twenty words per minute in Morse code. Now that summer was coming, it was time for us to go to a hot climate. In May, we boarded a troop train for aerial gunnery school in the desert at Yuma, Arizona. Temperatures rose from 40 degrees to 90 degrees on that three-day troop train trip to Yuma and aerial gunnery school. We had sleeping cars this trip and I got a top bunk under the ventilator. I woke up the first morning with soot from the train smokestack all over my face! I reversed my sleeping position the rest of the trip. In three days, we went from the frozen north to the land of orange and lemon trees. Yuma was boiling hot all summer. "How hot was it?" It was so hot that we were required to wear silver-painted helmet liners to prevent heat exhaustion. The cooling and humidifying systems in our barracks consisted of rain gutters suspended from the rafters under dripping water pipes. Fans circulated the moist air through the barracks. It was really a welcome change from that hot desert sun. Once again we faced heat, dust or sand storms like those at Amarillo. The temperature went down with the sun, and nights were cool and welcome..

Our training included indoor classes on .50 caliber machine guns and aircraft recognition. We practiced taking apart and reassembling those guns for weeks. Our final test was to take a .50 caliber machine gun apart and reassemble it in five minutes while blindfolded. It had approximately 150 parts. There were many hours of aircraft recognition. They taught this class with slide projectors flashing instant slides of German and Japanese fighters. The common joke around the barracks was, "We'll recognize the enemy planes 'cause they'll be the ones shooting at us!" We also learned to recognize all U.S. fighters. They wanted to be sure we would only fire at the enemy!

We endured the outdoor classes in gunnery all summer. First we used shotguns in "skeet" shooting. The "skeet range" was an oval track around twelve target shacks. The class took turns in the target shack loading and firing "clay pigeons" (targets) for the guys firing a shotgun at the targets sailing through the air. The country boys who had spent several years hunting took to the "skeet range" like a duck takes to water. However, many guys had never fired a shotgun and we had a lot of black and blue shoulders because of the shotgun's "kick" when fired. Later, we took turns riding around the track in the back of pick-up trucks with special braces to support the student and instructor. The object was to hit the flying clay pigeon while traveling 25-30 miles per hour. The "trick" was to lead the target by aiming "behind" it to compensate for the speed of the truck which imitated the speed of a bomber and the shot (bullets) would catch up with the target. Two of my toughest work duties were at Yuma. One day I drew K.P. in the big mess hall and they forgot to relieve me. I spent fourteen hours on duty. Another time they took our class to the flight line to unload .50 caliber ammunition boxes from a railroad car. The temperature inside that boxcar was really the hottest duty I ever experienced.

The last phase of our training was becoming familiar with aerial gunnery from a B-17 bomber in flight. This was what we had been waiting for! We flew in B-17s and fired machine guns from the waist gunner position at targets on the ground on the desert floor firing range. One day they asked for volunteers. They said a plane had crashed in the desert and we could get souvenirs. I passed (you never volunteer), but several of my buddies spent the day erecting air-to-ground targets in the hot desert sun! Our last training was air-to-air gunnery. We spent two weeks firing the .50 caliber machine gun at a long cloth sleeve target towed on a very long cable by another plane flying ahead of us. The waist gun was fed six-inch bullets in a metal belt hanging from an overhead ammo canister. Bullets in sections of the belt were painted different colors. Our gunnery instructor assigned a color to each of us. He could later examine the target sleeve to see how many "hits" were made by each man. The chattering machine gun, swagging ammo belts and brass shell casings spewing onto the floor added a new dimension to our training. I got a kick out of learning about the plane and radio room. Gunnery school was our first experience flying on a B-17. Twelve of us were on each flight and we were allowed to roam through the plane from the tail-gun position to the plexiglass nose. The big thrill was to walk across the narrow catwalk through the bomb bay when the bomb bay doors were open! You could see the desert scenery rushing beneath, several thousand feet below. It was especially exciting since we had no parachutes!

Yuma was an interesting sun-baked Western town. We were especially interested in the irrigated yards with grass---an unusual sight. Our first pass to town was an interesting experience. My buddy and I went into a nice air-conditioned bar for a couple of beers. We stepped out into the blazing noonday sun and almost went to our knees when that alcohol hit us. On our next pass we decided to try tequila but we stayed in the bar until it wore off. One sample was enough. We finished gunnery school in the fall and it was time for us to move north! Our destination was Lincoln, Nebraska where we would be assigned to a base for aircrew training.

The "fortunes of war" would decide my future assignment, but the uncertainty kept me on pins and needles. There were three "big questions". What type of bomber would I get? Where would I go for training? Which theater of war would I draw?

However, I was already on cloud nine. I had successfully completed the radio and aerial gunnery schools. I was as proud as a peacock. I had won my coveted silver (pewter) gunner's wings and there were Corporal's stripes on my sleeves! I was no longer a "buck private". I was ready for the next challenge.

Combat Crew Training

We left Yuma on a troop train to Lincoln, Nebraska for a few days of testing and reassignment. Here, I met Harold Brock, another man from my hometown and brother of the girl Jim Guthrie later married. August 1944, I arrived at Sioux City, Iowa for aircrew training and was assigned to the crew of Lt. Bill Templeton, and began flying in a B-17 Flying Fortress. The first "big question" had been answered!

Our crew of ten soon settled in at our new airbase and were eager to get into a bomber. We had all ridden in a B-17 during previous training, but now we were into the combat training phase. The B-17 Flying Fortress had proven its value in countless raids over Germany and that was in our future, so we wanted the best! The silver bird was 74 feet long with a 103 foot wing span. The four 1200 horsepower engines and three-bladed propellers insured that the plane had the power to get us to a target and back safely. Training was serious ---this was our last training before going to Europe or the Pacific for combat. The B-17 was a well-designed bomber. It was easy to fly and operated well at high altitude. Early raids had proven that the plane could take a lot of punishment and return safely to base. The B-24 was faster and carried a bigger bomb load, but it was harder to fly in the thin air at high altitude. Both planes were heavily armed. The Flying Fortress carried thirteen .50 caliber machine guns and could fire at attacking fighters from any direction. The Liberator was similarly armed with waist and tail guns and turrets that swiveled for protection. Designers had thought these planes could defend themselves while flying alone but German fighters disproved that theory!

Pilot Bill Templeton and co-pilot Dale Rector were in the cockpit. Navigator, Bruno Conterato and bombardier Walter "Benny" Benedict had desks in their plexiglass nose section. Engineer Ewing "Rod" Roddy had a jump seat behind the pilot and could step into his top turret in a second. My radio room was just behind the bomb-bay. The other gunners had seats in the waist area. Ball turret gunner, Wilber Lesh, sat where he could quickly open a hatch and climb into the cramped space of that ball that hung under the bomber. Waist gunners, Orville "Robby" Robinson and Bert Allinder, had benches at each window at their gun positions. Tail-gunner, Ralph Moore, had to crawl down past the rear landing tail wheel to his small seat behind the twin machine guns that provided an extra "stinger" for the bomber. The top and ball turrets also had twin machine guns and were powered to rotate 180 degrees. Gunners remained at their combat positions while over enemy territory.

Our crew represented a cross-section of our country as not one of us was from the same state. We ranged from Connecticut to Oklahoma and received our training in many sections of the country. For example Bert Allinder completed armorer school in Denver, Colorado, and gunnery school in Reno, Nevada. Ewing Roddy completed aircraft mechanic school in Amarillo, Texas, and gunnery school in Kingman, Arizona. Roddy and I, in a recent phone conversation, decided that he arrived at Amarillo about the time I was shipping out to radio school. We were all in training in the same time period and fate placed us on the same crew. I credit the guys on my crew for saving my life on those combat missions. They were a great bunch of guys and we adjusted very well as a crew. For the first time since leaving Fort Harrison I had a nice two-story barracks with indoor plumbing and a furnace. We all became buddies while learning our crew positions on the B-17 and preparing for overseas.

The radio area was perfect with its small desk and window. I even had a sunroof, but they had removed the machine gun. At last, I had my own office with scads of radio equipment on the desk and bulkhead (wall) in front of me. The Liaison heavy-duty transmitter and receiver for long distance sending by Morse code were bolted to the bulkhead behind my swivel chair. The receiver and telegraph key were fastened to my desk. There was also a transmitter and receiver for long distance voice communication, an FM set for inter-squadron voice use by the pilot, and an IFF (identification, friend or foe) transmitter. There was also a radio compass for use in navigation, and ten intercom stations for crew members. The plane had an electrically-operated winch to reel out a trailing wire antenna for the Liaison radio. We had three months of flight training to become a combat crew. We had ground training too, but it was those hours in the plane that we loved, flying over Iowa and South Dakota. We practiced take-offs and landings, bombing runs and night flights. Our final tests were long distance flights to "bomb" other air bases in Boise, Idaho or Dalhart, Texas. These were great exercises in preparation for the real thing. We came together as a crew and a cohesive unit knowing that our survival depended on our skills. We had to be a top team to bring a bomber home from every mission. I am thankful I was a member of Lt. Templeton's crew. Wilbur Lesh, our ball gunner, talked me into riding in his ball turret while we were on one of our night flights over Sioux City. It was really weird to be hanging under the plane in that goldfish bowl. It was a beautiful view of the city lights but I never tried the ball turret again.

Lesh and Robinson were the two married men in our crew. We met both of the wives when they came to Sioux City to visit their husbands. They were lovely girls and the rest of us were more than a little envious of our buddies. Our crew trained hard and enjoyed our weekend passes into town. Our favorite hangout was a place called the Town Pump. It was downtown just off the main drag, down an alley in a basement! It was a popular spot with enlisted men. The officers hung out in more expensive places. One night the officers decided to treat us to dinner and drinks at one of the fancy hotels. Their intent was to get the enlisted men drunk. That plan backfired and we ended up putting them on the bus back to the base. However, the bombardier "escaped" and was last seen following a couple of girls down the street!

Aircrew training included practice landings by the B-17s for the pilot and co-pilot. Once, on a day when we weren't flying, one plane came in for a landing too fast and crashed into another plane on the runway. The base fire trucks responded to fight the flames. We saw one fireman's hat blow off and they stopped the fire truck to pick it up! Several guys died in the accident. That didn't give us much confidence in the base fire department. Sioux City was a fine town and people were kind to us because they knew we would be overseas in combat before too long. It was mid-October, near the end of training, when the second and third "big questions" were answered. We were to be combat replacement crews for the Eighth Air Force and our planes were waiting for us in England. That was just the assignment we had wanted.

Well, I wasn't a pilot, navigator or bombardier, but I was still a VFT. I would just be sitting in the radio room behind the bomb bay instead of in front of it! We finished our crew training and received a five-day pass, not really long enough to go home to Bedford, Indiana. I had decided not to attempt the trip, but Bert Allinder encouraged me to go, even if I only got to see my family for one day before going overseas. I'll always be thankful that he talked me into that hasty train trip. I did manage a day at home for a family get-together and family portrait before I climbed back on the Monon and headed for Sioux City and overseas combat duty. My mother fixed a fried chicken box lunch for the train ride. That was the best cold chicken I ever ate.

A few years ago, my wife June and I drove past the Sioux Falls airfield where I spent the winter of 1943-44 learning Morse code and radio mechanics. We went on down the interstate to spend the night in a Motel 6 at the Sioux City airport. I think that motel was somewhere near the location of our old aircrew training barracks.

Off to Camp Kilmer and Overseas

The highlight of my troop train ride to Camp Kilmer, New Jersey was the fact that someone stole all the money out of my billfold while I was asleep. I was ready to go overseas just the way I was when I went into the army--broke! Camp Kilmer was just across the harbor from New York City. We country boys were really impressed with the harbor and that skyline full of skyscrapers so near and yet so far away. We heard rumors that we would get a 48-hour pass into the big city before we sailed. We should have known they weren't going to turn us loose in New York City. We could see the anchored Queen Mary in the harbor and that was all we were going to see.

On November 4 (my mother's birthday), 1944, I lugged my duffel bag up the gangplank of the Queen Mary in New York harbor. The band was playing a rousing march—it was "Our Director," the tune to Bedford High's school song! Talk about irony! We sailed past the Statue of Liberty, headed for the United Kingdom and the Eighth Air Corps. We spent six days on the high seas, with the icebergs, flying fish, German submarines, lifeboat drills, and Mickey Rooney! Mickey was with the USO, going to Europe to entertain the troops. He put on a great show on the boat for us. One day, while on the boat, I was leaning against the rail and found Fred Berretta's name carved in the rail. Fred was a Bedford boy, and an All-American basketball player at Purdue University in Indiana! The "Queen" was such a large and fast ocean liner that she crossed the North Atlantic without the protection of a Navy convoy. The German U-boats (submarines) were prowling in their deadly "Wolf Packs", but we sailed merrily along taking evasive action, dropping depth bombs and holding daily lifeboat drills. They would sound the drill alarm and every man had to grab his life preserver and fall into formation on the top deck.until the "all clear" sounded. I was completely fascinated by the large waves of the North Atlantic, and the fact that the ship didn't have enough lifeboats for all its passengers!

They had taken all the luxurious furniture and beds out of the staterooms to prepare it as a troop ship. We were on the "A" deck, and our room had been equipped with six hammocks for sleeping. They were tricky to climb into and we had to adjust to the roll of the ship through the waves. The large swimming pool area had been converted into a giant dining hall. We were served two meals a day. Breakfast was normal, but the mid-afternoon "dupper" was mostly boiled vegetables. They seemed to have a surplus of brussel sprouts. I swear we had them four or five days. I only got seasick once, but that was enough.

The Queen Mary and her sister ship the Queen Elizabeth each transported thousands of troops to and from Europe during WWII. Today, the Queen Mary is docked at Long Beach, California as a tourist attraction and convention center. A new Queen Elizabeth II was completed in 1969. The original ship which had transported thousands of troops was sold to become a floating hotel and convention center in the Florida Everglades. That business venture failed and the giant liner was moved to Hong Kong to become a floating university. It was refurbished and was ready to sail when it caught fire and sank in the harbor, January 1972. A new Queen Mary II, costing $780 million replaced the Queen Elizabeth II in 2004.

Basic Training Buddies in Amarillo
Front: L to R, Bill Irk and Art Carnahan
Back: Hutch and Don Goodfellow

Sioux Falls
Radio School barracks buddies:
Kneeling, author, George John, Stu Holcomb
Standing, Keen Umbehr

Yuma

Gunnery School pals: front; Farrell and Hirshdeirfer

Back; Johnson, Jobe, Hook, and Jones

Aerial Gunnery School – Yuma, AZ
I'm really in the Army now!

"Kilroy" Was Everywhere!

Sioux City, Iowa, Crew Training, Oct. '44
Enlisted men of the Bill Templeton crew
L to R, Front; Ralph Moore, Orville Robinson, Ewing Roddy
Rear; Wilbur Lesh, Bert Allinder, Lee Hutchinson.

PILOT BILL TEMPLETON VISITS OUR BARRACKS

Front row L-R Lt. Templeton, pilot; Bert Allinder, armor-gunner; Ewing Roddy, engineer-gunner.

Back row, L-R Wilbur Lesh, ball-turret gunner; Ralph Moore, tail-gunner; Lee Hutchinson, radio-gunner; Orville Robinson, waist-gunner.

Radio operator desk with code key

Long range transmitters in radio room

Chapter Four
Early Air War---The Eagles Gather

Great Britain and France declared war on Germany in September, 1939, to aid Poland. Hitler's armies had control of most of Europe. Poland surrendered after four weeks and German troops advanced across France. British forces withdrew back across the English Channel from Dunkirk and prepared to defend their homeland. New Prime Minister, Winston Churchill, addressed the House of Commons June 4, 1940 and warned that British citizens must mobilize to defend their country.

"We shall not flag or fail. We shall go on to the end. We shall fight in France, we shall fight on the seas and oceans, we shall fight with growing confidence and growing strength in the air, we shall defend our island whatever the cost may be, we shall fight on the beaches, we shall fight on the landing grounds, we shall fight in the fields and in the streets, we shall fight in the hills; we shall never surrender." (25)

France surrendered and six weeks later Hitler announced his plans to invade England with massive bombing raids and troop invasions across the English Channel. Operation "Sea Lion" was launched.

The Battle of Britain in 1940 was a crucial period when England fought off the German air raids designed to precede a German invasion. The young RAF (Royal Air Force) pilots in their swift Spitfire and Hurricane fighters fought valiantly against overwhelming odds. Hitler had ordered a "blitz", and German bomber air raids pounded London from July to October, bombing military and non-military targets. This was part of his plan to terrorize Britain into surrendering as most European countries had done once his troops and Luftwaffe attacked. Thousands of homes, businesses and factories were destroyed and casualties were very high. Blackouts were required every night; no lights, not even a cigarette was to be shown. Auto headlights were covered except for a small cross of light to warn pedestrians. Until the end of the war in 1945, many people slept in the tube (underground subways). Families would bring bedding for the steel bunk beds or sleep on mats on the concrete floor in the "Tube" (subway) every night because of the threat of German air raids. Air raid sirens would send all Londoners scrambling for the safety of bomb shelters or the subway.. More than a million British children were evacuated to safe locations, some to Canada and the United States. German leaders were using an aiming system of radio beams to direct their bombers to the target These directional beams were transmitted from the North Sea area and France and intersected over the target. The British began "jamming" those radio frequencies which eased the problem.

The Royal family refused to leave London and stayed to boost the morale of citizens in bombed out sections. When Buckingham Palace was hit in a 1940 air raid, the Queen remarked, "I'm glad we have been bombed. It makes me feel I can look the East End citizens in the face." The East End was one of London's most important German targets because of the shipyards, docks and factories. Hitler called the Queen the most dangerous woman in Europe because of her leadership and indomitable spirit in boosting British morale. The Blitz was a terrible ordeal for the British; it caused the destruction of thousands of homes, and was responsible for 40,000 civilian deaths and 6,000 seriously injured civilians. The early death of King George VI in 1952 demoted Queen Elizabeth to the role of Queen Mother. She lived to the age of 101 and was still loved by English citizens when she passed away March 2002. Historians credit her with being one of the most influential "Queen Mums" in England's history. I consider England's present Queen, Elizabeth II, to be one of my generation. Like me, she was a teenager during World War II.

This terrible bombardment of England in 1940 brought great sympathy from the U.S. who was already sending supplies and support to the British but had not yet entered the war (3). Sympathetic Americans sent "Bundles for Britain" containing blankets, medicine and clothing to aid the suffering bombing victims. The world had made the mistake of allowing Hitler to conquer Europe and now he was after Great Britain and Russia. German bombing raids had extensively destroyed sections of East London. Nazi bombers also punished the city of Coventry with saturation bombing. The city was an easy target for the German bombers on the night of November 15, 1940. Luftwaffe bombers dropped an estimated five hundred tons of bombs and destroyed over 60,000 buildings. The death toll was over five hundred, with twelve hundred injured. The city was literally wiped out (20). This was a brutal attack, as Coventry had no military importance. Germany's goal was to terrorize and break the spirit of the civilian population. In retaliation, the British bombers hit Cologne with equally savage raids. However, Prime Minister Winston Churchill later insisted that the RAF concentrate on military targets.

RAF Spitfire and Hurricane fighter pilots eventually turned back the waves of German bombers in the 1940-41 Battle of Britain. The Spitfire was a very good fighter and carried eight machine guns in its wide wings. It had a top speed of 370 mph with a 1000 HP Merlin engine and a five-bladed propeller. The Spitfire was very maneuverable in an aerial "dogfight" with enemy fighters. The plane was later adapted for use on British aircraft carriers. The Hawker Hurricane was slightly slower than the Spitfire, but heavily armed and very effective. It carried eight machine guns and four cannons and was very important in the defense of England. RAF fighter pilots were on stand-by and ready to "scramble" around the clock when enemy planes were sighted. Many flew five or six times a day to meet the Luftwaffe. Sergeant James "Ginger" Lacey, one of the top aces in the Battle of Britain, shot down 28 planes during this period. A German ace, Adolph Gallant, who eventually had 103 victories, recalls being shot down twice in the same day. In his book, *The First and the Last*, he credits RAF Spitfire pilots with being excellent fliers.

British fighter pilots shot down 1,600 German bombers and fighters. The German bombing "blitz" continued for several months. During this time British fighter pilots often flew five or more missions per day, and had an estimated eighty-seven hours of life expectancy in aerial combat. More than 900 RAF planes were lost (19). In his tribute to the heroic pilots, Prime Minister Winston Churchill said, "Never in the field of human conflict has so much been owed by so many to so few" (25).

The Royal Air Force (RAF) was composed of airmen from many allied nations. Approximately 70% of the RAF pilots were British or Canadians. The RAF Eagle fighter squadrons were made up of American volunteers. Late in 1940, American pilots formed three Eagle squadrons within the Royal Air Force. In September 1942, they became fighter squadrons 334, 335 and 336 in the U.S. Army Air Force (32). Pilot Officer W.M.L. Fiske of the Royal Air Force died August 18, 1940. Fiske was the only American airman killed in the Battle of Britain. He is commemorated by a plaque in St. Paul's Cathedral in London. These "Yank" Spitfire pilots fighting Germany before the United States entered the war later became leaders in our Air Force. There were also pilots from countries that had been conquered by the Axis powers (Germany and Italy). The RAF turned back the German aerial blitz and continued to protect their country until help arrived. Hitler's Operation "Sea Lion" had failed and he turned his attention to invading the Soviet Union.

The U.S. declared war on Japan December 8, 1941, and then on Germany and Italy December 11th. We immediately provided financial and military aid to England. So the lines were drawn with the Allied countries versus the Axis of Germany, Italy and Japan. The Eighth Air Force arrived in England in the spring of 1942. Allied strategists agreed that the U.S. heavy bombers would carry out daylight precision bombing missions while the RAF continued night raids. German territory was destined to be under attack around the clock!

By late 1944, the RAF Bomber Command had fifty-four airfields and ninety-eight squadrons. It could order up 1600 aircraft for raids on Germany. The RAF Lancaster and Halifax four engine bombers carried a seven-man crew which was asked to fly thirty combat missions. Statistics showed that less than 35% of the men completed their tour of duty, either because of wounds or death (20). The British bombers were escorted and protected by RAF Spitfire or Mosquito night fighters. The RAF heavy bombers, along with the two-engine Wellingtons, carried out night raids on German cities.

The Early Eighth Air Force Bombing Missions

The Eighth Air Force arrived in England in early 1942 and was faced with the task of proving that heavily armed bombers could carry out daylight precision bombing raids while defending themselves (18). U.S. heavy bombers faced the flak and Luftwaffe fighters alone in the early raids of 1942-1943 because allied fighters did not have the cruising range to escort bombers on long missions. In August 1942, Major General Ira C. Eaker led the first raid to Rouen, France. France had been conquered by Germany and was Hitler's base for invading England across the English Channel. Sixty B-17 Flying Fortresses were launched on this first mission. Bombing raids were carried out throughout the fall and winter by B-24 Liberators and B-17s with moderate success. The experienced German fighter pilots and improved anti-aircraft defense proved to be a very strong enemy. Spring brought six more bomb groups to England to beef up the Eighth in the aerial war. More crewmen and planes were needed to replace losses.

The B-17 was developed in the mid 1930's and immediately proved its ability, as the B-17B. It entered into military service in 1939 when the Air Force had 39 bombers. The Boeing aircraft company followed with improved models in the B-17C and later the B17D. The B-17D was in service at the time of Pearl Harbor. World War II brought the B-17E with a series of alterations from lessons being learned in combat. The large dorsal fin was added and armament was improved with turrets and ten heavy machine guns. The B-17F was modified with a plexiglass nose and ability to carry more machine guns and a much heavier bomb load. This model went into mass production by Boeing and Douglas and over 3,000 came off the assembly lines. The USAAF built its airfields among the farms of East Anglia, England and began forming plans for destroying Germany's war machine through precision bombing. This was the beginning of a two-year campaign to rule the skies over France before an Allied invasion could take place. Boeing aircraft plant workers were turning out 362 B-17 bombers a month by March 1944 (15).

Because of the heavy losses in early 1943, the Air Command was calling for replacement crews and more heavy bombers with modifications proven to be needed in combat. The growing U.S. aircraft industry was swinging into full force. By July 1944, the newest model, the B-17G Flying Fortress was ready. The B-17G was the final and most effective high-level bomber for the Eighth Air Force. A chin turret with remote controlled twin machine guns was added to the nose, along with additional ammunition for all guns. Engine turbochargers were also added to provide more power for heavier bomb loads. The assembly lines rolled out over 8,500 of the B-17G bombers, thus making a total of 12,731 Flying Fortresses for the war effort (15)! The waist guns were mounted in plexiglass windows which eliminated the freezing winds blowing through the plane. The plane now had thirteen heavy machine guns and carried over 5,000 .50 caliber bullets (15). I was lucky enough to serve my missions on the B-17G Flying Fortress. This improved bomber had a ceiling of 35,000 feet and a top speed of 300 MPH. The extra "Tokyo" gas tanks in the wings gave the plane a range of over 4,000 miles, and high altitude flying helped conserve gas. However, with a 5,000 pound bombload of "presents" for Hitler, it cruised about 160 MPH until "bombs away" over the target. The bomber formation used the extra speed to return to England and safety. Aircrew members considered the new nose turret and its two .50 caliber machine guns the most important modification. They now had more fire-power to greet those "twelve o'clock high bandits" who loved to swoop down out of the sun!

The Box Formation

The High Command devised a plan for heavy bombers to fly in a defensive "box" formation to maximize a wide field of machine gun fire power against German fighters. This "box" formation consisted of three squadrons of bombers flying a "stacked" formation of high, middle and low positions. Each squadron of twelve to eighteen planes maintained a 1,000 foot difference in altitude. The staggered formation allowed the group to drop their bombs while in formation. The middle squadron flew slightly in front. The formation's "command plane" flew the "lead" for the middle squadron. It carried the mission commander, pilot, group navigator and bombardier. The lead planes of the low and high squadrons also carried a "command pilot" navigator and bombardier. Later in the war a radar (Mickey) operator was added. The Eighth Air Force box formation presented a layered defense and every bomber was a part of the defense of the entire formation. Thus, squadrons were layered and staggered horizontally and vertically to allow simultaneous release of bombs and provide the widest field of fire against enemy fighters from any direction.

The average bomber "box" formation of three bomber groups would occupy space of a cubic mile in the sky. A tight "box" prevented German "bandits" from flying through the formation and allowed bomber gunners to focus a majority of their .50 caliber machine guns on the attackers. The formation's wide field of fire was a definite hazard to enemy fighters. We followed the same procedure every mission. To locate attacking fighters, aerial gunners used an imaginary horizontal clock dial, as if the plane were flying through it. Twelve o'clock was straight ahead, nine o'clock was to the right of the plane, the tailgunner kept watch on the six o'clock area and three o'clock was left and even with the plane outside my window. All crewmembers could report "sightings" to the pilot by a clock number and high or low if necessary. For instance, German fighters often made frontal attacks out of the sun at twelve o'clock high.

Early Bomber Losses

Germany had increased fighter production and anti-aircraft installations were more numerous. The Fourth Bomb Wing lost 200 men and several bombers in their first eight missions. However, their ninth mission to the submarine pens at Kiel was a shocker. The 94th and 95th Bomb Groups took the brunt of the Luftwaffe attack. Seven of the 95th group bombers were lost before reaching the target. General Nathan Bedford Forrest III, the newly assigned Group Commander, was an observer in the lead plane of the 95th which was lost over the target. He was the first Air Force General to die in combat. Only six of the sixteen 95th bombers returned to England. The 94th group was attacked over the North Sea on the way home and nine bombers were shot down (12).

The raid on Schweinfurt, August 17th, 1943, was another disaster. The Eighth sent out over 200 bombers and lost thirty-six. Another terrible example of the early bombing raids without escort fighters for the entire mission was the Schweinfurt raid October 14, 1943. This was a "maximum effort" mission designed to destroy this heavily protected target. Schweinfurt manufactured most of the ball bearings used in Germany's war machines. The P-47 Thunderbolt escort fighters, low on fuel, turned and headed for home and the German fighters (60-70) were there to attack the bomber formation all the way to the target. The Eighth Air Force sent 257 Flying Fortresses into Germany. Twenty-eight bombers were lost to flak and fighters before reaching the target. After "bombs away" another thirty B-17s were lost. A total of 64 planes did not return to England. Several others that made it home were damaged and were declared unfit for combat. Eighty planes were lost or destroyed. Almost 700 aircrew members were listed as missing in action over German territory (12). This became known as "Black Thursday". It was the Eighth's last long-range raid without fighter escorts. The Luftwaffe had proven that bomber formations definitely needed the protection of escort fighters. Fighter escorts on distant targets were not possible until late 1943. Allied fighters could escort bombers only so far; then they had to return to England or face running out of fuel. The hordes of German fighters would wait and attack the bombers after the escorts turned back which resulted in great losses of our bombers. Many were shot down before reaching the target. Allied Command knew they did not have "air superiority" which was necessary before the invasion of France could take place. It was estimated that the Eighth lost 40% of its bombers and crews during the bombing missions in 1943. Long range escorts were needed; fighters that could reach distant targets and fight off the Luftwaffe squadrons. The range of our fighters was increased with the use of auxiliary gas tanks that could be jettisoned when empty. The P-51 Mustangs, P-38 Lightnings and P-47 Thunderbolts became "little friends", escorting the bombers to the target and back and providing protection from the Luftwaffe.

The American industrial machine had to switch to the production of planes to support the war. In addition to more bombers, the U.S. workers cranked out P-51 Mustangs and P-47 Thunderbolts by the hundreds. By mid 1944, the Eighth Air Force had long-range fighters to escort and protect them on their missions, and the German Luftwaffe lost command of the skies. The loss of Allied bombers dropped dramatically and more aircrews survived their tour of duty. I'm glad my combat service was in the latter part of the air war over Europe when the odds of survival were a little better. The High Command, or "brass", had decided to concentrate strategic bombing efforts on oil depots and the German aircraft industry. The air superiority of the Luftwaffe had to be reduced before allied bombing raids could be more successful and the invasion of France could happen. The Air Force's "Big Week" came on February 20th, 1944, when weather cleared and bombing targets could be seen. The bombers were to hit all the "hot spots" Schweinfurt, Augsburg, Regensburg, Hanover and Kiel. These targets were all part of the German defense industry and were heavily protected by anti-aircraft, batteries and fighters. The Eighth and Fifteenth Air Forces concentrated on those targets and success was sweet. By the end of the month, the new Eighth Air Force Commanding General, Jimmy Doolittle, could announce that the Luftwaffe had been turned from an offensive power to the role of defending their country.

Target--- Berlin!

March 4, 1944, was the first raid on Berlin, or "Big B". It was to be a maximum effort but the clouds were too thick. The cloud banks caused the bomber groups to climb to a very high altitude. The poor visibility finally forced the Eighth Air Force Headquarters to send out a VHF (very high frequency) radio message recalling the bombers. Most formations turned and headed home, but Lt. Col. Grif Mumford, 95th group commander, chose to continue the mission. He knew that his bombers were already deep into enemy territory and believed that the Luftwaffe fighters were busy chasing the recalled bombers. He gambled that his group could bomb Berlin and slip on out of enemy territory without too many losses. Lt. William "Ed" Charles of Bedford, Indiana, was a navigator on this mission. Twenty-nine B-17s headed on to Berlin in the face of overwhelming odds.

Bombing "Big B" was one thing that would boost American morale and prove the value of strategically bombing. Early in the war, Reichsmarchschall Hermann Goering, head of the Luftwaffe, had promised the German people that Berlin would not be bombed again. RAF bombers hit the city in August 1940. This made the target even more important. The 95th and 100th bomb groups continued on and were attacked by about twenty ME-109 fighters, but our P-51 Mustang escort fighters drove them off and the formation bombed Berlin. The twenty-one 95th and eight 100th groups had made it, and had proven that Berlin was not invincible. They lost five planes to flak and fighters. The strategy had worked, thanks to the P-51 escorts.

Lt. Charles said that the top brass were waiting at the field when the group landed. Major General Curtis LeMay, Third Division Commander, was on hand to congratulate the first group to bomb Berlin. Lt. Col. Mumford, mission commander, was awarded the Silver Star, and lead pilot, Lt. Al Brown received the Distinguished Service Cross. The 95th Bomb Group was awarded its third Presidential Unit Citation. Life magazine featured pictures of the planes and crews who had survived the mission in its March 29, 1944 issue (12).

Lt. Chuck Yeager, a young P-51 pilot and later an ace, shot down his first enemy plane on that Berlin raid. Yeager became a test pilot after the war and in 1947 became the first man to reach MACH-1 (the speed of sound) in a Bell Aircraft X-1 experimental jet plane (19). Several test pilots had died when their planes broke apart trying to break the 760 MPH sound barrier. In October, 2002, Brigadier General, Chuck Yeager, age 79, again broke the sound barrier for the last time. He flew his F-15 Eagle jet at a speed of MACH 1.45, nearly one and a half times the speed of sound. This was more than fifty years after his first supersonic flight!

Two days later on March 6th the weather cleared and more than 700 B-17 Fortresses and B-24 Liberators headed for a follow-up mission to Berlin to capitalize on the propaganda value. They were escorted by a strong force of fighters. It was reported that the stream of bombers was so long that the middle formations had few escorts. They were hit by the Luftwaffe ME-109 and FW-190 fighters who shot down 23 bombers of the 95th and 100th bomb groups who had first bombed Berlin. In this raid, the Eighth suffered their worst losses of 69 bombers and over 700 men. Fifteen of those planes were from the 100th Bomb Group with only one plane returning to base! This was the third such loss by the "Bloody Hundredth". Only 25% of Allied bomber crews safely completed their tour of duty before D-Day, June, 1944 (16).

The Eighth bombers were back over Berlin on March 7th and 9th, 1944. The heavy losses continued but the new Eighth Air Force

Commander, Jimmy Doolittle, knew his raids were making progress. He called for more and better bombers and more replacement crews. The 95th Bomb Group had flown five Berlin missions in seven days. This air war was brutal but necessary to soften Germany for the invasion of France. Members of the 95th later published a book, *B-17s Over Berlin*, containing their personal stories and experiences. Lt. Ed Charles authored three stories in the book, and was named in several articles in the book.

The Memphis Belle

The Memphis Belle of the 91st Bomb Group was the first B-17 to complete 25 missions in the early air war over Germany. Bombers in the Eighth Air Force had an average life of fifty days, and crewmembers had a very short life expectancy. But the "Belle" made it and became a symbol of victory. The crew and plane survived those 25 missions in spite of overwhelming Nazi fighter attacks, heavy flak, and no fighter escorts. The famed flying Fortress survived serious damage and ground crews spent many hours replacing various parts and engines to keep it flying. Four of the original crewmembers died during the 148 hours of combat. The "Belle" dropped over sixty tons of bombs in those early days of the war. Crewmembers were awarded a total of 60 medals including the Distinguished Flying Cross. They also received congratulations from King George VI and Queen Elizabeth of England who made a personal visit to the 91st Bomb Group. They then received orders to take the Memphis Belle

Through These Eyes

back to the USA on a "26th mission", a morale and war bond tour. This mission was eventually a visit to 31 U.S. cities over a three-month period. On June 13, 1943, the Memphis Belle and her crew of ten happy men left England (3).

Completing 25 unescorted missions in 1942-43 was very unusual because bomb groups were losing 30 to 40 percent of their planes and crews on some missions. The "Belle" had suffered many hits from flak and fighters but always brought her crew home safely. Her crewmembers received credit for downing eight German fighters. The "Belle" crew and plane became the subject of a documentary film by William Wyler, "The Memphis Belle". Wyler and his cameramen flew several missions to record actual footage of the air war and the crewmembers in combat. Wyler was awarded the Air Medal. During combat, the Memphis Belle crew flew 20,000 miles, shot down eight German fighters and dropped sixty tons of bombs. The plane had 148 hours of combat and suffered many repairs. In that time she lost nine different engines and five superchargers, and both wings had to be replaced as well as two tail assemblies. The plane, named after pilot Bob Morgan's Memphis sweetheart, Margaret Polk, seemed invincible. Wyler's video of this award-winning documentary may be ordered from the Memphis Belle Association. It gives a vivid picture of World War II Eighth Air Force raids over Germany. There is also a recent Warner Bros. film "Memphis Belle" available on video.

The B-17 Memphis Belle was restored and displayed under a canopy on Mud Island facing the Mississippi river in Memphis,

James Lee Hutchinson, EdS

Tennessee for several years. Recently, a dedicated group of men and women completed the groundbreaking for a new climate-controlled museum. The plane was removed from Mud Island to undergo a complete renovation before being relocated in its new home in the Memphis Belle Memorial Park for the Second World War in an eastern suburb of Memphis. This new park will allow the Memphis Belle Memorial Association to continue to preserve the famous B-17 and other World War II planes for thousands of visitors each year. The Belle has been housed in Memphis since 1946 and it is hoped that the fund drive for the Memorial will succeed. If not, the bomber may be moved to the new WW II Aircraft building at the National U.S. Air Force Museum in Dayton, Ohio.

The groundbreaking ceremony was held November 11, 2001 (Veteran's Day). Col. Robert K. Morgan pilot of the Memphis Belle was one of the featured speakers. Also present from the original crew was Tech Sergeant Robert J. Hanson, radio operator. After completing twenty-five combat missions in Europe and the USA war bond tour Col. Morgan volunteered for the Pacific Theater. He completed twenty-five missions as a B-29 Superfort squadron commander and retired from the Air Force Reserve after Japan's defeat. Col. Morgan and his wife Linda remained active on the air show and lecture circuit for many years. He later recorded his life story in an excellent book *The Man Who Flew the Memphis Belle.* My younger daughter attended the ceremony, spoke with Col. Morgan, and purchased an autographed book for me. "To Lee, Best Wishes, Thanks for flying in

Through These Eyes

combat on a B-17". This book occupies a prime spot in my library. We visited the Memphis Belle in the summer of 2001. I told the guides in charge that I was a B-17 aerial combat veteran and they allowed my daughter, Susan, and I to board the Belle. We toured the plane and I sat at the radio operator's position once again. My daughter got some good photos and I got a memorable experience!

A historical marker outside the Memphis Belle pavilion on Mud Island listed the following information:

91ST BOMB GROUP (HEAVY)
UNITED STATES ARMY AIR FORCE

"The Memphis Belle was the first of the many B-17s assigned to the 91st Bomb Group, 8th Air Force, and the first bomber to complete 25 missions in the European Theater of Operation (ETO) during World War II. It was retired form combat in 1943. The 91st was formed and trained at Tampa, Florida and Walla Walla, Washington, before departing in September 1942 for the ETO. Based at AF Station 121, Bassingbourne, England, and supported by 2,000 ground personnel, the 91st officers and enlisted airmen flew 9,591 B-17 combat sorties on 340 missions from November 7, 1942 through April 25, 1945. In the air battles for freedom, the 91st lost 197 B-17s and destroyed 420 of Adolph Hitler's German aircraft. Lost were 1,010 combat crewmen (899) killed and 111 missing in action); and over 960 crewmen became prisoners of war.

> Two Distinguished Unit Citations were awarded to the 91st for missions on March 4, 1943 to Hamm, and January 11, 1944, to Oscheraleben, Germany. Another 91st B-17, named "Nine-O-Nine," completed a record 140 missions by V.E. Day. The plaque also honors the ground units that supported them."

Colonel Morgan passed away in May 2004 at the age of 85 years. He was honored by a final "flyover" of a B-52 bomber and a B-17 Flying Fortress with a P-51 escort fighter at his funeral in Asheville, North Carolina. The planes tipped their wings in a final salute to the famed bomber pilot.

Air Force Ground Crews

The ground crew mechanics, armorers and technicians kept the B-17s flying. They all had four to six months of training in their specialties. Each plane had a crew chief and a group of mechanics for service and maintenance. Their challenge was to keep their bomber airworthy and ready to complete a mission. After each flight they met pilot and crew at the hardstand to learn of any equipment malfunctions and to inspect for flak damage. They knew they had to "repair and prepare" for the next mission. Their regular tasks included everything from tire pressure to repairing the 1,200 horsepower Wright engines. A record of all repairs was entered into the plane's maintenance log. This included all those mechanical problems for which there were no explanations. Those problems were blamed on the "Gremlins"! Those mythical one foot tall creatures who caused

Through These Eyes

all the mysterious aircraft malfunctions were never seen but were believed to be passengers on all planes! Ground crews were capable of changing engines and turbo chargers or repairing the electrical or hydraulic systems of a damaged plane. Wings and tail sections could also be repaired or replaced. Mechanics used parts from planes that had been damaged beyond repair. It was exhausting work in all kinds of weather and there were only two hangars for the major work. Ground crews often worked all night on the flight line to get their "bird" back in the air and did a terrific job keeping bombers ready for missions. Each plane carried 6,000 pounds of bombs, 5,000 rounds of .50 caliber bullets, and the weight of 2700 gallons of 100 octane gas into the air (10). All four engines needed to be in perfect condition. Ground crewmembers were on the hardstand before the mission to check last minute preparations before take-off. Routine duties included pre-flight checks, starting the engine and checking gauges and controls. Many other support technicians checked the bomber's radios, radar, bombsights and oxygen systems. Armorers loaded and armed the bombs and ammunition for the .50 caliber machine guns. The ground crew could sleep while their plane was out on a bombing raid, but they were down on the field to "sweat out" the mission when the bombers were due to return. Medals were awarded crew chiefs whose planes flew many missions without aborting. The B-17 was a rugged plane that could take great punishment from flak or fighters and still make it home on "a wing and a prayer".

Ground crew members possessed vital technical information and skills to support their plane's crews. All had attended technical schools. Each bomber crew carried enlisted men who had at least 16 weeks technical training. On the Bill Templeton crew, there was Bert Allinder, armorer-gunner; Ewing Roddy, engineer-gunner; and Lee Hutchinson, radio-gunner. The other gunners and officers had also received technical skills and training to qualify them for their job descriptions.

There were three Lawrence county men stationed with the 95th Bomb Group at Horham. That field was only a few miles from Eye. They caught the train at Eye when they went on pass to London! I think it's ironic that I discovered this fact 57 years too late! Of course I didn't know them as I do now, but it would have been great to talk with someone from home. Sgt. Ralph Alexander, from Silver Creek, Georgia, served as a ground crew aircraft mechanic with the 95th. Ralph married a Bedford girl, Ruth Bolding, before going overseas. They became my oldest daughter's inlaws in 1968 when she married their son, Mike. We were "family" and friends for over 32 years. Our five granddaughters heard Eighth Air Force stories from both grandfathers.

My former golfing buddy Lt. Col. (Ret) William "Ed" Charles served with the 95th bomb group. He flew 25 missions in 1943 as a navigator. He received his "Lucky Bastard" certificate and volunteered to stay on as Captain and group navigator. Ed flew many more missions reaching the rank of Major. At war's end, he joined the Air Force Reserve and retired with the rank of Lt. Colonel. Ed also served as historian of the 95th bomb group for twenty-five years. A large library of books on the Eighth Air Force lines his office wall. He has also produced a video on the history of the 95th. Ed has provided information and pictures for many authors of books on the World War II air war.

My wife's brother, T/Sgt Doyle Byers, was a radio operator-gunner and flew 31 missions in the summer of 1944 when missions were really rough. Lt. Ed Charles and T/Sgt. Doyle Byers flew their tours in the early air war raids. They were involved in 25 of the same missions. They also participated in the group's shuttle bombing flights from England to Russia and on to Italy. These flights enabled B-17s to leave England, bomb distant targets, and land in Russia. There, they would load bombs and fuel and go after targets in Romania or Germany and fly on to the 15th Air Force base in Foggia, Italy. The leg of the shuttle was to reload and fly over the Alps to bomb southern German targets on their way back to England. Shuttle flights could last a week or so, depending on weather conditions. The 95th flew six of these missions. A few years ago both men received medals from the Russian government for their participation in those raids (12). Overall, the 95th Bomb Group flew 321 combat mission between May 13, 1943 and April 20, 1945 (24). They lost 156 bombers in combat. Both Charles and Byers were awarded the DFC (distinguished flying cross) and the Air Medal with four oak leaf clusters. Somewhere the 95th boys found time to win the Eighth Air Force basketball championship (12).

The Lucky Bastard Certificate was an unofficial award designed by various bomb groups. It was submitted to crewmembers who were lucky enough to complete their tour of duty. The certificate looked similar to the following:

ON THIS DAY _____

This crew member enters the LUCKY BASTARD CLUB

Name _____

Who today bearing his horseshoe after aviating in his B-17 Contrail Chaser on _____ raids of plastering der Fuhrer's map using bombs delivered by the 8th Air Force and furnished by people determined to exterminate the house painter's Third Reich.

Signed _____ and _____
       Col. Jones   Captain Smith

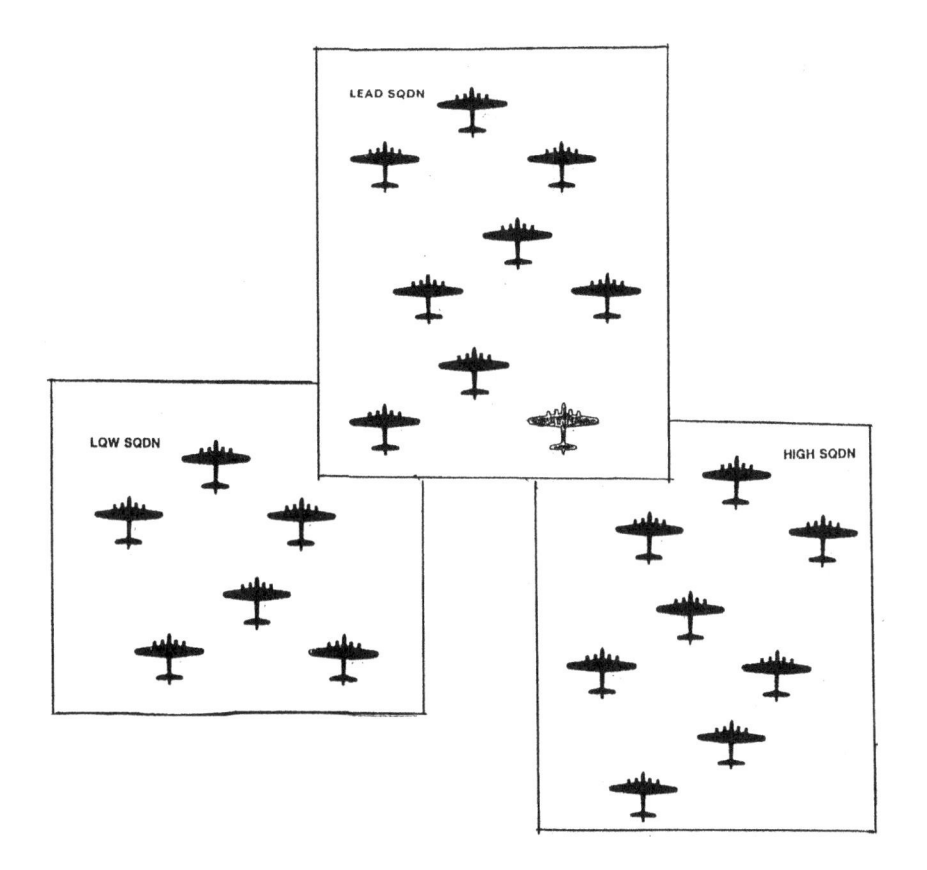

Box Formation

The combat flight pattern for protection against flak, fighters and allow all planes to bomb the target at the same time ---- (pattern bombing)

Death of a B-17 and crew! A direct hit by flak on a bomb run

The Memphis Belle – 2002

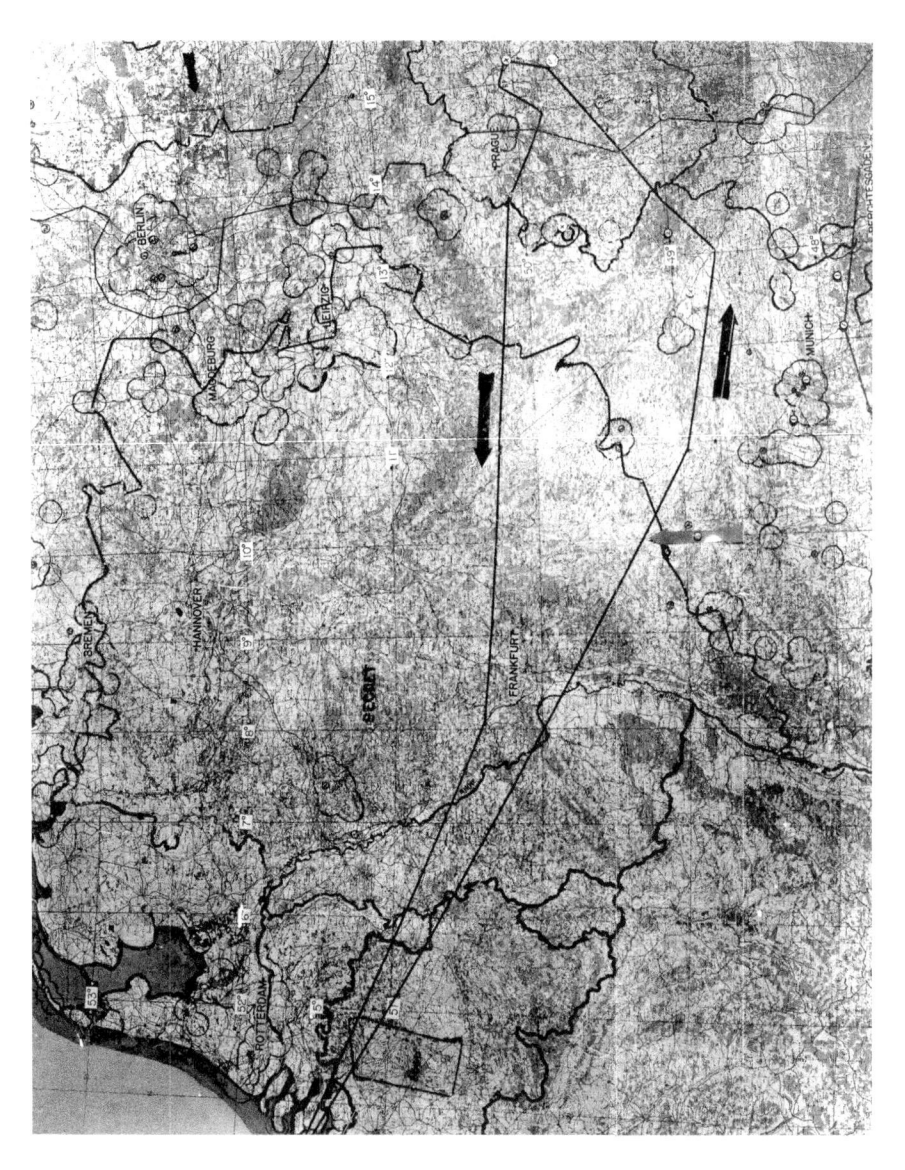

Briefing Map for a Czechoslovakia mission.
Arrows show safest to routes to avoid flak

Bombs Away

Chapter Five
England—The Combat Zone

The Queen Mary sailed up the Firth of Clyde, (my father's name), and docked at Greenock, near Glasgow, Scotland. We crossed the Atlantic safely in six days. That was my last ocean cruise! We disembarked and were billeted (housed) at a British Army facility. The huge red brick barracks were a welcome sight. Each man was assigned a steel cot with one sheet, two blankets, and three biscuits. The biscuits, much like sofa cushions, were to be a mattress. These biscuits required an adjustment in our sleeping habits. We had to place them on the cot, cover them with a sheet and tuck in all edges tightly. That night, we discovered that tossing and turning resulted in our rears hitting the springs, which caused an extreme draft. Our first impression of Scotland was great. We had good food and a bed that didn't swing. The next morning we boarded a small English train and headed for our airfield at Eye. We got our first look at the English countryside and the British Isles. I was amazed by all the fishing boats lying on their sides in the low rivers. This was a mystery to a kid from the Midwest until someone explained that they would float again when the tide came in. The train chugged through many small towns as we moved across England. Draft horses were used to move rail cars on the sidings because of the fuel shortage. We reached Eye in time for supper at the Mess Hall.

Eye, Our 490th Airbase

It was official, we were a replacement crew for squadron 848 of the 490th Bomb Group, the 93rd Wing of the Third Division. The Eye airfield, station 134 (code name Hangstrap), was one of the last U.S. airbases constructed in the rich East Anglia farmland. Aircrews called it the Brome Drome. It was nested in between the towns of Eye, Yaxley and Brome and only a mile or two from Diss. The field was basically a large triangle of concrete runways and hardstands surrounded by steel Quonset buildings. There was one 6,000 foot runway and two that were 4,200 feet in length. All runways were 150 feet wide. Fifty concrete hardstands (bomber parking areas) were built along the runways. Space was limited and a local road, A-140 between Ipswich and Norwich, had to be closed when bombers were using the east runway. I recently corresponded with a young English girl, Leah Amie, of Eye, who sent us a picture of a B-17 Flying Fortress taking off down a runway past her family's home.

Her father owns a restored P-51 Mustang and local pilots still use one of our old runways.

Construction was completed in the spring of 1944. Starting in May, the 490th group flew its first forty missions with B-24 Liberator bombers. The bomb group was switched over to B-17G Flying Fortress planes in August. This was the home of the 490th Bombardment Group (H) of the Third Division.

We arrived at Eye in late November, 1944. Cold winter weather had preceded us! The 490th was well established, having flown missions for five months. We were "replacement crews" for the aircrews which had either completed their tour of duty, (25 missions) or been shot down. We were to take over for the gallant crews who had survived the challenge of the Third Reich, and now realized that this was truly a grim business! However, we were required to complete two weeks of classroom instruction and flying in combat formation before we could fly a mission.

Home Sweet Home---Hut 29

Our base was one of 134 built among the farms and parishes of East Anglia (43 were for heavy bombers). They were concentrated in an area less than half the area of the state of Vermont. Living quarters for 420 officers and over 2,500 enlisted men were provided by concrete huts or steel Quonset huts on the east side of the field. The huts actually extended into the community of Brome. We referred to our hut as the Brome Dome 29. The hut was a sixteen by thirty foot steel Quonset hut with a concrete floor and a very small stove sitting in the center surrounded by twelve steel bunks. It looked like a giant gray trash can half buried in the ground with a brick wall in each end containing a door and two windows with blackout curtains. There was a smoking chimney through the roof.

The hut was our home for the nine months we were stationed in England---from November 1944 through July 8th 1945. Coke, a coal product, for the stove was rationed to a bucket a day unless more was delivered to our squadron. This meant very small fires and lots of extra clothing all winter unless someone in the hut could sneak out in the middle of the night and pick up an extra supply of fuel.

The 848th squadron enlisted men were housed in the same area. A latrine (showers and toilets) was in the middle of the huts. It was usually cold, and one never tarried when answering "nature's call". We used a steel helmet to heat shaving water on the barracks stove. We shared our hut with another crew who were veterans of ten missions and were a great help to us in learning our way around the base and flight line. We listened carefully when they described some of their missions. Officers had larger quarters closer to squadron headquarters and the mail room.

We spent many cold, damp winter nights huddled around the stove or "sacked out" in our cots wondering what the next day would bring. We solved the shifting "biscuit mattress" problem by using sleeping bags. Keeping warm was a challenge, you almost had to sit on the stove to feel the heat! Later, the experienced crew finished their tour and both replacement crews in Hut 29 became "lead crew", so we only had eight men and I was lucky enough to get a cot next to the stove! Brome was a nice area, I could step out our back door and peer across the road at an English manor house and a huge barnyard. I remember walking down the Oakley road past the house. An eight-foot brick wall bordered the road and the top of the wall had broken glass embedded in concrete to discourage trespassers. A small pond on our side of the road was a playground for farm ducks. The road behind our barracks went to the town of Diss. We visited the town several times during our pre-combat weeks of training and often during our nine-month duty in England. Diss was a larger town than Eye, located near the railroad between Ipswich and Norwich. When we received a three-day pass, we boarded the train for Ipswich and London. Diss also had a number of pubs and shops we could visit. The shops didn't have a lot of merchandise, but as soon as we mastered the value of English money (we didn't know a shilling from a quid), we went shopping. First, Rod and I purchased ledgers from the stationer's shop for our diaries. As soon as they became available, we bought bicycles to make transportation simpler to and from the barracks and around the airbase. I was also lucky enough to buy a 110 Kodak box camera (which I still own). I got a lot of good snapshots and several are included in this book. The butcher shop always intrigued me because of the lack of refrigeration. The dead chickens, rabbits, and ducks hanging in the open air still in their fur and feathers didn't look too appetizing. It reminded me of a scene from an old Charles

Dickens story. Diss also had a small lake in the village green with two white swans that glided gracefully across the water. It was such a peaceful scene in the middle of air raids and buzz bombs!

The "pubs" (public houses) were the social centers for the working class. Towards evening, people would gather at their favorite pub for a pint of ale and a few games of darts. Food was also available although the menu was limited. I was always amazed at the way they ate their beans! They would hold the fork upright and backward in their left hand and use their knife to mash the beans against the fork. They were very accomplished at this way of eating. My buddies and I tried it many times but no one got very good at eating beans backwards. People were very friendly and would often yell "'Ave a drink Yank" to welcome us. One lesson we learned quickly was to never play darts with them! I remember going into town when we had a few hours of free time. We travelled by "shanks mare" or bicycle past the White Swan pub a few miles down the narrow road. We went first through a lane with huge trees overhanging the road. I wouldn't have been surprised if Robin Hood and his Merry Men had dropped out of those trees to demand our money. Then it was out of the trees into the open road past the deserted golf course to town. There was little civilian automobile traffic because all petrol (gas) was needed for the war effort. Military vehicles, jeeps, buses and trucks were everywhere. The cars we did see were driving on the wrong side of the road! Night driving was really perilous because all headlights were covered except for a small cross of light so the car could be seen. Blackout curtains were required on all buildings so the town disappeared into the darkness at night. The countryside was pitch black on the way home. We sometimes saw flashes of big guns in the distance or a V-1 rocket on the horizon. It really is a small world because I recently met a doctor at the Veterans Administration Hospital who had owned a house near Diss for several years. She had lived there while studying for her medical degree.

Fish and Chips was a favorite finger food. Everyone liked the deep fried chunks of fish and French fried potatoes. The fries were much bigger, softer and thicker than we were used to at home, and the English called them chips. We often ordered Fish and Chips in the evenings while resting in the hut, especially if the mess hall chow hadn't been too satisfying. A local farm boy, Russell Etheridge, would go get them. Russell who was fourteen years old couldn't wait until he was old enough to join the Royal Navy. His mother did our laundry each week for a small fee and he was our pick-up and delivery boy and available to run errands for a small fee.

Fish and Chips were most delicious when sprinkled with vinegar, and we had many fine feasts in hut #29. On a cold winter night, eight Yank crewmen and Russell could make a large package disappear quickly. I remember the cook at the White Swan pub down the road always wrapped the order in newspapers and Russell would make it back to the hut while it was still warm. One night, he announced that his sister was getting married, so one of the guys managed to obtain a damaged parachute from the supply room to be made into a wedding dress.

English oldsters and youngsters were the only "Brits" we met because most of the young men and women were in the service or working away in the Home Guard. The Home Guard was an organization mostly made up of women, senior citizens and youngsters. They served in case of emergencies, air raids and other catastrophes. We Americans made up the bulk of the young adult population in the country during these horrible war years. England had suffered from German air raids and the threat of an invasion before the United States entered the war and turned the countryside into a giant airbase. They were grateful for the assistance of our Armed Forces, Air Force and Naval operations on the seas surrounding the United Kingdom.

The U.S. Air Force occupied many airfields in the United Kingdom by 1945. There were 43 heavy bombers bases. Fourteen were for the B-24 Liberators, and twenty-nine were dedicated to the B-17 Flying Fortresses. Heavy bomber bases required approximately 500 acres of the rich East Anglia farmland. There were seventy-five Eighth Air Force fighter squadrons (16) and numerous Royal Air Force bomber and fighter bases. A loaded B-17 required a speed of 110 MPH and 3,400 feet of concrete runway to take off on a mission (1). Two of our Eye runways were only 4,200 feet long so the pilots had to power all four motors as they coaxed those loaded bombers into the air. They also needed all the runway they could get when landing. The roar of each plane's four 1200 horsepower turbo-charged radial engines shook the English countryside every morning the weather was clear for a mission. Thirty or more bombers lined up and took off every 30 seconds from various airbases when on a mission (9). However, the "Brits" welcomed the noise and the thousand or so bombers assembling in the sky above to deliver their deadly loads to Hitler. The Eighth heavy bombers flew more than 55,000 missions in June and July of 1944 (9). Meanwhile the Royal Air Force bombers continued to pound the enemy during their night raids.

German Buzz Bombs

Our first night on the base, we heard the roar of the motor and/or exhaust of a buzz bomb. We all piled outside to watch a V-1 rocket hedge-hopping through the dark evening sky. The flames from its exhaust made it easy to follow across the horizon. It later ran out of fuel and exploded in the English countryside somewhere beyond the airfield. In June of 1944 the Germans had started launching unmanned V-1 rocket bombs, also called Buzz bombs or Doodlebugs, across the English Channel at London and strategic targets. The steering mechanism often failed or the bomb would run out of fuel, crash and explode in the English countryside on unsuspecting victims.

The V-1 rocket was another of Hitler's weapons to break the spirits of the English people. The rockets were terrorizing and nerve-wracking because they hit the countryside anytime, anywhere, and there was little defense against them. Thousands of V-1 rockets were fired at London from June 1944 to the end of the war. They killed hundreds of civilians

Through These Eyes

and destroyed or wrecked thousands of homes and businesses. The V-1 was slow, flew at a low altitude of around two to three thousand feet, and had a range of 150 miles. British Spitfire fighters could sometimes intercept and shoot them down. Prime RAF and Eighth Air Force targets included V-1 and V-2 rocket-launching sites in German occupied territories in France, Germany and Holland. It was estimated that Germany manufactured over 25,000 of these flying bombs.

A War-Time English Newspaper

I recently reviewed a copy of the October 16, 1944 <u>Evening Telegraph</u>, a Northamptonshire newspaper. The paper contained many short stories on local and war news. There was even a column on social events coming up. The size of the eight-page paper was reduced and it was printed in very small type. One article on buzz bombs caught my eye, and illustrated the calm British attitude:

"Three Fly-Bombs Down"
Casualties and Damage in Night Attacks

"During the night the enemy directed flying bombs against Southern England, including the London area. A.A. guns were more than usually active on the East Coast. Projectiles, which got through the barrage fell in scattered areas, and at least three were brought down after heavy explosions. Casualties and damage to property, including a cinema, have been reported.

A number of the flying bombs were destroyed by A.A. guns and fighters of the A.D.G.B (Aerial Defence of Great Britain). Ten people, most of whom lived in flats over shops, were injured, but no one was killed. Extensive damage was caused to the church, a school, a Post Office, a cinema and shops".

The V-2 rocket was much more powerful than the V-1 and there was no defense against it. The V-2 would soar a hundred miles high and plummet to the earth at over 2000 mph. It carried a 2000-pound explosive warhead and made a very large crater when it hit the city. The British nick-named them "Bob Hopes", because the only defense was to "bob down and hope for the best" (19). Well over 1000 V-2 rockets were aimed at London after September, 1944. V-2 missiles were manufactured in underground factories with slave labor. Therefore, they were more protected from allied bombing raids. Wernher von Braun, one of the German rocket experts who developed the V-2 rocket, turned himself over to the U.S. troops at war's end and came to the United States after the fall of the Third Reich. He became one our top rocket scientists and was very prominent in developing our space program located in Huntsville, Alabama. He later headed NASA's Space Flight Center and directed the building of our Saturn V moon rocket.

The B-24 Liberator

The Eighth found that the B-24 Liberator was difficult to fly in close formation at high altitudes. The narrow wings made it hard to control in the cold, thin air. B-24 pilots said they developed extra strong arms from fighting the controls. The bomber was more difficult to fly in a tight formation and some planes and crews were lost in mid-air collisions during training and combat.

The Eighth Air Force equipped the First and Third bomb groups with B-17 Flying Fortresses as they became available, and the Second Bomb Division became an all B-24 Liberator operation. Headquarters could now assign bomb groups to missions best suited to their performance and bombing ranges. Both bombers were very successful for long-range missions with the Eighth. The Fifteenth Air Corps flew B-24 bombers from Africa, flying the Mediterranian to carry out successful raids on the Ploesti oil fields in Romania, and targets in Italy. They were even more successful once they gained airbases in Italy and could hit targets in southern Germany by crossing the Alps.The B-24 was also very effective in the Pacific Theater.

Our 490th Bomb Group had trained with and flown B-24 Liberator bombers for the first 40 missions. It was switched to B-17 Flying Fortresses after August, 1944 and was organized into four squadrons, 848, 849, 850 and 851, and the crews competed to see who would be the first combat ready squadron. Much time was spent in practice take-offs and landings before attempting rendezvous and flying high altitude formations. Take-off and getting into bombing formation took special skills. This was a chore to be mastered before crossing the English Channel. The group practiced bombing missions on various English cities. The training was completed and the first B-17 combat mission was July 27, 1944 with 39 aircraft, but the mission was recalled. I recently discovered that our 490th Bomb Group Commander Colonel Frank B. Bostrom was the B-17 pilot (then Lieutenant) who flew General MacArthur Douglas from Hawaii to Australia in 1942 after the fall of Corregidor and Bataan (1).

Generally, only three squadrons flew on a mission. This allowed a rest period for the men and planes. This practice was followed by all Eighth Air Force groups and allowed for more frequent raids. On November 30, 1944, our crew had not yet been cleared to fly missions, but the 490th sent out 36 bombers on a mission to Merseberg. The target was the heavily guarded synthetic oil refineries. The Division lost seventeen bombers on this raid but all our planes made it back safely. However, there was a great deal of flak damage and several crew members were wounded or killed on this seven hour mission. This was the heaviest flak our group had faced.

Nose Art and Plane Markings

Bomb Groups had distinctively painted markings for identification in the air. One was the national insignia of the white star in the blue circle and white bar. This was on each side of the fuselage and on each wing. The 490th group markings were red bands around each wing and horizontal tail. The top third of the vertical tail was also red. Our 848th squadron ID was on the vertical tail and was a black bar before the letter "N". Most of the bomber photos in this book are of planes from the 490th

Bomb Group. Oddly, the ME-262 jet fighters that attacked us on the March 21, 1945 Plauen mission had much the same red markings. There was also the distinctive nose art. Ground crews stenciled a small bomb on the nose of each plane for every completed mission, and a swastika for German planes shot down by gunners. Aircrews chose names for "nose art" on their bombers. Some picked names of cities or girlfriends, while others chose more provocative names. A majority of the artwork pictured nude or scantily clad beauties copied from the "Petty" or "Vargas" girls in our pin-up calendars. There were also cartoon characters or animals. Examples were: Memphis Belle; Picadilly Lily; Daisy Mae; Bad Penny; Ascend Charlie; Tinker Toy; Raiden Maiden and Eight-Ball. Crewmembers with A-2 leather flight jackets often duplicated the picture and name on the backs. Lead crews never had assigned planes. We flew whatever PFF (radar dome) B-17 had been tested and was ready for "lead ship" duty. The Templeton crew flew twelve different bombers according to flight records provided by the 490th Group historian, Eric Swain of London. Near the war's end, I bought a used A-2 jacket. I told my crewmembers that we were the "Hot Dogs", and painted a picture of Disney's Pluto in helmet and goggles with eighteen bombs beneath. I wore that leather jacket for several years after returning to Indiana. However, it eventually became too small!

Moment of Truth

We were on pins and needles the night before this first mission. The veteran crew in our hut thought it might be the Merseberg oil plants again with all that heavy flak. We were scheduled for a 2:30 wake-up call and that meant a long mission. The wake-up call came on schedule. We donned fatigues and our heavy flight suits and hurried to the Mess Hall. The cooks served a hot breakfast of fresh eggs, bacon and all the trimmings. We learned that crews always got a big breakfast on mission days because they went without lunch and needed all the energy they could get. Trucks waited at the Mess Hall to haul crews to the big "briefing hut" for the enlisted men's briefing. The group intelligence officer stood in front of a huge wall map of Germany to give information on the routes to and from the target. It was Berlin, or "Big B"! The suspense was over—we were starting at the top. Hitler's capitol hadn't been bombed since October and was heavily protected by anti-aircraft batteries and fighter squadrons. The shivers we felt were not all because of the cold weather!

Our flight routes to the target and return were plotted on the wall map so that we would avoid as much anti-aircraft and fighter danger as possible. However, the Germans also had mobile anti-aircraft mounted on trains and river barges! Officers attended a separate briefing and met us at the plane. The equipment hut was our next stop. We were issued oxygen masks, chute harnesses, helmets with headsets and throat mikes, Mae West life jackets, electrically-heated suits to wear under our flight suits, and other equipment. Then it was on to the parachute hut for a chest-pack chute. Those jokers had a sign over the counter, "If it doesn't work---bring it back".

Part of the equipment on each B-17 was an emergency duffel bag filled with extra clothing, first-aid kits, and oxygen masks. Bomber crewmembers carried a .45 automatic in case they had to bail out over enemy territory. I also carried a ten-inch Bowie knife I had purchased in Sioux City. We were told to tie a pair of G.I. shoes to the parachute harness. Those wool-lined leather boots we wore over our electrically-heated boots would pop off with the jerk of a parachute opening. Nobody wanted to be barefoot if they survived the jump. We were also instructed to bury the parachute if we landed in enemy territory so the Germans could not pinpoint our location. A small "escape kit" tied to the parachute harness contained a compass and a morphine syringe. They also issued a K-ration box or high energy candy for our snack. We all carried an ID card in Russian saying "I am an American" in case we landed among advancing Russian troops.

A jeep hauled our crew and equipment to the hardstand where our plane had been fueled and loaded with bombs. Our flak jackets, steel helmets and flexible flak panels were on the plane. The .50 caliber guns had been installed at all positions. While the rest of the crew checked their guns and battle stations, I tuned my radios to the assigned frequencies, called the tower for a radio check and studied the bomb code for the day. The bombs had already been loaded and armed with fuses. The pilots and navigator arrived from their briefing, started the engines and checked all flight instruments. We had finished our formation flying training and were classified "ready for combat". The combat crew training at Sioux city had taught us to do our jobs. Now, we knew we had to rely upon each other and the training we had just completed to keep us alive. I went into the U.S. Army Air Force in August, 1943, and now in December of 1944 the moment of truth had arrived. I was nineteen and a half, just under the age of 20 which was average for Eighth Air Force crewmembers. I was now a Buck Sergeant and glad to have those three stripes on my sleeve! This was the job we had volunteered to do when we became VFT's in the Air Cadet program many months ago.

First Mission   Berlin   December 5th, 1944

Combat Mission Diary

Alerted Monday night, awakened at 0230 Tuesday morning, had breakfast and briefing. Briefed for 300 or more guns at target. Take off 0730, IP 1029. Was so busy tossing chaff, I didn't see any flak, felt a big burst though, right below us! It gave us 4 holes. Bombed with PFF, saw several dogfights between our P-51 escorts and German fighters – thought I saw a couple go down. They (anti-aircraft guns) shot pretty accurate and our exact altitude.

Mission was 7 hours long, 5 hours on oxygen, flew at 25,000 feet, heated suits worked fine and "flak suit" and helmet were good morale boosters!! Threw 336 bundles of chaff in 21 minutes, not a bad job, keeps your mind off flak.

Dropped bombs at about 10:45, got only 4 flak holes, 2 in the wing, one in nacelle number 3, and one in the nose. Cut out Bert's interphone!

Landed at 15:30, interrogation, coffee and cookies, and shot of Scotch! Had supper, Roddy and I had to go back and clean the guns. Had 3 letters from Mom when I got to the hut.

Pretty good mission to start with, hope they are all as good and safe!! Flew 849 ship number 490-E, hardstand 8.

[Briefing Order: Crew stations 6:05 – Start engines 6:30 – Taxi out 6:35 –Take off 6:45 – Group assembly at 11,000 feet on red and yelow flares – Target Berlin – Bombing altitude 25,000 PFF – Chaff to be dispersed two minutes before IP and continue on bomb run. Radio channels and code-words were listed for all units on the mission.]

Taking off in the early morning with the bomb group was different than practice flights. Planes taxied out and lined up for take-off. With a full bomb load, ammunition and ten men, we had about 56,000 pounds to get into the air (the plane weighed 26,000 pounds). Early dawn take-offs required planes to pull off their hardstands (parking areas) and into line on the runway. There was a terrific roar over the countryside as pilots of thirty or more bombers gunned their four motors and carried out pre-flight checks to make sure they were prepared to get into line and lift their loaded B-17s into the air. Take-off was always a dangerous event because the pilot had to reach a speed of over 110 mph before he dared lift off the runway and climb into the crowded skies over England. Planes took off every thirty seconds, often climbing through the "zero visibility" sky to assemble in squadron formation and on into their groups at their assigned altitudes. Lead planes used various colored flares to identify their bomb group assembly location. Rendezvous or assembly over England was a perilous business. Planes often flew up through clouds and overcast skies that would ground today's civilian planes. The air control plan involved the use of radio beacons or "bunchers". Each bomb group had an assigned climb pattern guided by radio beams from the ground. A pilot was required to stay on his "radio beam" and climb safely up through the hundreds of planes in the sky. Crewmen referred to a good pilot as being, "on the beam". There were many "near misses" every mission. A bomber straying into another group's climbing pattern could result (and sometimes did) in a mid-air collision. This usually meant flaming wreckages of planes and live bombs falling back to the East Anglia countryside and twenty lost men!

Accidents were bound to happen, and one dark morning we were lined up on the take-off runway when the ball turret guns in a plane ahead of us started firing and bouncing .50 caliber bullets off the concrete runway. You can imagine our panic with bullets ricocheting in all directions amidst thirty B-17 bombers with 5,000 pound bomb loads! We never found out what happened. Take-off and landing accidents could and did happen at the many airfields. There were planes that failed to make lift-off and crashed at the end of the runway. Damaged planes limping home from bombing missions often crash-landed. Many planes and men were lost due to accidents. Ambulances, fire trucks and crash trucks were kept busy on mission days.

Later on one of those early missions a bomber in our formation radioed pilot Bill Templeton to tell him that our bomb bay doors were not fully closed. Our toggleleer, Bert Allinder, volunteered to go into the open bomb bay and check out the problem.. It was a very dangerous job because we were flying at a high altitude on oxygen. He had to go out into the bomb bay at 40 below zero with a portable oxygen tank. He discovered that the lowest bomb on one rack was only hanging by its rear shackle (bombs had two shackles to keep them level). This allowed its nose to rest on the bomb bay door, forcing it slightly open. We were armed with ten 250 pound bombs with spinner fuses which would spin 250 times when dropped and explode above the target. Bert later said he didn't know if, nor how many times that bomb's spinner had rotated but he knew he had to act fast! He hooked his parachute harness to a bomb rack and worked with both hands. I watched from my radio room as he freed the bomb from its rear shackle and it plummeted into the North Sea near the island of Helgoland off the southern coast of Denmark. We never learned how many fish he killed.

The B-17G Flying Fortresses rose into the dark morning sky to rendezvous with the rest of the squadron at around 5,000 feet. Each squadron had to find their group based on various colored flares and maneuver into the formations in their assigned positions. The group's lead plane fired a green flare when the formation was in place and ready to start the mission. They moved out across the English Channel once the combat formation took shape and then rose to the assigned bombing height of 25,000 feet or so before entering enemy territory. As a new crew, we flew tail-end Charlie. This meant I had the radio trailing wire antenna which I could reel out behind the plane in case it was needed to send reports back to Eye. The trailing wire was a long cable with a steel ball on the end to keep it taut. (This not something desired in the middle of a tight formation).

There was heavy flak on the bomb-run and the lead plane of the high squadron was hit. It fell out of formation with a feathered prop. Our formation tightened up and headed for home as our P-51 escort fighters intercepted the Luftwaffe (German Air Force) fighters. The Nazi fighters came up through that hole in the clouds and a great aerial battle was fought at 25,000 feet. The Eighth fighters had a "turkey shoot" and shot down 80 Luftwaffe fighters in that battle above the clouds (9).

This Berlin mission of around 500 bombers had been scheduled as a maximum effort, and we were heavily escorted by P-51 and P-47 fighters. The 490th sent out 37 B-17's and Major Cochran led this mission. Our Fortress flew "tail-end Charlie" (last) in the low squadron. This position was also called "Coffin Corner" because it didn't have the protection of planes flying beside it and was more vulnerable to enemy fighter attacks who often attacked the last planes in the formation. The B-17 was a very tough plane, and could take a lot of flak and fighter attacks and keep on flying. The Fortress could maintain its place in formation on three engines. A Fort could fly on two engines and still make it back to England if the Luftwaffe didn't get it after it fell out of the formation. By December 1944 these wounded stragglers would often get lucky and be escorted and protected by our escort fighters (little friends) until they could land in liberated territory in France or Belgium.

So there I was, my first mission was to "Big B" and it was one to remember. This was a long mission and they had told us to expect German fighters to be protecting the target. We had a scary episode after we entered Germany, because our number three engine began to lose power and we were lagging behind the formation! Templeton, Rector, and Roddy were going through all the procedures to correct the problem as we saw the group gradually pulling away. The situation was serious because we had come too far to abort the mission. A lone bomber over enemy territory was a "sitting duck" for German fighters. Finally, the engine regained power and we slowly caught up with the formation to take our place as "Tail-end Charlie" in the low squadron! There was a heavy cloud cover, but the sky cleared just before we reached the target and we were able to bomb visually. Our bombardier, Walter Benedict, had been transferred to the 851st squadron and the Gamble crew, and Bert Allinder, our armorer-waist gunner, was assigned to ride in the nose as "toggleleer". His job was to throw a toggle switch and release our bombs when our squadron's lead plane's bombardier dropped its bombload. We were on the bomb run when Bert saw the lead ship's bombs drop. He threw the switch and yelled "Bombs….", but nobody heard the "away" because at that minute a piece of flak cut his intercom line! We knew our bombs had been released because we felt the "lift" of the plane when we dropped 5,000 pounds! I thought Bert had been hit! The navigator reported him okay, and helped hook him up to another intercom. Flak on the bomb run was heavy but the excitement came after "bombs away" as the lead plane in the high squadron was hit by flak and fell out of formation and our group split. However, the formation got back together and our escort fighters intercepted the Luftwaffe planes coming up to get us.

The guys in our formation had a ringside seat, and we saw a terrific series of dogfights between our P-51 fighters and the enemy FW-190 attackers. This aerial battle continued behind us as we headed for England and safety, courtesy of our escort fighters. Ralph Moore, our tail-gunner, had an excellent view of the action. However, the lead plane of the high squadron had been heavily damaged over the target and fell behind the formation. It was later attacked by the FW-190 fighters and crashed. The crew was listed as MIA (missing in action). The Eighth Air Force lost only four bombers in the 500 plane raid and one was from our 490th Bomb Group.

Lutzkendorf (Aborted)   December 6, 1944

Awakened at 03:30 – breakfast, briefing at 04:30, take-off at 07:45 – take-off "Chicago 4" (delayed).

Our plane "aborted" over Holland with engine trouble – saw flak and a rocket during time over Holland. Called MF/DF and then HF/QF for QDM. Returned to base. 849 ship 135-B.

On our second mission (we thought), we developed engine trouble and had to abort. We were headed for Lutzendorf, Germany, but the plane gave us so much trouble that over Holland our pilot decided it was not air-worthy. We saw some flak and a rocket but left the group and returned to the base with a cancelled mission under our belts. Twelve planes, led by Captain Kavanaugh, carried out the mission to bomb a synthetic oil plant.

Practice Flight   December 7, 1944

Pearl Harbor Day was no different than any other; it was a clear day and we had a practice flight scheduled. The skeleton crew of pilot, co-pilot, navigator, engineer and radioman were to check the plane's performance and equipment. We slow-timed the plane for about four hours to check the motors. Our pilot, Lt. Bill Templeton, let me "fly" the plane. I climbed into his seat and Bill gave me the controls and said, "Keep all the needles where they are now". I was completely dumbfounded by the plane's instrument panel. There were needles and dials everywhere! Bill laughed at me and my mistakes. Rod was heckling me too. We all had a good time, including co-pilot Lt. Dale Rector who kept his seat and actual control of the plane! After I climbed out of the pilot's seat, I told them to come back to the radio room and I would show them around.

London Pass   December 10, 1944

Our crew received a three-day pass to London after our first mission. We caught the train at Diss and stood up for a few hours until we reached Liverpool Station. Our immediate goal was Piccadilly Circus, the entertainment hub of London. The "tube" (subway) was crowded and our tail-gunner, Ralph Moore, missed getting into the car with us. Ralph was "as a wet hen" as the doors closed in his face! He caught the next tube and met us at the Piccadilly Station.

The American Red Cross operated the Rainbow Corner Canteen for U.S. servicemen. The canteen was located on Shaftsbury Avenue just off Piccadilly Circus. The Canteen was within easy walking distance of Leicester Square, Marble Arch, Hyde Park, Trafalgar Square and Buckingham Palace. The Red Cross staff was very helpful. They provided food and activities and made us feel welcome. Fred Astaire's sister and first dancing partner, Adele, volunteered at the canteen and often helped with cablegrams and phone calls home.

Rainbow Corner was also a great place to watch for guys we had known in our stateside training days. I met a couple of fellows from our VFT basic training barracks in Amarillo! They knew of several gunners who had finished their missions and gone home. Unfortunately some others didn't make it. We could also check the guest register and note board for names and addresses of buddies stationed at other airfields. We all registered by name and crew before going to our room.

The staff at Rainbow Corner had assigned us a room at the Columbia Club, a hotel for American servicemen. The YMCA type facility was only a flew blocks from Piccadilly Circus. The room was clean and cost four shillings (80 cents) each for two nights. The four of us stored our bags and headed out for our first night in London. We walked back to Piccadilly Circus and had supper at the Corner House – a big ritzy place –where all the old waiters wore "tails" and starched collars. The waitresses wore the traditional black with white apron and cap. The orchestra members were very old and their favorite song was "Lady of Spain". I think it was the Reggie Dare band. It was quite a place and carried the high society name of a "brasserie", which is French for a beer garden that serves food. You can guess what the G.I's called it! We had a nice table and ordered what they had on the menu, which was very limited; a few vegetables and fish or sausages. I liked the sausages and was really surprised when I later read in the "Stars and Stripes" that the British meat supply was improving and they were going to put less sawdust in their sausages!

Oh happy day!!! They had "American" beer. After a month or so of "mild & bitters" at Diss pubs, we finally got cold beer! The English drink beer warm, and wherever they served cold mild, they called it "American Beer". Well, we ate our meal and begged a few more beers from the waiter before they chased us out!

After supper, we roamed the streets around Piccadilly Circus and let the "commandos" (prostitutes) hit on us and bargain for prices just for the fun of it. In England, prostitutes were licensed and inspected for diseases, so it was a legal profession! We didn't take them up on their offers, and got back to the Columbia Club about midnight. It was evident that those "VD films" in basic training had the desired effect! There was a worn-out tale about a naïve serviceman who was picked up by a commando. The story went something like this:

> She: "Hey, Yank, how about going to my place?" He agrees and when they get to her apartment she says, "How about a drink?" He agrees and then she says, "How about going to bed?" He agrees and the next morning she says, "How about a big breakfast?" He says, "That would be great". As he was leaving she says, "How about five pounds ($20)?" He says, "Oh, no lady, you've done way too much —I couldn't take your money!"

London had suffered greatly from German air raids, and there were many bombed-out buildings. Now the German "buzz-bombs" were coming in regularly, especially at night. I had an uneasy night's sleep as bomb explosions sounded in the distance. When you went to bed in London, you never knew if you would wake up! Some guys wouldn't take a London pass! Luckily, all went well and we got up when the old chambermaid knocked on the door. She wanted to make the beds, and while we were dressing, she told us her life story. She was a fat old lady (everyone looks old to a 19 year-old) and was very nice. She had been buzz-bombed out of her home and was working to have a place to live. She said we Yankees had quite a name to live down. Then she told us a poem.

> "Old Father Hubbard went to the cupboard
> To get himself a hanky.
> When he got there the cupboard was bare,
> And so was his wife with a Yankee!"

It was really funny with her Cockney accent. Then she asked why our hair was cut so short. She said the English called G.I. haircuts a "four-penny bob" because for four pennies they cut all your hair off – it's easier that way!

London Passes

Our bi-monthly three-day passes were looked forward to with great anticipation. We would pack our overnight bags with the bare necessities and hop on a "pass truck" to catch the London train at Diss. A "pass truck" met every train at the station. It was a quick trip into Liverpool Station. Across the street from the station was a three-story house with Dirty Dick's bar on the first floor. It was a very convenient place to "wet your whistle." The unusual décor of Dirty Dick's included a stuffed alligator and dried out carcasses of "road kill" cats and dogs on the wall. The place hadn't been dusted in years and really lived up to its name! Later we would head for the Rainbow Club at Piccadilly Circus to secure rooms. We learned much about London's sights on these trips. We took a tax-cab tour on an early trip and saw Big Ben, Parliament, Tower bridge, St. Paul's cathedral, Number Ten Downing Street, and Tower of London. We also saw the many bombed-out sections of the city.

Leicester Square, the theater section, was within walking distance of Piccadilly. It was eerie to sit in a beautiful theater and hear V-1 "buzz bombs" bursting in the area. Plaster and dust fell from the ceiling when the explosions were too close. At one theater before the show started, the organ player would rise from the orchestra pit in front of the stage playing "God Save the Queen". The organ would then sink into the pit and the movie would begin. We only went to see American films, and a large part of the audience was composed of servicemen and women on leave.

Our visit to Westminster Abbey was a memorable event. Three or four of us caught the subway and emerged in front of the historical building. Visitors were welcome, so we entered and were awed by the eternal flame on the British Tomb of the Unknown Soldier. We turned to look down the aisle to the beautiful golden façade and altar in the front of the church. I went down the aisle for a better look and was trapped by the singing choir as they marched toward the altar. I couldn't get back to a side aisle, so I fell back into a pew as the somber choir passed by without a glance in my direction. They were probably amused by the predicament of a green country boy from Indiana.

We went back to the Rainbow Corner Canteen and spent the day walking the streets of Piccadilly Circus (the restaurant area), Leicester Square (the theater area) where there were good movies playing, and Trafalgar Square (the cultural center). It was easy to find our way around the area. The British were very helpful to guide us and their directions usually ended with "you caun't miss it!" The Trafalgar battle monument was really inspiring. It is a large stone column with a statue of Admiral Nelson on top and a plaza where we could rest and feed the pigeons. We also went into the British Art Museum.and made the greenhorn mistake of getting too close to the artwork. We observed the English visitors and learned to stand back from the pictures to get a better perspective of the paintings.

We had supper again at the Corner House (brasserie) and argued with the old waiter until we got some cold beer. The waiter was an RAC (Royal Army Corps) veteran of World War I, and it was fun to talk about the world situation.

The next morning we got up and went shopping for who knows what, because. the shops had very little merchandise due to war rationing. We roamed and window-shopped before going back to Piccadilly for a late lunch or early supper. Later, we went back to Rainbow Corner and sent cablegrams to our parents. Then we checked out our bags and took a wild taxi ride to Liverpool Station. Two of the guys had a bottle of scotch and were feeling pretty good. One opened the sliding top and stood in the back seat with head and shoulders out the top! We took turns standing and looking at the city, waving and yelling to pedestrians as we went down Victoria Street to the Thames river, Bishopsgate and the station. Our train ride back to Diss was uneventful and boring after our London R and R (Rest and Relaxation). We received London passes about every two weeks, but that first trip was the most memorable.

Back at the base the weather was miserable, and there was no flying; only a few classroom training classes. We huddled around our little "coke stove" trying to keep warm and remembering our London pass. There had been an accident (while we were on pass) due to fog. The group was returning from a mission and one plane landed on top of another on the runway, both were destroyed and few crewmembers survived.

Articles in the "Stars and Stripes" kept us well informed on the war news and stories on our bombing raids and many of those stories of our missions are pasted in my "war diary". I especially enjoyed the cartoons like "Sad Sack", "Hubert" "The Count" and "Willie and Joe."

One of the most popular cartoon characters in Stars and Stripes was "Sad Sack".He suffered all the trials and tribulations of the typical army private at the very bottom of the chain of command. "Sad Sack's" advice was very simple:

> If it moves, salute it,
>
> If it doesn't move, pick it up:
>
> If you can't pick it up, paint it! (19)

Bill Mauldin the World War II soldier's cartoonist, passed away at the age of 81 January, 2003. His early cartoons, based on his experiences as a rifleman in the 180th Infantry, earned him a position on the staff of "Stars and Stripes". Mauldin's "Willie and Joe" depicted a realistic view of the foot soldier's life in combat. The ironic humor of those two characters applied to all fighting men. Like Ernie Pyle's news stories, Mauldin's cartoons reflected the common G.I.'s view of the war, whether in a foxhole, tank or a B-17 Flying Fortress.

Bill Mauldin was awarded his first Pulitzer Prize in 1945 at the age of 23 for his book "Up Front with Mauldin." He later became a noted political cartoonist working on newspapers in St. Louis and Chicago. He authored several more books and was awarded a second Pulitzer Prize.

The "Stars and Stripes" was our main news source. The Army paper was started in April 1942 and reached a circulation of 1,200,000 before the war ended in May 1945. Rod, Robby, Bert and I had chipped in to purchase a thirty dollar radio in Diss to hear the current news over the British Broadcasting Corporation (BBC) and U.S. Armed Forces Network.

German propaganda was broadcast by two American traitors. William Joyce, "Lord Haw Haw," an American born in Brooklyn, New York, was on the air for over five years. He was captured, tried for treason after the war, and hanged in 1946. "Axis Sally" was an American-born English teacher named Mildred Gillars. She was convicted of treason and spent sixteen years in prison. Both broadcasters played a lot of popular American records and used all kinds of messages to destroy our morale (19). We enjoyed the music and ignored their propaganda.

James Lee Hutchinson, EdS

Letters From Home

Mail-call was always well-attended because letters and packages from home brought welcome news for lonesome guys in the service. The dreaded "Dear John" letter was one that nobody wanted. It was that letter from a wife or girlfriend notifying a soldier that she no longer loved him and wanted to date other guys. Any guy who received such a letter had the sympathy and comfort of everyone in the squadron! I recently read about a Dear John recipient who got his revenge. His girlfriend had asked that he return her photo. He mailed her picture and those of four other girls and asked her to pick out hers because he had forgotten who she was! Mail was especially important when we were on combat duty in England. My family's letters kept me informed about relatives and the home situation. My mother included newspaper clippings and snapshots of interest. There were also letters from girls in my high school class with news on how the school year was going without me! Of course the teachers were encouraging students to write letters to keep up the morale of the fighting men. It worked, and I really enjoyed those envelopes with their three cent stamps and the penny postcards with the news they contained. When I returned home, I soon realized that I was more interesting to those girls when I was thousands of miles away!

I answered all my mail. Servicemen spent a lot of time writing to friends and family. However, we were warned to be careful about what we wrote. All our letters were censored by our officers to be sure we didn't give away any military secrets! As if we knew anything of

Through These Eyes

great importance. The censored letters were photographed, reduced in size and sent back to the USA by a process called V-mail. Prior to the war, Eastman Kodak had developed the V-mail system to reduce the weight of air-mail letters. Approximately a ton of servicemen's letters could be reduced to twenty pounds of film (19). I managed to preserve a few from Mom's mementos. You'll notice I drew cartoons in those days (note the Hot Dog). Just think, down through the years, I've progressed from V-mail to E-mail!

I was beginning to feel as if I knew what I was doing now. Here I was, a small-town Hoosier kid from Indiana, nineteen and a half years old, flying and helping to win the war. I was drafted out of Bedford High only six hours short of graduation. I received my draft notice the day after my 18th birthday! We decided the war must be going badly in June of 1943----they needed everyone. Two years later my diploma was presented to my mother in May 1945 while I was still in England.

But in reality, the air war was fought and won by teenagers and young men. The average age of air crewmembers was twenty. Prior to the war, our Army Air Corps was but a handful of men and the pre-war planes were nowhere near those developed during the war years. The United States industrial machine had to be rushed into high gear and we were lucky to have had time to build our armed forces into a powerful force to win wars on both fronts. For example, the B-17G that we were flying barely resembled the B-17 the Air Force was flying before the war. The plane had been refined and redeveloped as the war progressed. The Norden bombsight was a highly secretive invention that enabled us to carry out strategic bombing missions and destroy the German oil, industrial and transportation systems.

The civilian population was back home experiencing rationing of food and fuel, and the automobile industry had switched to making jeeps, trucks, and tanks for the war effort. No civilian automobiles were made in 1943 and 1944. The suggested speed limit was 35 miles per hour to save gas and tires. I was so young that I went into the service unable to drive a car. Our family had no car so I had never learned to drive. It was eighteen months before anyone in the service asked me to drive. I remember that embarrassing moment well. Our crew was standing on a hardstand at Eye getting a B-17 ready for an equipment flight test. We were short a parachute and the pilot said, "Hutch, take that jeep and run back and pick up a chute!" I had to confess that I couldn't drive. I had ridden trains, trucks and buses all over the states, the Queen Mary to England and spent hours in test flights and combat missions. But, I didn't learn to drive a car until I returned to Indiana!

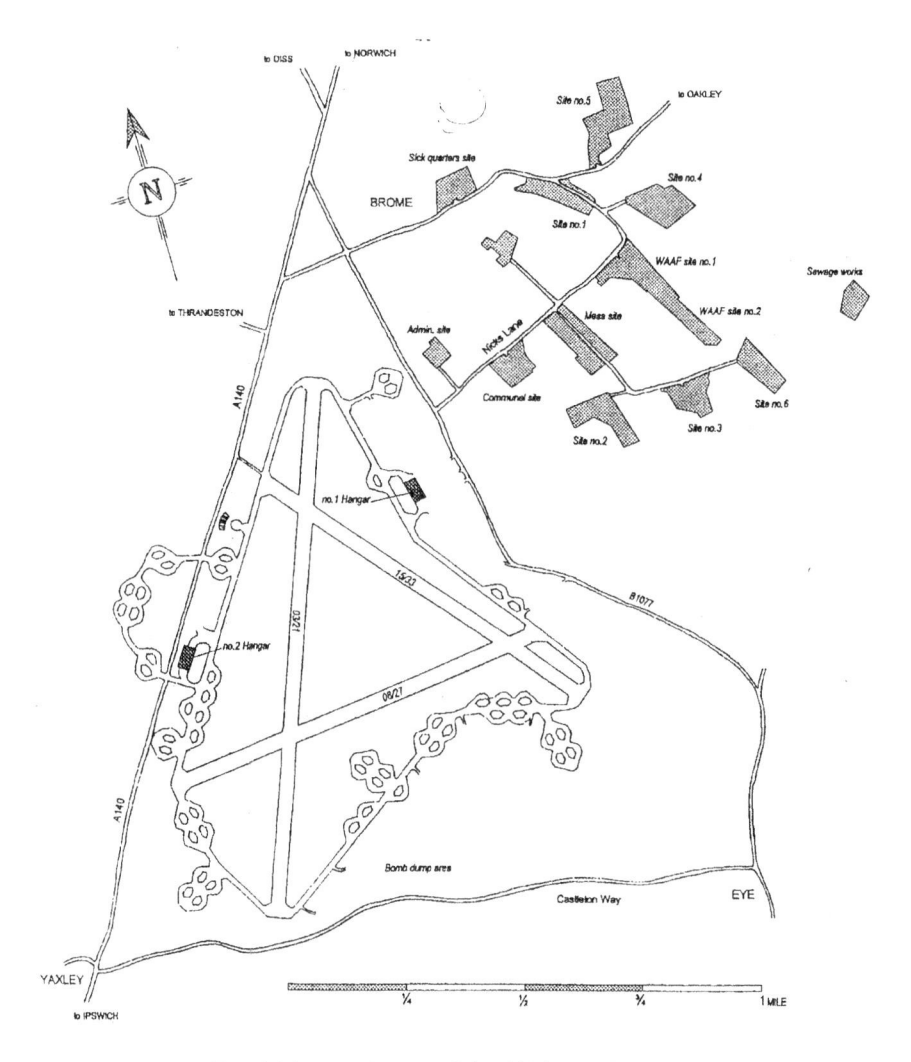

Eye Airbase – Home of the 490th Bomb Group

We flew into flak over the target!

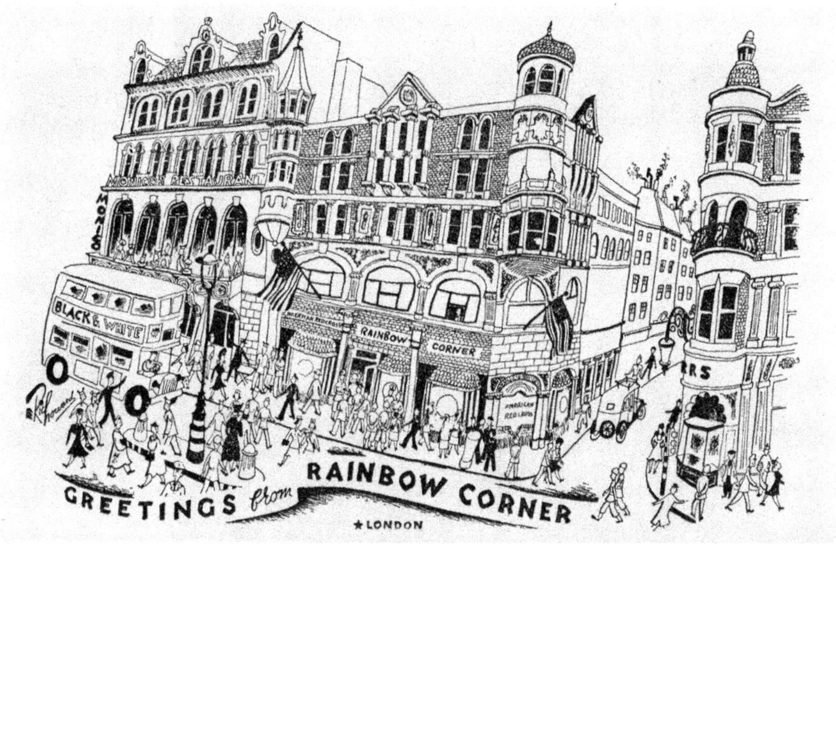

Bert Allinder and Ralph Moore hanging out in London

Piccadilly Circus with Paul Covington

German factory in the Norden bombsight

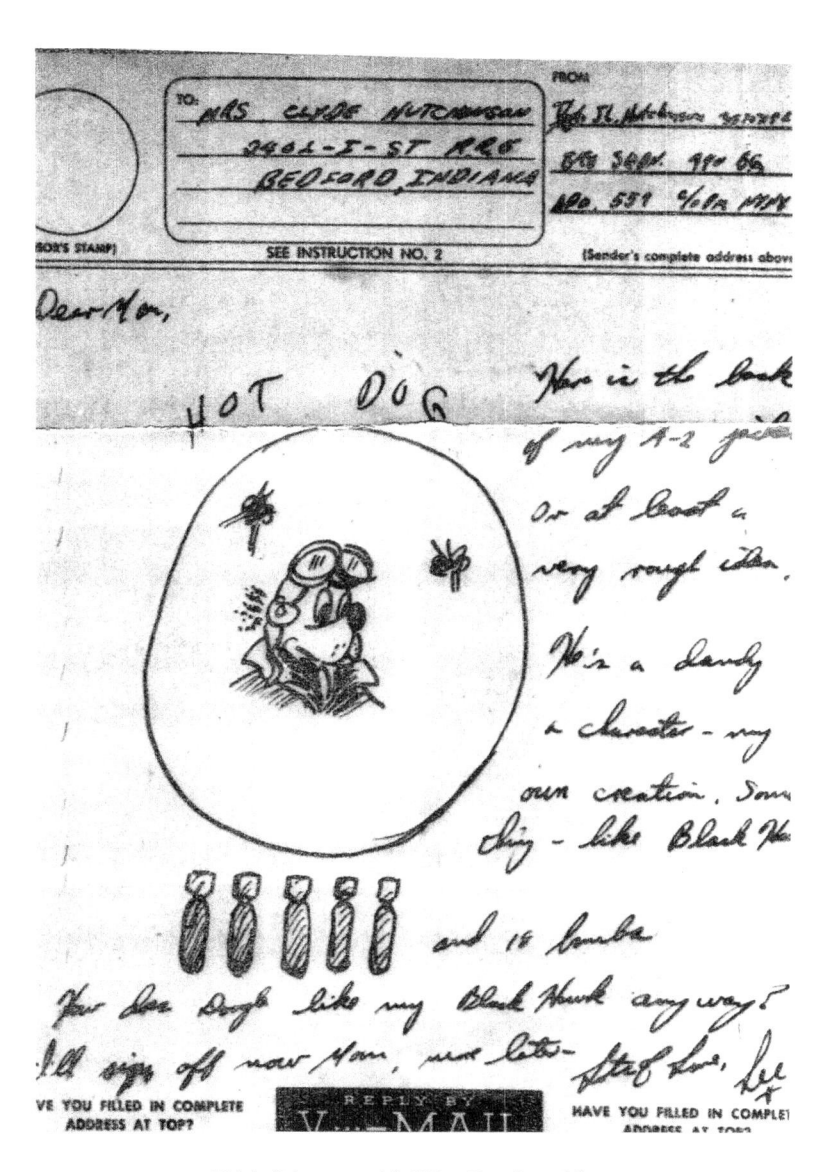

V-Mail letter, with "Hot Dog" emblem

Chapter Six

The Wild Blue Yonder

Mission Two   Hanover   December 15, 1944

Another good breakfast of ham and eggs and off to briefing. We took off at 8:30. We had good sight on our waist guns. We were loaded with 500-pound bombs and a couple of incendiaries too. Another mission, not much flak at all, practically a milk run. I threw chaff for 12 minutes over the target, about 288 bundles. We bombed at 24,500 feet by PFF, saw several German rockets but they weren't effective. Our target was the Hanover marshalling yards – not much flak. Rod got a hole in his turret. Flak was rated moderate but accurate. This mission was 5 hours and 45 minutes long and we were on oxygen 4 hours.

There were 39 planes on this raid led by Major Blum. The "Stars and Stripes" news stories later said this mission of 650 Flying

Fortresses escorted by 550 Mustang P-51s and Thunderbolts attacked Germany's rail and industrial plants. The Eighth lost four bombers and two fighter planes. The 15th AF B-24 Liberators flew in from Italy to hit targets in southern Germany. The strategic bombing campaign was planned for the U.S. Air Force to bomb specific targets during daylight. Our Norden bombsight was very effective for pinpoint bombing, and the B-17 was a top-notch offensive weapon. England's RAF (Royal Air Force) bombers pounded German targets at night, while B-17s bombed heavily during the day.

The December weather had cleared and our group had flown three more missions while we were on leave. This time we flew in the rear of the middle (lead) squadron. This was also the third time that the formation's target was a railroad marshalling yard. The weather had eased again and as the Army Air Corps song said, " Off we go into the wild blue yonder, climbing high into the sun". Our problem was to climb safely up through the overcast in order to see the sun!

The group formation was easy and we were on our way for mission number two.

When we set up on our bomb run over the target, the planes had to hold the course until bombs were released. This made our formation a good target for German anti-aircraft guns. Once they found our altitude, they could fire away and the air would become black with bursting shells (flak). Close explosions would shake the plane and pieces of flak (small, steel chunks of metal) would come flying at the plane. The Eighth had a defense for that. An entire squadron of twelve or more bombers would be loaded with cartons filled with bundles of 7x8 sheets of aluminum foil This squadron would lead the formation over the target area. The bundles of chaff were fed into metal chutes on the plane and sucked out into the airstream. The sky was filled with the fluttering metallic sheets which fouled up the radar on the anti-aircraft guns below. Two minutes before reaching the IP, (bomb run) we were ordered to begin tossing the chaff and all available crewmembers helped. It was something like feeding bundles of paper towels into a paper shredder. We kept at it for twelve minutes through the bomb run and helped hide our formation by knocking out their ability to find our planes.Actually this meant that the "chaff" squadron was unprotected while flying head-on into the barrage of bursting shells! German fighters were another matter, and we kept a sharp eye for these "bandits". They usually came at us from 12 o'clock high right at our noses and out of the sun if possible! Our escort fighters protected us on this trip and we saw no German fighters. Once the lead bombardier yells "bombs away", the lead pilot takes control of his plane and the formation turns toward England.

B-17 gunners had been trained to avoid shooting our own fighters or spraying other planes in their formation. Aircraft recognition classes were part of our training. Short bursts and watching where those balls of fire (tracer bullets) were going was the key. About every fifth .50 caliber bullet was a tracer. The German Focke-Wulf 190 carried cannons and loved to come in from 12 o'clock (front) high and rake the formation with his machine guns and cannons as he swooped

Through These Eyes

past. Eighth Air Force gunners blasted many German fighters from the sky. The B-17 carried the fight to the enemy. The wide field of fire provided by the box formation protected the bombers. But large numbers of Luftwaffe fighters could overwhelm unescorted bombers. Our escort fighters, P-51 Mustangs, P-47 Thunderbolts and P-38 Lightnings gave us the protection we needed in the fall of 1944. British Spitfires were wonderful short-range fighters. Now our P-51D Mustang fighters equipped with extra fuel tanks could fly escort all over Europe with our formations. The P-51D now had a speed of 400 MPH and a combat range of 750 miles.

The B-17G was the latest model. It had a remote-controlled nose turret with two .50 caliber machine guns which were very effective in discouraging frontal attacks. The name "Flying Fortress" described the strength of the B-17. The plane could fly 160 miles per hour with a full bomb load for a radius of 800 miles. There were thirteen .50 caliber machine guns to protect all angles of approach by enemy fighters. The B-17 had a ceiling of 36,000 feet but usually flew missions at 23,000 to 28,000 feet.

My radio room was over the left wing and just behind the bomb bay door. A small desk fastened to the bulkhead (wall) held my radio receiver and Morse code sending key. On the bulkhead behind me was my large liaison radio with all its tuner units stored beneath. I pre-tuned these units to assigned secret frequencies before take-off and could call the control tower for a radio check. Radio operators were issued new cryptographic code charts (BOMBCO) and group radio frequencies before each mission. Changing frequencies in flight simply required taking out one pre-set tuning unit and inserting another. Coded strike reports or messages could be sent back to the base. The radio reports I sent were in Morse code with the BOMBCO for the day. All planes were required to maintain radio silence because the Germans could pick up radio transmissions. Not only could they intercept our messages but they could pinpoint our formation's location and relay it to their fighter and anti-aircraft batteries. Crewmembers communicated with the intercom system. Pilots had VHF (very high frequency) sets for communication between planes if absolutely necessary. Additional radio equipment included a radio compass for the navigator and an IFF (identification friend or foe) set which emitted a continuous signal to identify us to other Allied friends. We also had numerous three-letter "Q signals", a type of Morse code shorthand. Each represented a statement or request for information. For instance, QTF was short for "request a fix location". In voice radio between planes, the words "Roger" or "Wilco" were used at the end of a message to signify, "Okay, I understand" or "will comply". Planes in distress used the dreaded vocal "Mayday", or sent an SOS by Morse code. I had a small window next to my desk and another across the aisle. I could observe the wings and engines one and two on the left, and three and four out the right. A plexiglass sunroof overhead gave a very good view of the sky behind and above me when I stood up. The B-17G no longer carried a machine gun in the skylight of the radio room. I had become a radioman instead of a radio-gunner! I was in the middle of the plane and all crew traffic from the tail to the nose passed through my domain. However, at high altitude traffic was greatly reduced because it required hooking up to a portable oxygen tank. There was also the extreme cold until you could plug into another electrical outlet. Frostbite was always a possibility when we were five miles high at –40 degrees!

Flying a six or seven-hour mission was demanding, especially since we were on oxygen much of the time. We always had an excellent breakfast to carry us through the day. Our lunch was often an army K-ration dinner about the size of a cracker-jack box. If and when we found time to eat, we would have a small can of Spam or cheese spread, crackers and a chocolate bar. On some missions we received a small box of high-energy hard candy as a change of menu. Aircrew members often saved left-over candy for the children living around our airfield.

Our only toilet facility was a "relief tube" for urinating. It was simply a funnel attached to a hose leading outside the plane. It was located in the waist gunner's area of the plane. Few men dared to use it at 40 degrees below zero. Most guys preferred to "hold it", although one crewmember failed to make it and shorted out his electric suit. He nearly froze before he could get to the dry clothing in the emergency bag.

Hazards of Flying

Today's airliners are oxygen pressurized for high altitudes. Ours were not, and ears and the common cold could cause a problem in high altitude flying. Pressure on a flier's eardrum was equalized by the Eustachian tube from mouth to inner ear. This was accomplished by yawning or yelling as the plane descended rapidly. If your tube was clogged by a cold you would get an extreme earache. A lot of screaming seemed to help. I had a few colds but I never missed a flight because of "sick call". World War II planes carried oxygen tanks that were located near each crewmember's station. Portable tanks were also available so that crewmembers could move about if the need arose.

Oxygen masks were required once we started our climb to bombing altitude. Six thousand feet was the maximum height without oxygen masks. An oxygen mask failure could occur if ice particles froze the valve. We were warned to periodically squeeze the rubber mask to break up any ice particles. The lack of oxygen, or anoxia, caused a giddy, euphoric feeling. The crewmember who was not aware of an oxygen mask failure felt fine, but could be dead of anoxia in less than twenty minutes. Pilots used the plane's intercom to check crew positions to make sure their men were alert and on the ball. We had portable oxygen tanks to allow us to move about the plane. If a plane's oxygen system was knocked out, the plane had to drop out of formation and go down to fly at a low level.

Fire was the most dreaded accident and usually meant disaster. Flak or a fighter's bullets could start an engine fire. The wings held the plane's gasoline tanks, and that combination meant danger. Crash landings and mid-air collisions usually resulted in fire and explosions. A fire anywhere on the plane was a good reason to clip your chest pack parachute onto your harness and be ready to bail out.

Engine failure was serious whether it was a mechanical failure or flak cutting oil or hydraulic lines in one of the plane's engines. In this event the pilot had to cut off the engine and "feather the prop" quickly. This was a process to adjust the propeller so it would not "windmill" and shake the entire plane, or fly off its shaft and damage the plane. "Feathering" the prop meant changing the position of the blades so they would cut into the wind and remain still. It was a simple procedure if all went well; the pilot pushed the "feather button" for the damaged engine and closed its fuel valve. The B-17 could keep up with the group on three engines when necessary. There were several times we had an engine failure on our test flights over England.

The below-zero temperature forced all crewmembers to wear electrically-heated boots and suits under our heavy flight suits. The electric shirt, pants, shoes, gloves and caps were all connected by plugs. We could plug into the 12-volt adjustable outlet at each crew position. It was necessary for the -40 degree temperature at 25,000 feet. Any failure of the suit or taking off of gloves could result in frostbite or bare flesh sticking to metal. Sending Morse code messages on the code key at this altitude was also tricky. I removed my heavy glove and used my electric glove to key IP and strike reports. A mechanical failure on a bombing mission was a serious problem. Ground crews did their best to keep their "bird" in good condition. Once a bomber crossed the channel any pilot with a problem had to make a quick decision on continuing the mission or dropping out of formation (aborting) and returning to base. Engine failure over enemy territory usually resulted in disaster because the German "bogies" (fighters) picked off the strays.

New group commander, General Curtis LeMay, became Third Air Division Commander. He was a strong advocate of flying tight formations. This was an extremely difficult task and required great skill from bomber pilots in the middle and rear positions. They had to fight the turbulent air currents created by the "prop wash" of planes leading the group. The B-17 became much lighter after it dropped its bombs. The group then turned and followed the designated route back across the English Channel and to Eye. German fighters (bandits) were always on the prowl for "loose formations" or stragglers. Flak-damaged bombers or those with mechanical problems were in serious trouble unless some of our "little friends" could escort them to safety.

Mission Interrogation

Our mission was not over when we returned after six or seven hours on a raid. We still needed to clean and turn in our machine guns, parachutes and equipment and go to interrogation. The G-2 intelligence personnel collected information from all returning aircrews and they quizzed us on everything we had observed on our route to the target and back. They were especially interested in details on enemy fighters and flak locations. All information was compiled and forwarded to the Eighth Air Force central intelligence. The goal was to provide better briefing information to all bomb groups for safer missions. The Red Cross girls were always on hand in the interrogation room with coffee and cookies to give us a lift after flying six or seven hours. There was also a shot of scotch available for those who needed a boost after many hours of fatigue and stress. That alcohol really gave us a lift. Some guys gave their drink to their buddies and there were some who were "lifted" pretty high by the time they got to the Mess Hall!.

Mission 3   Stuttgart   December 16, 1944

Awakened at 4:30, breakfast, briefing at 5:15, take off at 8:30. Our group assembled over the North Sea and flew across Belgium. I set up my radio and put on my flak jacket (a bullet-proof vest). We had a couple of fighter alerts on the radio. German fighters, "bandits", were reported in the target area. We threw 450 bundles of chaff in 19 minutes over the target. We were camera ship for this mission. We hit the railroad marshalling yards dead center, and our squadron was complimented by General Partridge, head of the Third division. Mission was 7 hours long, 4 hours on oxygen. Flak was moderate but accurate. There were no holes in the ship when we landed. We carried ten 500 pound bombs and two 500 pound clusters of incendiary bombs, the same as the Hanover raid yesterday. We flew over the battle lines at Saarbrucken and

Strasburg. Bombing altitude of 23,000 feet. The temperature was –32 degrees.

We sent up 36 planes on this raid which was led by Major Gell. Railroads were a high priority to protect our troops by preventing Germany's forces from sending supplies and reinforcements to the front. The weather almost cancelled this mission, but the group took off and flew by instruments through fog (pea soup) to an altitude of 21,000 feet. Needless to say, all crewmembers sweated out our climb,with practically zero visibility. We were all relieved when we cimbed above the overcast and joined our formation. The weather cleared somewhere over France and we went on to hit our target. Our camera ship was located in the middle of the formation and we carried a special camera to record bombing results if the weather was clear over the target. The "big brass" loved it when the formation hit the bullseye and had a photo to prove it! However, there were some anxious moments on the trip home. The overcast sky was still over England and after learning of the weather at the base, the group leader decided we would go in under the clouds. Our formation did some low-level flying across friendly territory, the English Channel and landed safely at the Brome Dome.

The "Stars and Stripes" reported that the weather hampered the Eighth, but they sent up more than 300 Fortresses and lost three. The night raids of the RAF (Royal Air Force) hammered synthetic oil plants in southern Germany. The 15th Air Force out of Italy also hit the oil plants, and their P-51 Mustangs and P-38 Lightnings engaged Nazi fighters in over 50 dogfights.

This was the day we learned that Major Glenn Miller, director of the popular Armed Forces Band, had been lost due to the same bad weather. A light plane left Miller's headquarters in Bedford, England, for Paris to arrange a concert for troops on December 15th. The plane experienced stormy weather and was never heard from again.

Battle of the Bulge   December 16, 1944

The Allied armies had moved across France and Belgium and prepared to cross the Rhine River into Germany. Hitler reorganized his troops in a massive counter-offensive to break through the Allied lines and move to Antwerp to capture Allied fuel dumps and supplies which were badly needed. Twenty-four divisions of German troops, ten of which were Panzer tank divisions or special armored forces, succeeded in breaking through Allied lines. This created a dangerous bulge in the American front in the Ardennes, and the "Battle of the Bulge" lasted almost six weeks. Hitler's successes were aided by snow and overcast weather, which covered his troop movements and also grounded Allied bombers and fighters and prevented them from assisting our surrounded forces. The Germans used captured American equipment, and English-speaking German soldiers dressed in American uniforms to create havoc by changing road signs and giving false directions to our advancing troops.

James Lee Hutchinson, EdS

General McAuliffe and the 101st Airborne division helped stop the German advance by holding the city of Bastogne, Belgium until General Patton's Third Army tanks could come to their aid. Hitler had ordered his officers to strike hard and fast and create panic and fear in the thinly spread Allied forces. The German atrocities in this offensive strengthened the determination of the American troops to fight even harder and seek revenge. At Malmedy, Belgium, German troops captured 70 American soldiers, marched them unarmed to a large field and murdered them with machine guns. In another incident, one hundred and thirty Belgian civilians were also murdered for sheltering American troops (21).

Mission 4   Frankfort   December 24, 1944

Woke up at 4:00am   *Take-off 09:35*
Briefing 05:45   *Mission of 8 1/2 hours*

We bombed Frankfort airfields to keep the Luftwaffe on the ground. Our bomb load was 38 one hundred pounders. We threw chaff at two different places when we crossed the enemy lines and again at the IP (initial point). I saw all kinds of rockets. Our tail gunner, Ralph Moore, saw a jet fighter. We flew high squadrons at 25,000 feet. What a Christmas Eve. We landed about 17:00 (5:00 pm) and got back to the hut about 20:00 (8:00pm). This was the biggest mission ever completed by the Eighth. We flew everything that had wings. By the time we got home, it was dark. We landed first and beat the crowd to the mess hall! We were last cleaning our guns and got to the hut about 8:00pm. Only got about two holes in the plane, one big one in the end of the left wing.

The Mighty Eighth launched a massive raid on Christmas Eve---all four of our squadrons flew on this day. There were 50 planes in our group. A Frankfurt airfield was our target and we hit a squadron of German fighters on the runway before they could get airborne.

The 490th sent out all four squadrons (50 planes) on this mission. I later learned that the plane of a boyhood chum who was a B-17 tail gunner had been shot down on that raid. He was a member of the 487th Bomb Group on a mission to assist our troops in the Battle of the Bulge. A recent newspaper article reported his memories of that experience when his bomber received a direct hit and broke up over Belgium. He survived by riding the tail section down until it cleared the wreckage of the doomed bomber. He then bailed out and did a "free-fall" for several thousand feet before pulling his ripcord. He landed in enemy territory, buried his chute and eluded capture for several days before he reached American lines and safety. Crewmen who had to "bail out" of downed planes over enemy territory were sometimes able to "walk out" with the aid of the "underground workers". They could claim the honorary "Order of the Flying Boot".

It was Christmas Eve, and the Mighty Eighth gave German targets tons of bombs. The weather had broken at last and the Air Force could fly again. We were to pound German forces attacking our American forces at Bastogne! U.S. forces at Bastogne had been cut off and surrounded for several days. The weather had prevented

U.S. air strikes, but as the skies cleared, our bombing raids began in earnest. Our group flew 13 missions in December despite the bad weather. It had been very frustrating to "stand down" during these days, unable to aid the troops at Bastogne.

Over 2000 B-17 Flying Fortresses, B-24 Liberators and 900 escort fighters bombed airfields, communication centers, bridges and railroads to prevent German supplies and troops from reinforcing their position. This was the biggest air raid carried out by the Allies up to this time. Planes were still taking off from England when the first groups were bombing their targets! I remember bombing our target, going home to England and passing our bombers still headed for Germany! Allied fighter escorts shot down seventy-six Luftwaffe fighters (9).

The fighter planes and light bombers like the B-25 Mitchells and B-26 Maranders of the Ninth Air Force were flying low and blasting tanks, trucks, V-2 rockets (buzz bombs) launching sites and railroad cars to hamstring German troops. The tactical bombers flew 1,175 missions in support of the 1st Army division at the front on the Rhine. They destroyed 116 Nazi tanks, 778 armored vehicles and 56 railroad cars, according to reports in the "Stars and Stripes". They also knocked out a major fuel dump and two bridges.

This Allied aerial offensive continued for three days, and the Eighth and Ninth Air Forces took out 218 Luftwaffe fighters in aerial combat while losing 38 bombers and 40 fighters. Eight of the eleven German airdromes attacked were put out of service. The cost was high but the offensive drive resulted in a greatly weakened Germany (20). Mark Twain once said, "Thunder is good, thunder is impressive, but it is the lightning that does the work". Our planes made lots of "thunder" over England but we saved our lightning for Hitler's war machine.

Allied ground forces were advancing, and the Air Force was able to bomb visually because of the good weather. This fourth mission was the start of an all-out effort, and the Germans met it with heavy flak, rockets and fighters. We saw plenty of rockets and lots of flak on this raid. Thankfully, the P-51 Mustang escorts kept the "bandits" away. Ralph Moore, our tail-gunner sighted two German jets, but they sought other prey. Our P-51 fighters had a speed of 448 miles per hour with a range of 1300 miles. They had two machine guns, eight rockets, and two bombs. Today's F-16 fighters cost approximately 35 million dollars and have top speeds of 1500 miles per hour. We could have used a few of them when the Luftwaffe introduced their ME 262 twin-engine jet fighters late in the war. Hitler's counter-offensive was eventually defeated by superior forces and a shortage of fuel for his tanks, armored vehicles and trucks. German troops had planned to capture Allied fuel supplies but failed and were forced to retreat. It was reported that some abandoned their vehicles and walked back to their lines. The Eighth Air Force had flown through snow and bad weather to bomb those German oil dumps, marshalling yards and bridges. This was Hitler's last big push. I am proud that I flew six of the thirteen missions of the 490th Bomb Group in December of 1944.

Germany's Fighters

The Focke-Wulf FW-190D was another of Germany's top fighters. Its speed and maneuverability made it a fierce enemy of Allied bombers and fighters. The plane was bulky and resembled our P-47 Thunderbolt and was heavily armed with four 20mm cannons and two machine guns. It could also carry bombs. Like all fighters, it went through several stages of development. More than 20,000 FW-190s of all types were built. The FW-190 had a top speed of 420 MPH and a 500-mile cruising range (29).

The ME-109 was Germany's best fighter defense against the waves of Allied heavy bombers raining hundreds of tons of bombs on targets critical to the war effort. The plane had a 1400-horsepower engine and a top speed of 350 mph. It was armed with two 20mm cannons in the wings and two machine guns on the nose. The ME-109 was easy to maneuver and a quick climber. Bombs or rockets could also be hung underneath. Allied forces estimated that Germany had over 30,000 ME-109 planes by 1944. The Germans kept improving this plane and it was a formidable foe for the RAF and the Eighth Air Force fighters.

The ME-262 Jet Fighter was the first German jet our crew encountered, and it was sleek and fast. We were attacked by these planes on the 14th mission to Plauen. The ME-262 was a twin-engine fighter with great potential and a top speed of 540 miles per hour. However, its flight time was limited because it only carried enough jet fuel to fly about twenty minutes. The limited range of the ME-

262 aided our Ninth Air Force tactical fighters and medium bombers to locate and destroy the jet airfields. Armament included four 30mm cannons along with their machine guns. The German High Command had failed to realize the capabilities of this experimental fighter and didn't push development. They finally produced 1,300 ME- 262 fighters and put them into service in 1944, shortly before the end of the war. Our side was grateful that this plane wasn't developed earlier.

Special Targets and the German Anti-Aircraft

All missions were dangerous but there were special "targets" that were very important to the Germans such as oil supply refineries, tank and plane factories, V-bomb launching sites, submarine pens and Berlin. These targets were highly protected by anti-aircraft guns and fighters. Bomb crews knew that raids on these targets meant heavy casualties. Regensburg was the site of the Messerschmidt fighter plane factory and, of course, the ball-bearing plants at Schweinfurt were dreaded targets. It was a simple fact; Nazi Germany needed to protect all their fuel and industrial centers and the Eighth needed to destroy them to ruin the Third Reich's war machine (18).

Crucial German industrial sites, airfields and oil storage depots were protected by heavy concentrations of 88mm anti-aircraft gun batteries. Places like Augsburg, Berlin, Regensburg and Schweinfurt were some of the "hot spots" or "flak cities" dreaded by bomber crews. Thousands of anti-aircraft guns and troops were installed to protect critical targets. Approximately a third of the Nazi armed forces had to be devoted to bomber defense (20). The 88mm gun was very versatile and could be used as an anti-tank or anti-personnel weapon. The German army could have used those anti-aircraft guns on the battlefield, but our bombers kept them busy day and night. (The RAF night raids complemented our daylight bombing). The Germans even mounted the 88's on railroad cars and river barges for mobility. By the summer of 1944, the anti-aircraft guns were improved with radar sighting and shells which could reach higher altitudes than our bomber formations flew. Germany also constructed huge concrete and brick "flak towers" for concentrated defense of critical targets. The Ruhr valley industrial area was heavily protected with anti-aircraft batteries. Some targets had as many as 200 batteries of six to eight 88mm guns. Once they determined the path of the bomb run, they could box out a large flak area ahead of the bombers. Eighth Air Force crewmen nicknamed the Ruhr Valley area "Happy Valley" which reflected a "devil may care' attitude because it was one of the most deadly target areas. Hundreds of Allied planes and crews were lost over "Happy Valley"!

By 1944, German gunners had the ability to fill the sky with 88 shells that exploded into puffs of black smoke sending iron shrapnel (flak) ripping through the attacking bomber formation. Flak fragments would tear through planes, wounding or killing crewmembers and damaging planes. A direct hit by an 88mm meant a downed plane. Bombers that lost engines, oxygen or hydraulic systems, or were otherwise heavily damaged had to drop out of formation and risk an attack by German fighters. By 1945 our escort fighters could often provide protection against "bandits" and escort those planes to safety in Allied airstrips in Belgium or France.

Disabled bombers could signal surrender by lowering their wheels, thus allowing crewmembers to "bail out" before the plane went down in flames. This procedure was seldom used. Damaged planes making it to the neutral countries of Switzerland or Sweden were safe but the planes and crewmembers were interned until the end of the war.

By 1944-45, bomber crewmembers wore flak vests (bulletproof) and steel flak helmets specially made to allow the use of headsets. Those flak jackets weighed twenty pounds but we welcomed the protection. Flak curtains of flexible steel covered with canvas were also used on the walls and under our seat or gun position. These 3 x 5 panels gave us a sense of security because we knew the thin aluminum walls of the plane offered no protection. Each plane carried a first aid kit with burn jelly, morphine, bandages and instructions for treatment and there was also the small first-aid kit on every man's parachute harness. Orville Robinson, our waist gunner, was hit by a piece of flak on his helmet on our tenth mission to Hohenbudburg. He was severely wounded and lost his eye, but the flak helmet saved his life and medical treatment eased his pain until we returned to Eye. Orville got the Purple Heart and a ticket to the USA.

Our briefing sessions before each mission included a map of anti-aircraft "hot spots" to avoid on the way in and out of Germany. The German anti-aircraft guns used a strategy of "tracking flak" while bombers were on the way to the target. Our formation could use evasive tactics to avoid heavy fire. Once the group started the bomb run to the target, the Germans switched to the "barrage system" and filled the sky ahead of us with shrapnel! The radar-equipped guns could zero in on our altitude once a bomber formation started on the bombing run (12). Planes had to hold the course for several minutes for the bombardier and his Norden bombsight to be effective. The formation flew into and through the flak over the target. Exploding shells shook and rattled the plane and sometimes the black smoke from bursting shells was so thick you could walk on it! (This was a common aircrew expression). We were "sitting ducks" until "bombs away", when we could close the bomb bay doors and break away. Then, it was "business as usual" as we tightened the formation and our "little friends", (P-51 Mustangs), escorted us back to England and safety.

"Little Friends" P-51 escort fighters

Bombs Away!

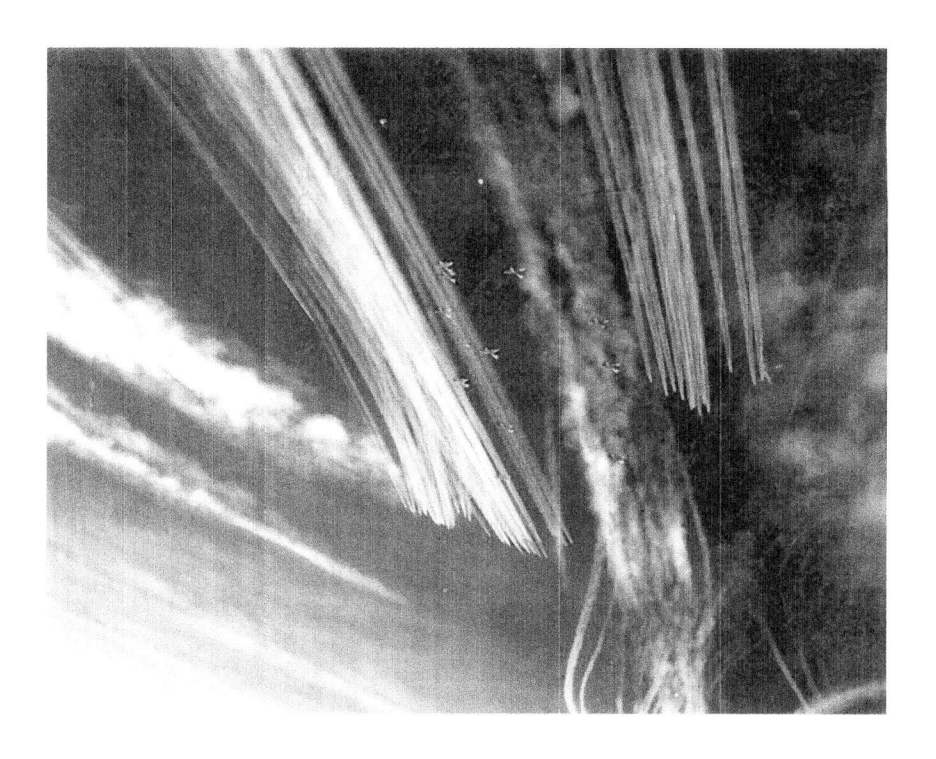

Bomber contrails during mission group formations

Dropping incendiary bombs

Ralph Moore in his tail-gun position

Full flight gear with chest-pack chute

Bill Rhiel (on bike) and Jim Collins

Chapter Seven

Lead Crew – Taking the Point

Mission 5   Bad-Kreuznach   January 2, 1945

Wake up 0300   *Take off 0700*

Briefing 0515   *Mission 7 hours*

We flew as deputy lead for the 3rd Division. We were PFF ship and it was our first mission with the new Bombardier, Command pilot, and Mickey operator and without Ralph Moore and Wilbur Lesh. It was a pretty easy mission close to the front and not much flak. We destroyed a bridge and town-- pretty much of a "milk run" but not easy at all. Had a bomb load of 10,500 pounders, and two big incendiaries. Bombed visually. Thirty-eight aircraft on this raid.

Today, our target was a bridge and supply dump. We were now getting to a point where the U.S. strategic bombing ability was really helping Allied armies on the front. Bad-Kreuznach was a small town but an important railway center for the enemy. The sky cleared and were able to bomb visually. The Norden bombsight had again proven effective. The majority of the planes in our formation carried toggleers who released their plane's loads as the lead bombardier dropped his bombs. We were "saturation bombing" the target area. We received an "excellent" rating for the raid which knocked out the flow of German troops and equipment to the front.

The daytime strategic bombing ability of the Eighth Air Force was greatly improved when the PFF radar (Mickey) equipment was made available to our planes. The radar dome replaced the ball turret under the B-17G on lead planes. A radar officer replaced our ball turret gunner. This "Mickey" operator was seated across the aisle from me in the radio room. He operated the radar equipment with the aid of radar maps made from actual photos of German targets taken by USAAF planes. The Air Corps could now bomb through the clouds without seeing the targets! This made it possible to carry out more bombing missions in overcast skies when the target was invisible. This also meant more dangerous flying for the Flying Fortresses that took off and flew up through that "pea soup" and snow storms to rendezvous with the group over the channel and head for Germany to bomb through the clouds.

Lead planes were equipped with a PFF (Pathfinder Force) radar domes which replaced the ball turrets. The PFF radar could penetrate clouds and pick out the target city outline of concrete and steel. The dome could be lowered when we neared the target and retracted for landing. Switching to a squadron lead ship after four missions was a feather in our cap, but it also completely re-arranged the make-up of our crew. The average bomber carried a crew of four officers and six enlisted men but group and squadron lead planes carried a command pilot, navigator, bombardier and radar (Mickey) operator. A lead crew's four enlisted men were engineer gunner, radio operator and two waist gunners.

Pilot Bill Templeton was joined in the cockpit by a "command pilot". Co-pilot, Dale Rector, became our tail gunner with the title of squadron gunnery fire control officer; Bruno Conterato, our navigator remained with the crew, and a lead bombardier and a Mickey operator were assigned for each mission. Our toggleleer, Bert Allinder became waist gunner with Orville "Robby" Robinson, Ewing "Rod" Roddy was flight engineer and top turret gunner, and I remained as radio operator Tail gunner, Ralph Moore, and ball turret gunner, Wilbur Lesh, were reassigned to the 490th Bomb Group gunnery pool and flew as "substitute gunners" with various crews. So, Lt. Bill Templeton's lead crew was now just the reverse of a regular B-17 combat crew. My job as lead plane radio operator had become more important and I always gave it my best shot. Today, I've been scaled down to a cell phone and CB radio. I occasionally end my phone conversations with, "Roger, and out" just for old times' sake!

Flying lead plane position was an honor but it also had a downside. As in all wars, the primary plan was to kill the enemy's leaders and win the battle. The lead planes carried the squadron or group commanders and were therefore the first targets of the Luftwaffe fighters seeking to break up our formations. However, I liked the battle plan of the Army Air Corps. Everyone from the buck sergeant gunners to the high-ranking squadron commanders and at times, the general in charge of the entire Third Division, flew combat missions. There were none of those "Wish I could go with you boys, but I am needed here at the base" speeches. Everyone knew what B-17 bombing raids required of the crews who flew them through the flak and fighters. We were all in the same position and "rank" was not important as long as we all did our jobs to the best of our abilities. Most of our officers had come up through the ranks and had flown many missions. One guy said it best, "If you survive, you get promoted!" Our goal was to fly safely and bomb Germany into submission. We were now a more important target!

Training Flights

Training and practice flights were necessary to train new crews as they were assigned to our 490th Bomb Group. Also lead crews flew many practice flights over England or Scotland to check out planes and radar equipment, and train replacement crews. We would practice take-offs and landings and flying group formations. These were dangerous flights, as we often flew up through fog and clouds to gain altitudes of 20,000 feet or more. These flights were made during the morning hours after other groups had taken off on combat missions. Flying through clouds with very little visibility was always a nerve-wracking experience because of the ever-present danger of mid-air collisions. We enjoyed solo test flights in clear weather. When flying an "equipment check" flight each man was required to check out all equipment at his station. All mechanical equipment had to be ready for a combat mission. I remember long glides and practice landings on the clouds. One phase of checking out the engines was quite a thrill. The pilots would put the plane in a "stall". This was accomplished by going into a steep climb until the engines reached their limit and "stalled out". The B-17 vibrated and shook like a wet dog until the pilot tipped the nose downward and the engines regained power. At that point we crossed our fingers and there was always a sigh of relief when the "stall" was finished and the motors "roared" again. We sometimes managed to combine business with pleasure and go sightseeing. I remember low-level flights over Oxford, Cambridge and Stratford-on-Avon. During one flight, we were up over Scotland when number one engine on our left wing malfunctioned. We headed home and number three on our right wing started spewing oil and it had to shut it down to avoid a fire. We had dropped to about 4,000 feet and were now flying with two dead engines with "feathered" props. Things were getting serious and wearing a chute suddenly seemed very stylish. Everyone from the radio room on back hooked on their chutes and got ready to bail out if a fire broke out in one of those engines! We had an anxious flight back to base as we stood in the waist gunner area near the rear exit, knowing that we might have to jump at any time. We made it to the field and just as we landed a third engine was acting up. It was better for this to happen over English territory than over Germany. That was one lead plane that needed a lot of work before it was ready for a bombing mission. I later witnessed a tragic mid-air collision on a training flight for tight formation flying.

There were many "stand downs" (cancelled missions) during the winter months. The fog and rain often gave us "pea soup" or poor visibility situations. However, the German Battle of the Bulge started in mid-December and bombers had to fly to help our troops on the ground despite bad weather.

A Bed-Time Story

Cancelled missions meant unloading the plane and going back to the hut. Snowstorms or fogs often caused "stand downs". This was always disappointing after we had gone through "briefing", loaded guns and equipment and readied our planes for action. When the weather report made us "stand down", we had to reverse the process and return all gear and chutes to the equipment hut. Even though the mission was cancelled, we had still lost several hours of "sack time" so we would go back to the hut to catch up. We needed our sleep to stay alert on those strenuous bombing missions. This was a special problem when we had two missions in a row.

Sleep or "sack time" was coveted by all combat crews. Rising early for a mission and flying many hours on oxygen at sub-zero temperatures drained a lot of energy. A six-hour mission normally required thirteen to fourteen hours. Crews were rousted from the "sack" at 3:00 am for breakfast, briefing and preparation for an 8:00 am take-off. At the end of the six-hour mission, at least three hours were required for equipment check-in, interrogation and supper. Flying two days in a row really brought on fatigue. Flying planes for performance and equipment checks was also demanding because of the threats of mid-air collisions or engine failures. Sleep provided an escape from the stress of our situation. The possibility of death, wounds or a POW camp faced us during every mission. The foggy weather was conducive to mid-air collisions on "take-off" and "assembly." Flak and Luftwaffe fighters were distinct possibilities once our formation entered enemy air space. I always had a great feeling of relief when our mission was over, our plane landed safely and the stress was gone. It was back, of course, as soon as the next "mission alert" was announced!

The "sack" was also a great place to escape the cold, damp weather in England during 1944-45. Our small stove with its rationed coke supply put out very little heat. Luckily, my cot was near that little stove. However, the latrine was out the back door and thirty feet to the left. It was usually unheated except for the hot water, and that was available only a few hours a day. Boy, did I miss our nice Sioux City barracks!

Our first hut-mates finished their thirty-five mission tour of duty in January and went back to the states. We considered ourselves a veteran crew since we had finished five missions and had become a lead crew. The new crew assigned to our hut arrived in mid-January.

These guys were still in training and hadn't experienced the stress of combat missions. They stayed up late at night and ignored our crew's request to "hit the sack" and turn out the lights. The situation quickly came to a head one night. Our crew had just flown an eight-hour mission and were alerted for another raid the following day with a 3:00 am wake-up call. We got no action on requests for "lights out", so at 9:00 pm. Roddy pulled out his .45 automatic and shot out two ceiling lights before someone hit the light switch! It was just like a Saturday afternoon western when the hero shot out the saloon lights. We had a couple of holes in the roof, but a rule was established. It was "lights out" when requested when either crew was alerted. We all became good friends as the war progressed and the missions kept coming.

Fortunately, we had a base theater and a library. The group Special Services department provided the latest films available for the Piccadilly Playhouse movie matinees. The library had many books, magazines and comic books. I remember reading several classics. During the Revolutionary War, Thomas Paine wrote "The American Crisis", and the book made quite an impression on me. Many of his statements are as true today as they were in colonial times, and WWII. The statement I remember most was:

> "These are the times that try men's souls, the summer soldiers and sunshine patriots will, in this crisis, shrink from the service of their country. But he who stands as of now, deserves the love and thanks of man and woman" (25).

Paine was lamenting the fact that many of the soldiers in Washington's army fought in the summer and went home to harvest crops in the fall but stayed all winter.

The base dance band, named the "GI Wolves", played for special dances at the Aero Club three or four times a month. Girls were brought in from surrounding villages to provide dancing partners. I remember that the Special Services and the Red Cross girls organized a big Christmas Party at the Aero Club, December 23rd, for the children of surrounding villages. It was a great production, complete with Santa Claus and a large Christmas tree. Movies, gifts, and refreshments for the children made for a war-time Merry Christmas for everybody (1).

The Norden Bombsight

The Norden bombsight was a top-secret weapon never to leave the plane unless it was guarded by authorized personnel. Actually, it was a gyroscope and computer, an extremely accurate instrument which should never fall into enemy hands. I seldom ventured into the plexiglass nose of the plane where it was placed, and even then I was nervous about looking at it! They said the bombsight was only as good as the bombardier who supplied it with necessary data to make it possible to hit the target from an altitude of 25,000 feet or better. Once the B-17 squadrons started their bomb run over the target, the bombardier was in complete control of the plane. The bombsight was connected to the plane's automatic pilot and controlled the plane's flight direction. He had to adjust for wind speed, ground speed, altitude, wind and other basic data before releasing the bomb load. The famous Norden bombsight was manufactured in a small factory in Indianapolis, Indiana.

The plexiglass nose cone of the B-17 was nicknamed the "greenhouse". I rode in the nose several times during crew training at Sioux City. It was similar to sitting on an extremely high ledge in a stone quarry back home and watching the landscape slip underneath. I never envied the bombardier and navigator their work stations in the "greenhouse".

Air War Success

Thanks to the hundreds of heavy U.S. bombers who delivered thousands of tons of bombs on their targets, Germany was being defeated. The Allies were able to keep German fighters out of the skies by destroying their airfields, and fuel supply and oil storage facilities. The pinpoint bombing knocked out bridges and railroad yards, and cut major highway transportation routes. Bombing factories and industrial cities broke the spirit of the civilian population, similar to what Germany had done to the British. The morale of the German troops was fading, as they were prevented from receiving supplies and reinforcements. The winter of 1944-45 saw the beginning of the end for Hitler's Third Reich. The USAAF strategic bombing was literally destroying the German war machine. When the war ended, generals of the Nazi high command credited the massive bombing raids as the "chief cause of their defeat." American Supreme Commander General Dwight Eisenhower was quoted as saying, "The Allied Air Force achieved the impossible". The British people were very appreciative of the sacrifices made by the young men of the Eighth Air Force. Of the RAF, Winston Churchill said, "The fighters are our salvation, but the bombers alone provided the means of victory".

Early in 1945, the Allied Bomber Command concentrated on destroying Hitler's transportation and aircraft industry. The Eighth Air Force in England and the Fifteenth, based in Italy, flew daytime raids on strategic targets with precision bombing. The RAF bombed the same targets at night. Bomb groups with the longest missions were protected by escort fighters. In mid February 1945, the Allies launched a 1,000 plane raid on Germany with light losses of bombers and very effective results. The following weeks brought larger raids and more bombing successes as our Air Force fighters shot down a large number of Luftwaffe fighters while protecting American heavy bomber missions (9). Hitler and the Nazi party had gained complete control of Germany by 1935 and proceeded with plans to rule Europe, Russia and the British Isles. Those who protested or questioned Nazi policy were murdered or placed in concentration camps so there was very little resistance from church officials or leaders of countries annexed by German armies. However, by 1944, it was obvious to many of Hitler's officers that he was leading their country to complete destruction and there was an attempt to kill Hitler and many high-ranking officers at a staff meeting. A suitcase bomb was placed under the conference table but was moved by an aide before it exploded. Colonel Claus von Stauffenberg and General Rommel were leaders of the failed assassination plot to save their country. They and a dozen others were executed or allowed to commit suicide and the madman went on to lead the Fatherland to ruin! (15)

By early 1945 the Germans had a serious problem because they could no longer replace lost planes or trained pilots. The weakened German air force was forced to conserve fuel and concentrate on protecting their strategic industrial locations. This gave American bombers more unprotected targets. The Allies had gained "air superiority" and American losses of planes decreased sharply. The Eighth continued bombing and our aggressive fighters baited the Luftwaffe to come up and fight. The Allies had gained their goal of having less resistance from German planes on our massive bombing raids.

Mission 6   Aschaffenburg   January 3, 1945

Woke up 0315   *Take off 0730*
Briefing 0400   *Mission 8 hours*

Really starting the new year right. Third morning we've been awakened in a row. We flew this one (had been "scrubbed" last two mornings), so now we have 6 missions in, which gives us the Air Medal and an "excellent" rating. This was our second mission in a row.

We were lead crew of the low element (squadron) today. We bombed P.F.F. and got a marshalling yard. I had to send a "strike report" and was kept pretty busy. The mission lasted 7 ½ hours with 3½ on oxygen. A "milk run" (easy mission) if there ever was one. We didn't see any flak at all and only two rockets. We had ten 500 pounders and two incendiaries (fire bombs) and probably hit the target square! Had a command pilot since we were lead plane on the low squadron.

This mission of 38 planes was led by Capt. R.A. Barraclough. The heavy snow was still a problem and was very unusual for this part of England. All crewmembers wore headsets and throat mikes for the intercom system. Once we formed our group over England, we crossed the channel into friendly French territory and climbed to the specified height for the bombing mission. I was required to send back radio reports as our group passed certain checkpoints on our designated route to the target. More importantly, I had to keep those headsets on and monitor the assigned frequencies in case there were messages from our base in England.

Our target was another railroad yard and this one was at Aschaffenburg. The previous day's raid on Bad Kreuznach's railroad junction had completely destroyed it and was another blockade that stopped German military transportation of men and equipment to the front. That raid had earned another "excellent" rating for the Bomb Group and we were trying to duplicate it. This was our sixth raid which earned the Air Medal for our crew. It was presented later at a base parade formation for awards by our commanding officer Col. Frank P. Bostrom.

Today, I have my Air Medal, Good Conduct and three campaign medals with my gunner and crewmember wings in a special display case hanging by my fireplace.

Mid-Air Collision   January 5, 1945

Thirteen replacement crews had been assigned to our group in late December. They were as welcome as the flowers in May, but there was one big problem; these crews had gone through combat crew training in the states on B-24 Liberators! Switching to the B-17 was a big challenge. After flying only a few hours in their new planes, the crews would face the final phase of the switch-over which was learning to fly the tight "box formation" used on combat missions.

Group training officers decided that skeleton crews of combat veterans would fly with the new crews as instructors. An experienced pilot, co-pilot, navigator, engineer and radio operator was assigned to each of the thirteen bombers to help the new skeleton crew adapt to the B-17. Our crew felt lucky to have completed our sixth mission, but many of the "instructors" were much closer to completing their tour of duty. We were all leary of flying with a bunch of "rookies". The odds were against us on every bombing mission and we dreaded any extra risks. It turned out that those fears were justified! The winter weather that threatened to cancel the exercise cleared and we roared down the runway and lifted into the fog. The near-zero visibility lasted until we climbed above the clouds into gray skies. The squadron practiced getting in and out of the "box formation" at

25,000 feet and it quickly became a dangerous situation as the new pilot jockied their planes in and out, or up and down to maintain position. I hooked my chest-pack parachute to my harness early in the day!

We were leading the top group so we had planes on both sides, but at least we didn't have to worry about a bomber dropping down from above. I explained the radio equipment and mission procedures to the "student" who was seated at the radio desk. I was glad to be standing so I could watch through the plexiglass roof and side windows for any planes that were getting too close. The new pilots were doing a lot of "dipping" and dropping in and out of the formation. Bill Templeton had warned crewmembers to keep their eyes peeled and the intercom clear for emergency warnings!

The twelve plane formation practiced simulated bomb runs for two hours. One important skill of formation flying was to spread the formation during the bomb-run and to close up after leaving the target. A tight box formation was the best protection against fighter attack. We wanted these new pilots to master this exercise because they would soon be flying missions in our formations! There were several near collisions during the training session but everyone survived and we dropped to a lower altitude and headed back to Eye. I was still on watch on the way home and saw the collision below and to our right. A B-17 stacked in the middle formation lost altitude and dropped down on a plane below. The lower bomber was cut in half but three of its crew parachuted to safety before both planes burst into flames and crashed near Bury St. Edmunds only twenty minutes from Eye. There were no other survivors. Many men lost their lives due to a careless mistake when someone relaxed a few minutes before the job was finished.

The following information was taken from an article in the Historical Record of the 490th Bomb Group H:

> "The instructor pilot in the lower bomber escaped because he was wearing his back-pack. He recalled a terrific jolt from the impact, just before his plane went down. He was thrown out of the wreckage, pulled his ripcord and floated to earth amid the falling debris of the crash. The instructor bombardier and navigator also survived (1). The 490th had flown nearly a hundred missions, but this one accident cost almost three times the number of lives which had been lost in combat. This crash really lowered morale at Eye. Those "instructor crew" members who perished had safely completed many combat missions. Word went out: flying training missions with "green crews" could be hazardous to your health!"

It was a very quiet flight back to the base. We flew four more combat missions in January and several more equipment check flights.

Airmen Downed in Combat

Bomber crews led stressful lives day in and day out "sweating out" each mission they were flying and those to come. Would the next mission be their last? Would they ever finish their 35th mission and join the "Lucky Bastards Club"? This was an unofficial club for those who completed their tour of duty safely and went back to the States. Early in 1943, the average crew lasted six missions! But by 1944, the life expectancy of a crew member was fifteen missions, and the aircrews were now required to fly a 35-mission tour of duty. We manned our guns as we crossed the English Channel and were on combat alert until we crossed again on the return trip. Many flyers suffered nervous breakdowns under the pressure. A typical mission lasted five to six hours from take-off to touchdown. Crewmembers were always close to death, and everyone could remember talking with a crew or a buddy one day only to learn of them being killed or "missing in action" on the next mission.

All bomber crewmembers were volunteers. Somewhere between joining or being drafted they had signed onto the VFT (Volunteer Flight Training) program. As VFT's we had the opportunity to enter the Air Cadet program and become pilots, navigators or bombardiers, officers and gentlemen. The majority ended up in aerial gunnery school.

Memories of planes in our formation being shot out of the sky by flak or fighters cannot be easily forgotten. There were also many damaged aircraft that made it back to England with dead or wounded boys on board. Bombers with wounded crewmembers fired red flares and were allowed to land first. Ambulances and fire trucks were standing by after every mission. The thought of "bailing

Through These Eyes

out" (parachuting) from a disabled plane over Germany was mind-numbing. We had read too many stories about German civilians or SS, troopers, killing the airmen who had just demolished their town. That is why we carried the .45 Colt automatic. POW, prisoners of war, camps were also dreaded like the plague. I also strapped on a holster with a ten-inch hunting knife that I had purchased in Sioux City.

The SS troops (Schutzstaffel) were originally formed to be Hitler's bodyguard, but later grew into hundreds of special units in the black uniforms to carry out the cruel duties of the Nazi party. The fanatical members of the SS were required to prove they were pure Aryans who would fight to the end for the Fatherland. Sixty years after WW II I learned how the cruelty of the SS affected a former member of the Templeton crew!

Crewmembers who were forced to "bail-out" or crash land in enemy territory suffered many horrible experiences. Those who survived the jump were usually captured by civilians or German troops and imprisoned in POW (prisoner of war) concentration camps. Parachuting from a disabled or burning bomber over enemy territory was seldom an option . When "bail-out" time came you grabbed your chest pack, clipped it onto your parachute harness, and jumped. I took no chances, I wore my chute the entire mission whenever possible. Every crewmember feared a chute failure, fatal wounds and landing in the hands of the enemy. Airmen were warned to delay pulling the rip cord until they had fallen far enough to clear the plane to avoid flames, flak and debris in the air. It was best to "free-fall" a few thousand feet because pulling the ripcord too soon left the chutist floating down in the thin cold air without oxygen. Crews of crippled planes were also advised to bail out above 6,000 feet. Most of this advice fell on deaf ears because in an emergency you jumped when necessary. If time allowed, crewmen could assemble in the radio room and exit by the open bomb bay or bail out the nose or waist door. There were also stories of German fighters shooting at parachutists or buzzing them to cause the chute to collapse on the way down. There were many stories of pilots who kept flying the wounded bomber until their crews could bail out. They often gave the crew the option of bailing out or staying with the plane to try for a friendly airbase or the English channel. However, if the bomber was going down, it was "everyone hit the silk" time.

Capture and a POW camp (stalag) meant poor treatment, bad food, and terrible living conditions in crowded barracks. Camps were surrounded by barbed wire fences and guards armed with machine guns in the watchtowers. There was no escape, and prisoners watched and waited for the war to end. Two movies, "Hart's War" and "Stalag 17" made shortly after the war, gave realistic views of the POW camps for downed airmen. Food shortages were common and Red Cross packages made life bearable. However, by 1945, the hungry prison guards would steal the food from the Red Cross packages. Many prisoners suffered life-threatening diseases and mental illnesses after their releases, while others returned home after the war to live productive lives. I recently read an article in our local paper about a local man who was an engineer and top-turret gunner on a B-24 Liberator. His plane was hit on its twentieth mission. He was unconscious from a flak wound, so his buddies revived him and shoved him out of the plane before it went down. His chute opened and he landed safely and spent a year in a POW camp.

Early in the war, parachutists who landed in enemy territory were hidden and helped by civilians. This was true in the occupied countries of Belgium, Holland and France. These "resistance fighters" set up an underground system to continue harassing their conquerors by sabotage. These brave men and women were very skilled at hiding aviators and helping them back to friendly territory. Underground members provided clothes, false identification papers and transportation. These people knew they faced torture and death if discovered by the Gestapo (Secret Police). Therefore, they only used first names so that if captured and tortured they could not identify other group members. These patriots did much to help win the war against Germany.

Recently, I met an Eighth Air Force B-24 pilot who served with the 487th Bomb Group. His plane was hit on the fifth mission in May, 1944 and his crew bailed out over Belgium. Seven were captured, but the pilot and two others were hidden by the Belgium Resistance Fighters. They managed to stay "underground" with false identity papers for six months before making it to the American lines.

Crippled bombers that made it back to the English Channel without being picked off by German fighters could "ditch" the plane in the water. Crewmembers preparing to "ditch" lightened the bomber by throwing out all heavy equipment, including machine guns and ammunition. Every plane carried a rubber raft and crewmembers wore bright orange Mae West lifejackets under their parachute harnesses. Ditching the 26,000 pound Fortress called for great skill by the pilot and co-pilot and required a long, low glide with nose up and tail down and pancaking the plane into the water. The plane would sink in less than three minutes, so everyone scrambled into the raft or the water. Ditching was really tricky if there were wounded aboard. British Navy boats and friendly fishing boats made many rescues. The B-17 carried a "Gibson Girl" battery-powered emergency radio. The watertight radio was shaped so you could clamp it between your knees and crank out a pre-set S.O.S. signal once you were afloat in the raft.

Closer to Heaven   January 10, 1944

Our crew did not fly today but the 490th lost three planes due to extremely heavy flak over the target! The group bombed a railroad bridge on the Rhine river at Cologne. The destruction of Germany's transportation system had become a top priority for Allied air forces. Railroads, bridges and river barges became prime targets. The Germans had reinforced the usual landbased anti-aircraft batteries by towing in several barges mounted with anti-aircraft guns to reinforce the land-mounted batteries to protect the bridge. Three planes from squadron 849 were lost over the target. The lead plane of the low squadron received a direct hit and two others were hit. Several parachutes were reported as surviving crewmen bailed out. One plane managed to limp back to safety in friendly territory. This was the hundreth mission for the 490th.

Flying in aerial gunnery school over the desert in Yuma, Arizona and crew training on B-17s at Sioux City, Iowa proved to me that I was in a dangerous line of work. Combat brought me to the realization that I needed God's help on every mission. As the saying went, "There are no atheists in the sky". My mother was raised in the church, and she had joined a neighborhood church when I went into the service. Her many letters to me ended in prayers for my safety. Prayer came easily in combat after we began counting flak holes in our plane after every mission. I was literally much closer to heaven up there in the "wild blue yonder". The concussions of 88mm anti-aircraft shells bursting under and around us shook our bomber and sent jagged pieces of steel flying through our formation. Our pilot, Lt. Bill Templeton, was an excellent man to have at the controls on these missions when we were five miles high at 50 below zero with no place to hide. The heavy flak and Luftwaffe fighters were taking down Forts in groups ahead and behind our formation. These losses really came home to me as I witnessed B-17s in our group dropping out of formation and going down in flames. I watched the crew bailing out and counted the parachutes as they popped out of the plane, praying that everyone would get out of the burning plane and survive the jump. We were all aware of the high mortality rate in our occupation.

We knew that death or disaster was always near; there were so many ways it could happen. The high cost of daylight bombing raids was evident in the loss of crews and planes. The personal belongings of those crews missing in action or dead were inventoried and boxed for eventual shipment to the United States. They could be claimed by next-of-kin or those men who survived and returned safely. Replacement crews were assigned to squadrons as they arrived. They filled huts vacated by MIA crews, or "Lucky Bastard" crews who had completed their tour of duty. The new crews were often warned by those going home, "Don't unpack and get too comfortable kids, it's rough up there"!

Today, as I enjoy my retirement and family and old age gallops upon me, I again feel closer to heaven.

The Life of Riley

I had a "missing man" experience when I visited a buddy at the 486th Bomb Group at Sudbury. Keen Umbehr and I were buddies the five months we were in radio operator school at Sioux Falls and we exchanged visits in the spring of 1945. I used a 48 hour pass to get to his airbase near Sudbury, and we had a great time. However, at bedtime he had to find a place for me to sleep. A crew in the next barracks had failed to return from a mission that day. There were six empty bunks, and that night I slept on a "missing man's" bunk! His name was " Riley" and he was the MIA crew's radio operator. I didn't turn down the covers---just flopped on the bunk. It was an uncomfortable night with all the photos of "Riley's" family staring down at me. The next morning we learned that the plane had made a forced landing in safe territory and the crew would be returning to base. I felt much better when I boarded the train to go back to Eye. "Riley" was safe and would soon be sleeping in his bunk again. Later, when Keen visited my base, I put him in the bunk of a guy on a pass to London. Thank heavens we didn't have any missing crews. Keen and I have exchanged letters recently, and like me, he returned to his home community after the war.

I believe the prayers of my mother and family members helped bring me through the war. Mom joined the church and never lost her faith in my safe return. I also had the support of many others at home. My Aunt Gladys in Chicago sent me a St Christopher medal and a New Testament with an armor-plated cover inscribed with the words. "May the Lord be with you". I carried the Book in my shirt pocket over my heart on combat missions, and added the St. Christopher medal to my dog tag chain. I also wore a silver chain ID bracelet engraved with my serial number and gunner's wings – just in case I lost my dog tags! These items were my "lucky charms" and and helped me believe that I would survive. Most of the guys also had special routines, clothing or items they carried for luck. Roddy, our engineer, recently reminded me that he always wore his number 14 high school quarterback shirt under his flight suit. He felt safer wearing that old maroon and white jersey. We knew it was superstition, but we needed all the help we could muster and we couldn't ignore " lucky charms" that might provide extra flight insurance.

One short poem says it all:

Life is short
Death is sure
Sin's the cause
Christ is the cure.

Battle statistics after the war revealed that ten percent of all WWII casualties were in the skies. The bombers took their punishment and often returned to England on a "wing and a prayer". This was the title of a popular song referring to the many flak-damaged planes returning to base. They often carried dead or wounded and had first landing priority---some crash-landed. More than 12,000 B-17s were built and approximately 5,000 were destroyed by flak, fighters or accidents. The average life of a B-17 in combat was six missions without crashing, going down or facing major overhaul. Many shot–up bombers making it back to base were "cannibalized" for parts to repair other planes that could be repaired to fly again.

Mission 7   Derben   January 14, 1945

Woke up 0300   *Take off 0830*

Briefing 0445   *Mission 8 hours*

We led the high element (squadron). Had a big time. German fighters were reported in the area. Blew up a big underground oil storage dump – got rid of lots of oil for the Jerries. Bomb load of ten 500 pounders, five hours on oxygen. Bombed visual. Our fighter escorts had a busy day too.

Through These Eyes

We had 38 aircraft on this mission in spite of the unusually heavy snow. At one point in January the ground crews organized a "snow shoveling" brigade and worked several days and nights to clear the runways. However, the weather caused several "scrubbed" (cancelled) missions after we were briefed, loaded, and ready to go. The 490th flew only eleven missions in January and our crew flew six. We were especially wary on this raid because our group lost three bombers on the previous mission.

Snow and fog made for poor flying conditions, and we often took off with only 500-600 yard visibility. Each squadron flew up through the "pea soup" to assemble on Vary pistol flares, much like Roman candles, fired from their lead plane. Flying blindly through the thick fog was eerie and every crewmember held an inter-com mike, while sitting near a window, on alert for any other planes. We were very aware of the possibilty of a mid-air collision. Our flare "colors of the day" were red and yellow and when we broke out into the clear, our plane united with our squadron. We then joined the group formation on radio signals from a "splasher" (radio station). Group formations would then "rendezvous" over a "buncher" radio station to start the mission across the English Channel or North Sea. Planes of each mission filled the sky, leaving their snow-white contrails streaking across the horizon. Moisture particles in the engine exhaust froze at high altitude. The contrail patterns of hundreds of bombers in the English skies was a beautiful sight. It was ironic that they were headed across the English Channel to rain destruction on Germany.

In turn, the German anti-aircraft gunners loved those cloudless days but I imagine the people at the target weren't to happy!

We were anxious preparing for this mission because flak had shot down three of our 490th bombers during the last mission, January 10th, over Cologne. The take-offs and landings were almost as dangerous as the mission itself. The following day, the "Stars and Stripes" reported that more than 850 Mustangs and Thunderbolts flying escort for 900 Fortresses and Liberators on this mission shot down 149 German fighters. Gunners on the bombers also shot down 31 bandits during attacks. The bombers hit oil refineries and oil storage depots. The headlines were "8th Fighters Hit Luftwaffe for Record Kill".

U.S. Air Force Fighters – Our "Little Friends"

U.S. fighter pilots were an elite group of young men who faced and defeated the German Luftwaffe. However, the Army Air Force was in its infancy in 1941 and had very few fighter squadrons at the start of World War II. Aircraft production and pilot training became a desperate need after Pearl Harbor. There were some American pilots who had combat experience with the Flying Tigers in China's war with the Japanese in 1938-41. This was a group of some three hundred pilots and ground crewmembers hired by the Chinese government to fight Japanese planes. These mercenary fighters were mostly Americans under the leadership of General Clair Chenault. Pilots flew the Curtis P-40 Warhawk with white shark's teeth painted on the nose. Pilots were paid $600 a month and a $500 bonus for each Japanese plane shot down. The Flying Tiger's main task was to protect the China supply line from the West, the Burma Road. When the United States entered the war, these pilots became the nucleus of the Fourteenth Air Force in the Pacific Theater.

There were also American flyers who joined the RAF (Royal Air Force). Eagle squadrons of U.S. pilots were flying British Spitfires against the Germans in the Battle of Britain. Once the U.S. entered the war and the Eighth Air Force was stationed in England, three RAF Eagle squadrons were transferred to U.S. groups. The Eighth had 96 fighter groups by 1945.

The Lockheed P-38 Lightning

The P-38 was very easy to identify because of its twin bodies and tail booms and twin contrails at high altitudes. The fighter was powered by two 1300 HP engines. With a top speed of 414 miles per hour, it became more effective when gas drop tanks were added to increase its range for bomber escort duty. Armed with a 20mm cannon and four machine guns, it could carry two bombs and was later adapted for rockets for air-to-ground raids. Lockheed produced over 9,900 of these fighters (7). The P-38 was especially effective in the Pacific war. Major Richard Bong became the top American ace with forty victories (8). He was awarded the Congressional Medal of Honor, America's highest award (19). The P-38 Lightning with its twin body was the most easily recognized U.S. Air Force fighter in the skies. It was also very deadly, and the Germans called it "the fork-tailed devil". Only four or five P-38 fighters remain in flying condition. However, a recent Associated Press article reported on the P-38 "Glacier Girl" which crash-landed on a Greenland glacier in 1942. The plane was recovered from an icy tomb after fifty years and restored to flying condition at a cost of several million dollars. Brad McManus, the pilot who crash-landed the plane in 1942, was among the crowd of more than 10,000 who gathered to watch the P-38 fly again at a Middlesboro, Kentucky airport in the fall of 2002.

The Republic P-47 Thunderbolt

The P-47 was our heaviest and bulkiest fighter, almost twice the weight of sleeker fighters. It was very effective in aerial combat. Many of the leading "aces" in the Eighth Air Force flew the P-47, such as Colonel Francis "Gabby" Gabreski, our top ace in the European Theater with 28 "kills" (8). The P-47, or "Jug" as it was often called, was credited with the destruction of over 3,700 Luftwaffe aircraft in aerial combat (8). Fighters also destroyed over 3,200 German planes on the ground in bombing and strafing missions. Powered by a supercharged 2000 HP engine and four bladed "paddle propellers", it could reach a maximum speed of 515 miles per hour. It carried four .50 caliber guns in each wing and two bombs as necessary. Later, it was armed with rockets. Two 150 gallon drop tanks extended its range for bomber escort duty. Over 15,000 Thunderbolts were manufactured, many parts were made at an Evansville, Indiana plant.

The North American P-51 Mustang

The Mustang was the best escort fighter for the Eighth Air Force heavy bombers. The P-51 was an excellent plane and most effective in downing Luftwaffe foes. They shot down over 4,000 German fighters in aerial combat, and protected heavy bombers on long range missions. It was always a thrill on a bombing mission to look out and see those sleek fighter escorts flying on our wings. Late in the war the P-51 Mustang was also used in low-level strafing of trains and truck convoys. The North American P-51 Mustang was first used in combat in 1942. Like all other planes, it was redesigned and modified several times before it became one of our best fighters by 1944-45. The P-51D with a 1500 HP engine and a four-bladed paddle propeller could reach speeds of 450 mph. (8). Pilots loved the "bubble" canopy which allowed a 360 degree view of the sky, a distinct advantage in combat. Its gasoline drop tanks gave it a range of 1250 miles and it could escort bombing formations to Germany, jettison its employ fuel tanks and engage the Luftwaffe fighters in aerial combat. The Mustang carried six machine guns in its wings and racks to carry eight rockets or two 500-pound bombs in place of the drop tanks, making it very effective in air to ground missions. Over 15,000 Mustangs were produced. I shudder to think what our Eighth Air Force bombing missions would have been like without the protection of the P-51 Mustangs.

British Fighters

RAF Spitfire

The Spitfire was credited with winning the Battle of Britain. It managed to fight off the German Luftwaffe in its two-month assault on London, and prevented the invasion of England. The Spitfire was armed with two 20mm cannons and eight machine guns. The supercharged 1000 HP Rolls Royce Merlin engine had a speed of over 450 miles per hour. The British produced over 22,000 of those sleek elliptical winged fighters. Many called the plane the most famous fighter of all time (7). The Spitfire was not the only RAF plane, and many pilots preferred the Hawker Hurricane. This fighter was easy to fly and was heavily armed with eight machine guns and four cannons. The Hawker Typhoon was a big and powerful fighter; perfect for strafing and low-level tactical support of the troops. It carried four machine guns and eight rockets, or two 1,000-pound bombs. There were also twin-engine fighter bombers which the British used very effectively.

The Bristol Beaufighter plane carried six machine guns and four cannons. Its radar and ability to carry a torpedo made it a threat to enemy shipping and seaports. The de Havilland Mosquito was a long-range night-fighter, equipped with radar. It carried four cannons and six guns in its nose.

Building the Arsenal of Defense

Our armed forces had been severely reduced during the Depression. Army, Navy and Marine units were poorly equipped and under-manned. After our declaration of war against the axis powers of Germany and Japan there was a desperate effort to mobilize for the defense of our country. The production of planes, ships and armored weapons were achieved by concentrating our industrial facilities toward one goal---victory!

The Armed Services created the largest technical training in history. All servicemen needed training before going to war. The Selective Service Act enabled the military forces to build powerful defenses. One of the top priorities was increasing our air power. Building planes and training pilots and aircrew members were most important. The first strategy of the top commanders was for strategic bombing of German industrial targets. Heavily armed bombers with the ability to defend themselves was the basis of this plan. The valiant efforts of the B-17 Flying Fortress, B-24 Liberators and the British Lancaster and Halifax heavy bombers are well documented. However, the heavy losses early in the war proved that bombers needed fighter plane escorts. The extremely strong and experienced Luftwaffe pilots controlled the sky over German territory. Allied heavy bombers had strong firepower to protect themselves but could be overwhelmed by flak and the large number of German fighters. The losses of U.S. bombers and crews was extremely high in the early raids. At times, there was a severe shortage of planes and aircrews. However, an Eighth Air Force bombing mission was never turned back from its target by the enemy. Early in the war, the Luftwaffe pilots watched and waited until U.S. fighters had to turn back. They then attacked the bombers on the way to their target, often shooting down several bombers before "bombs away". By the early spring of 1944 our fighters were much improved, with extra gasoline drop tanks to increase cruising range. Additional armament was also added to the later models of the P-38 and P-47, and the P-51 Mustang had become a formidable long-range fighter to protect our bombers. U.S. Air Force fighters were winning many more aerial combat "dogfights". The heavy bombers were bombing with more success now that they were escorted to and from their target. U.S. fighters also flew many bombing and strafing missions against German airfields to destroy planes and equipment on the ground. Germany was losing air supremacy. The allied forces knew they must have air superiority in preparation for the invasion of France. Operation Overlord, (D-Day) went on schedule June 6, 1944 largely because of the successes of the Allied Air Forces.

The Eighth Air Force had become very strong by late 1944 and early 1945. With the latest models of heavy bombers and fighters, the allies were gaining control of the skies and pounded Germany, destroying Hitler's Third Reich. Hitler's refusal to recognize defeat brought needless suffering to the German people. The war intensified and more good men lost their lives as the air war over Europe continued. The Eighth Air Force suffered the loss of many bombers and aircrewmen between January and the war's end in May of 1945. Our 490th Bomb Group flew missions every day that the weather was clear, and many times when it wasn't! The winter of 1944-45 was one of England's record-breakers for snowfall.

I always pictured our U.S. fighter pilots as the "cowboys of the skies". They seemed so free and easy as they zipped and zoomed around our bombing formations on a mission. A fighter would often pull up on our wing tip and fly along beside our B-17. We could look out the window and the pilot would be very close. We could see his face and read his name painted under his cockpit canopy. Often we could see the small "swastikas" painted on the fuselage over the right wing to indicate enemy "kills".

We would exchange signals or waves before he "peeled off" in a swooping dive to continue his patrol of the sky. Bomber crewmembers really appreciated our "little friends" who protected us from German fighters. Several Eighth Air Force bomber pilots volunteered for a second tour of duty as fighter pilots. I guess they just wanted to get even with those Luftwaffe fighters who had been harassing them on their bombing missions. A fighter pilot tour of duty was 300 hours of combat flying.

The USAAF had dozens of fighter and support groups as well as forty-two Bomb Groups in England by 1945. A native Hoosier, Lt. General William Kepner, headed the Eighth Air Force Fighter Command during World War II. The Ninth Air Force also had many fighter and medium bomber groups in England and at air bases in France after D-Day. Fighter groups were assigned to escort and protect specific sections of the "bomber streams" into Germany on each mission and pilots often referred to their escort duty as "ramrodding" the bombers to and from the target. Fighter squadrons had distinctive identification markings with various colors or patterns, checks or stripes, or solid colors on their nose cowls and tail as well as the air force insignia. Squadron ID letters or numbers were painted on the horizontal tail fins. Fighter pilots often named their plane for wife or girl friend. A fighter became an ace when he had shot down five enemy planes. "Kills" could be verified by their gun cameras, other pilots in the group or the pilot's word. A small swastika emblem was painted on the plane under the pilot's name to indicate a victory. There were more than twenty U.S. pilots with twenty or more victories.

Our loaded B-17 bombers usually cruised about 160 miles per hour. The early bomber armadas had an escort of Spitfires, P-47's or P-38 fighters which had a limited combat flight range. However, by 1945, fighter pilots could leave their base an hour later, catch up and take over the escort duty to the target and return.

The top ace of World War II was Major Richard Bong who was credited with downing forty planes with his P-38 Lightning in the South Pacific. Bong switched to the new jets in 1945 and died in a P-80 crash. Joe Foss, a marine P-47 fighter pilot, shot down twenty-six planes in the Pacific and was awarded the Congressional Medal of Honor for his defense of Guadalcanal. Francis Gabreski was the top ace in the European theatre by shooting down twenty-eight planes with his P-47 Thunderbolt. He destroyed three more while strafing German airfields. He later crashed on a strafing mission, was captured and spent ten months in a prisoner of war camp. During the Korean War, he switched to the F-86 Sabre jet and shot down six North Korean jets. Colonel Francis "Gabby" Gabreski lived until the age of 83, and died February, 2002.

Tactical Bombers and Fighters

The Ninth Air Force directly assisted the Allied ground forces advancing across Europe. These pilots were in radio contact with the troop commanders on the ground who could direct the planes to targets blocking their progress. The fighters and/or twin engine B-25 Mitchell and B-26 Marauder bombers then blasted the designated targets. The fighters also dropped bombs and used their machine guns to strafe enemy trains, troop convoys, armored units and airfields. Many of Germany's locomotives were blown up and hundreds of Luftwaffe planes were destroyed on their runways. This destruction destroyed supplies and prevented German troops from reaching the front. U.S. fighter pilots delighted in catching enemy fighters on the ground. However, low-level bombing and strafing could be a dangerous task. Flying debris from their own bombs and explosions from the target had to be avoided, especially if it carried ammunition or explosives!

One of the most effective fighter outfits in the Eighth Air Force was the 56th Fighter Group. Five of the top aces in the ETO were P-457 Thunderbolt pilots in the 56th. They included Francis Gabreski, 28; Robert Johnson, 27; David Schilling, 22; Walker Mahurin, 20; and group commander, Hubert Zemke (19). A majority of the U.S. aces in Europe flew either the P-47 Thunderbolt or the P-51 Mustang. The D-Day invasion forces made rapid gains and as the war roared on, the German Luftwaffe began to weaken because of aircraft losses to the steadily growing U.S. fighter forces. More than 275 pilots became "aces" flying the P-51 Mustang whose speed and maneuverability made it a top fighter. Germany's air force was forced into a defensive role, often using pilots with little or no training (18).

German Aces

Early in World War II the German Luftwaffe had the advantage of battle-tested pilots and planes. Germany had been preparing for war for several years. German pilots fought in the Spanish Civil War and the Battle of Britain. However, as the war progressed, they faced the fact that they had no "tour of duty". They were to fight until they were killed, disabled, or the war ended. Allied bombing raids and improved fighters won air superiority because Germany lost planes, pilots and fuel supplies which could not be replaced. Adolph Galland is an example of Germany's experienced fighter pilots. He flew 280 combat missions in the 1936 Spanish Civil War when Hitler was secretly aiding General Franco and building a nucleus of pilots for his air force (20). Galland had thirteen "kills" in the twenty-seven day war with Poland, forty by the end of the Battle of Britain and 103 by war's end. He had flown every type of German fighter and was shot down three times (34).

In November 1941, Galland, then thirty, was promoted to Major General and assumed control of the entire Luftwaffe fighter force. One of the biggest victories for Galland was the Allied Schweinfurt raid on October 14, 1943, when Luftwaffe fighters downed sixty B-17s and damaged 138. Eric Hartmann was another top Luftwaffe

ME-109 pilot. It was reported that he flew over 1,400 missions and shot down 350 Allied planes in aerial dogfights. He survived being shot down sixteen times. The top twenty German aces had all shot down more than 180 planes (19).

Early in 1945, Germany's desperation brought about the formation of the Luftwaffe "rammer squadron". It was reported that more than 300 pilots volunteered for this near suicide plan. The strategy called for German pilots to fly directly at a bomber with guns blazing. They were not to pull out of their dive but rather to use the wing of their fighter to cut the bomber in half at the waist or clip off the tail just before they ejected from the plane. Our crew always believed that some of these "rammer" pilots hit the 490th Bomb Group on our sixteenth mission, the April 7, 1945 raid on Parchim. Eighth Air Force bombers and fighter pilots had first encountered a jet plane, the Messerschmitt 163, in July 1944. The ME-163 single-engine jet flew at a top speed of 500 mph but could only stay aloft about ten minutes. They would soar up to attack the bombers, make a pass or two and dive back down to their base. However, in September, the Luftwaffe revealed the ME-262 twin engine jet fighter. This plane might have prolonged the war, but Hitler waited too long to put it into production. The ME-262 was much faster than the P-51 Mustang but couldn't make sudden changes of direction. Our fighters could catch them in a turn by using a maneuver called the "Luftwaffe stomp" which involved stalling their P-51 fighter and turning at the same time to get behind the enemy and gain the advantage in combat (19). The ME-262's inability to maneuver quickly and its limited fuel supply was a definite handicap in aerial combat. However, they were very effective against heavy bomber formations and shot down twenty-five planes in March, 1945. The German High Command had also ordered General Galland to form a special ME-262 jet fighter squadron. The top aces, including Generals and Colonels were selected. This elite JV-44 squadron was a last-ditch effort to stop Allied bombers and fighters. The heavily armed jets were also equipped with wing racks which carried twenty-four rockets. Thank heavens this group wasn't ready for combat until April, and Germany was on the verge of surrender! German jet airbases became prime targets and many were destroyed on the ground. Germany eventually produced about 1200 of these difficult to fly twin engine jets.

Mission 8   Augsburg   January 15, 1945

Wake-up 0300   *Take off 8:50*
Briefing 0430   *Mission 8 ½ hours*
                       Oxygen 4 hours

Bombed our secondary target – a big marshalling yard – 100 flak guns. Flak was barrage type and moderate. Our bombload was ten 500 pounders – one hung up and Rod kicked it loose.

[Briefing Order: Templeton crew led lead squadron – Command pilot, Major Lightner – command navigator, Captain Everett Kallstrom – Crew stations at 0755 – taxi, 0825 – take-off, 0845 – Estimated Return Time (ETR), 1340.]

Through These Eyes

The Battle of the Bulge had failed and the Germans retreated and prepared for a last-ditch stand with their ground forces. However, this meant more anti-aircraft guns to protect remaining targets! The Luftwaffe also prepared for a desperate defense against tactical and high-level bombers. The "Stars and Stripes" continued to carry encouraging news of Allied victories on land, sea and air. The Templeton crew was unaware of the trials they faced in the closing months of the war. The Battle of the Bulge was the biggest and bloodiest battle of WW II, lasting slightly over six weeks. More than 76,000 Americans were killed, injured or reported missing, and Hitler's army was decimated.

The 490th sent up 38 bombers to the target, the railroad marshalling yards at Augsburg. We flew as lead crew of the high squadron at 13,000 feet. Major Adams was mission commander. This, again, was two missions in a row. We had released our bomb load and turned for home when we discovered that one of the 500-pound bombs didn't release from the bomb rack! Our engineer, Ewing Roddy, volunteered to go into the bomb bay and work on the shackle to release that last "hung bomb". Bombs were loaded into the bomb bay and attached to two shackles one above the other in two columns. Roddy had to get a portable oxygen tank and get out on the catwalk with bomb bay doors open to loosen that bomb! We certainly had to get rid of it before we could land back at the base. Luckily, Rod freed it quickly and got back to his regular oxygen hook-up as the bomb bay doors closed. We later teased him for bombing an "undesignated target" and credited him with a direct hit on a dangerous Nazi barn!

RAF Augsburg Raid

The Submarine diesel engine factory at Augsburg was first bombed April 1942 with a low-level raid. Augsburg was also the location of an important ball-bearing factory for the German war machine. In 1942, the British RAF had drawn up a plan to pull a long-range surprise raid to show the Germans that no place was protected. This was much like General Doolittle's raid on Tokyo after Pearl Harbor. The RAF carried out the raid at a very high price in men and bombers. The raid was the subject of a book entitled The Augsburg Raid by Jack Currie(4).

Mission 9   Sterkade-Rheine   January 20, 1945

Awakened 0200   *Take off 0730*
Briefing 0400   *Mission 5 ½ hours*
Altitude 27,000   *Oxygen 4 hours*

We were chaff ship – we were lead chaff ship – that made us first into German territory and first over the target. In other words, we were at the head of all the bombers. We even passed the tail-end of our bombers coming into Germany as we were going home. We were loaded with chaff and no bombs. Our group hit synthetic oil storage tanks at Sterkade, and bombed PFF. We also hit a secondary target. This was a short mission and we were back by noon and through cleaning our guns by 1500. It was 57 degrees below zero and everything on the plane froze. Lesh went with us today to help throw chaff. He and Bert threw from the waist gun positions and Lt. Russell (Mickey operator) and I from the radio room. Since we were leading and out by ourselves, we had a group of P-51 Mustangs to protect us alone.

[Briefing Order: Templeton crew led a flight of six bombers loaded with "chaff" to disburse at the IP and on the bomb run to foul up German anti--aircraft guns.]

Severe weather had kept our bombers grounded since January 16th. This was the Eighth Air Force's first raid in four days. The Eighth sent up 1,000 Fortresses and Liberators escorted by 250 P-51 Mustangs which still had to battle severe weather conditions. Targets included synthetic oil plants, railroads and bridges. This raid came one day after the Eighth's third birthday. The railroad marshalling yards at Sterkade-Reine were our secondary targets on this mission. We sent up 34 B-17s from the 490th Bomb Group, and the mission Commander was Captain Martin.

Our ship was loaded with boxes of chaff, and we had been briefed to be aware of a heavy concentration of 300 anti-aircraft guns, or more, over the target. Needless to say, once we started the bomb run, we threw out chaff (packages of 7" x 8" aluminum strips) like crazy to foul up the German radar on those guns. We were flying at 27,000 feet, it was minus 57 degrees and some of the guns froze. Other planes in the squadron later reported the same problem. Wilbur Lesh, flew with our crew as an extra helper on this mission. It was great to have him along, but it was the last mission he flew with our crew. Many years later we learned that Wilbur had been volunteering for extra missions in order to finish his tour of duty and return to his family.

Our engineer, Ewing Roddy, had an eye injury on this mission. A Vary pistol flare shell exploded in his top turret and a small piece of the shell casing hit him in the eye. He managed to apply a bandage as we continued on to the target. An ambulance took him to the hospital for treatment as soon as we landed and he was cleared to fly on our next mission a few days later. I knew Roddy was determined to fly with us, because it was bad luck to miss a few missions and have to finish up with a different outfit. This was the reason crewmembers seldom went on " sick call." I remember a few times when I flew with a sinus cold and clogged Eustachian tube which hampered equalizing air pressure on my eardrum and caused extreme pain as we changed altitude. The immediate remedy was to scream and pound my desk. I knew the yelling would equalize the pressure until my ears popped. My ears still pop when I ride a fast elevater. One morning, we were riding out to the plane in the back of a canvas-covered army truck and waist gunner, Dwight Parrish, was sitting on the tailgate. The truck hit a snow bank and he fell out onto the concrete runway! Luckily he was well-padded by his flight suit and he was determined to fly the mission in spite of a few bruises.

We had earned another pass to London, and this time we were looking for suspected Black Market eating spots that served meals usually not available in the enlisted mens' Mess Hall. Our buddies had given us directions on using the tube (subway) to find our targets. Both restaurants were in bombed-out areas, and the first was up a dark stairwell over a closed store. They served steak and fried potatoes! We later decided it was either horsemeat or stolen meat from Army supplies. The second spot was down a dark alley among several bombed out buildings. They even had a peephole in the door so they could look us over before we were admitted. This cafe served bacon, toast, jelly and fresh eggs. These places definitely had a direct supply of black-market food from a British or U.S. Army mess hall and they had a brisk business in spite of all the secrecy.

London passes were especially great when several of our buddies got passes at the same time. We enjoyed sharing memories and experiences around the little stove in Hut 29 cold winter nights. The memories were often better than the original trip!

Lt. Bill Templeton's crew completes twelfth mission 2-22-45

Earns second Oak Leaf Cluster to Air Medal

This was the core of our "Lead Crew" A command pilot, bombardier, and radar operator were added for each "Lead Crew" mission. We never knew who, until mission briefing.

Front row, left to right---waist gunner, Dwight H. Parrish; flight engineer, Ewing G. Roddy; radio operator, James Lee Hutchinson; waist gunner, Bert B. Allinder.

Back row, left to right---navigator, Bruno P. Conterato; pilot, William D. Templeton; co-pilot, Dale F. Rector

Two "Lead Crews" of Hut 29

Front L to R – Roddy, Hutch, Parrish – Back, Bert, Mantley, Anderson, Perrin, Ginsberg (Lucky was our mascot)

"Flak so thick, you could walk on it!"

490th B-17 planes were marked with broad red bands around wings and tails and a red-tipped tail

Bomb-run View of the Target

Chapter Eight

Our Crew's "May Day"

Lady Luck had been with our crew for nine missions, but then came number ten! We had no premonition of impending trouble. We hadn't flown a mission in a week and were anxious to get on with it and get credit for another raid on our tour of duty.

Mission 10   Hohenbudburg   January 28, 1945

Diary Entry

We awakened at 4:15am and after breakfast and briefing we picked up our parachutes and equipment. The guns were installed, bombs loaded and we took off at 8:30am for a mission that would last approximately six hours. We climbed quickly and were on oxygen for four hours. Our target was the railroad marshalling yards at Hohenbudburg. Major Lightner was group commander.

We took off into a snow storm and only 18 of the 25 planes managed to get into the air. We led the wing today and I was busy as the devil with the radio, sending control point and strike reports. We had a good bomb load and it was a short mission. The sky cleared over the target and the Mickey operator, LT. Russell said we hit the target. Flak was very heavy and accurate. We picked up many holes in the plane, and waist gunner Robinson was hit in the head. Luckily he was wearing his steel flak helmet which saved his life. We managed to get him bandaged until we could get back to England.

As we approached our airbase a snowstorm was closing in below us and we could not land. We were directed to another field ahead of the storm. Rod fired the red flares as we landed, indicating we had wounded. An ambulance met us and picked up Robinson.

The weather cleared the next day and we took off for our base, leaving Robinson in the hospital. We visited him before he was sent back to the U.S. and learned that he had lost his eye. That was a Purple Heart medal and a ticket home for him.

Our squadron landed back at Eye, and waist gunner Bert Allinder and I cleaned the guns and went in for supper. This was the first time we flew as a group leader with a command pilot and bombardier. Lt. Oliver was bombardier and Lt. Russell was radar officer. Our group had 18 aircraft led by Major L.S. Lightner. We flew lead squadron today.

James Lee Hutchinson, EdS

Flak Casualty --- "May Day!"

The winter weather had kept us grounded for too many days. The 490th flew only thirteen missions in December and only nine so far in January. We were alerted to fly "lead" position on this mission. Our crew didn't realize that Orville Robinson, our waist gunner, would be wounded. It was the tenth mission for the Templeton crew and we had flown four of the last six missions. We took off in a snowstorm and only eighteen planes were able to get airborne before the storm closed the runway. However, our "reduced" squadron joined the bomber stream heading for Germany. We carried twelve 500 pounders and bombed at 27,000 feet. There was heavy flak over this well protected target! No planes were lost, but many received flak damage and several crew-members were wounded

The bomb group had released their bombs and was leaving the area when a piece of flak hit Robinson's steel flak helmet and its jagged edge cut him above the eye. Bert Allinder, the other waist gunner was able to treat him with bandages and a morphine shot from the plane's First Aid kit. Bert said he knew Robby's head wound was serious, but because of the temperature at that altitude, the blood had frozen and it was easy to apply a bandage. We never doubted that the steel flak helmet had saved Robby's life. We were on our way home but there was still the threat of flak and fighters. I sent the "strike report" back to our base and was ready to take over Robby's waist gun position if fighters were sighted in the area. The ground crew later reported that our plane had over a hundred holes in it. Other crews reported higher numbers. I guess some of those trains had anti-aircraft guns mounted on the flatcars. The snowstorm beat us back to Eye and we couldn't land. It was eerie to watch that blizzard blot out the runways just before we could land. We had to hurry to land at another base, check Robby into the hospital, leave our planes and take trucks back to Eye. The next day the weather cleared and the trucks took us back to pick up our planes and visit Robby. Bert had found the piece of flak in our plane and gave it to Robby for a keepsake! His head injury resulted in the loss of an eye. He was later transferred back to the states and awarded a Purple Heart. He was the oldest man on our crew at age twenty-six, and a great guy. Our crew was glad he had survived, but sorry to lose him as a crewmember. It seemed ironic that he lost his eye while stationed at Eye. "May Day" was the intercom word for emergency and carried the same meaning as an SOS sent by Morse code. The Templeton crew had its emergency on this mission and word of the hit quickly spread over the intercom.

Bert and I met again in May, 2003 to visit and talk about our WW II Eighth Air Force days. Bert said that the piece of flak he found and gave to Robinson was shaped like it came from the bottom of a shell. We decided that the shell had barely missed our left wing and gas tanks before it exploded above our plane. A few feet either way and it would have instantly destroyed our B-17! Far too many Eighth Air Force bombers received those direct hits and went down in flames. Flak hit our plane many times on our eighteen combat missions. I remember one time a slug came zinging through my radio room over my head and out the other side over the Mickey operator's head! The ground crew patched more than 100 flak holes in our plane after that raid.

The London edition of the "Stars and Stripes" gave the Eighth bombers huge headlines for this raid. This was the second biggest bomber raid on Germany since the Normandy invasion on June 6, 1944. It pinpointed the German rail and canal systems. Generally, the weather had cleared and the Eighth Air Force, the Fifteenth Air Force and the RAF bombed targets around the clock.

The Eighth Air Force had sent out more than 1,400 B-24 and B-17 bombers escorted by 800 P-51 Mustang and P-38 Thunderbolt fighters to smash Nazi transportation. The heavy bombers used a new technique for the first time. Instead of bombing from their usual height of 25,000 feet, some of the big bombers swooped down to as low as 1,500 feet! Bombers blasted more than twenty-four marshalling yards over a 38,000 square mile area in the heart of the Third Reich. Our bomb load was twelve 500-pounders (9).

Mission 11   Frankfort   February 17, 1945

Diary Entry

Our target was the railroad marshalling yards at Frankfort. We flew a seven hour mission at 21,000 feet and were on oxygen for four hours. We led the high squadron today and I sent the "control point" radio reports. We received a message that changed the target to Plan B. I forgot to receipt for it and I got "chewed out" good by the group communications office (a major) when we landed!

We hit the target by PFF and got good results. Dwight Parrish flew waist gunner to replace Robinson, whose eye was injured, and they sent up plenty of flak for him. Lt. Campbell was our bombardier and Lt. Klein, Mickey operator. The twenty-four aircraft mission was led by Major W.C. Cochran. We broke the jinx today and got in another mission. We hadn't flown a mission since January 28th. We had been left on the hardstand for eleven days because of weather and cancelled mission. The "Stars and Stripes" ran an interesting article stating the aircrew chances of survival were now double those of crews in 1943!

Our crew had been worried at take-off on this mission. We were flying lead of the high squadron and had a new waist gunner to replace Robby. The group had flown only six missions in the first two weeks of February because of bad weather and hazardous flying conditions. Five bombers and many crewmembers had been lost in that period. A flak damaged B-17 had made a forced landing in Poland on the February 3rd mission to Berlin. The crew returned to fly again. Three days later, four bombers were lost in mid-air collisions during the Chemnitz mission. The first bomber collided with a plane from another group during formation assembly over England. A second crashed due to engine failure and two others collided over France on the way home!

A short guy in fatigues was in the plane as soon as we parked on the hardstand. He tore me out for failing to receipt that I had received that "change of target" message. After flying a combat mission for seven hours, I was in no mood to be "chewed out" by some "ground pounder". I let him have it with both barrels, pointing out that we had bombed the right target and admitted that I had not sent a "strike report". He calmed down about the same time I saw the gold leaf of a Major on his collar. Of course, I calmed down even faster. He was the group communication officer! I was a Staff Sergeant radio operator and I wanted to keep those stripes. I shut up, paid close attention to his criticisms, and said "Yes, sir" several times!

The Eighth Air Force continued on its course to destroy bridges and railroads, and disrupt the German communications system. Air power's job was to prevent and/or slow down the enemy's ability to move trips, supplies and equipment to their ground forces sat the front. In addition to railroad marshalling yards, bombers also targeted German fuel supplies. Often the weather over the targets allowed "visual bombing". Clouds covered targets on several missions forced the Bomb Group to bomb with radar.

During the latter half of the month, the Mighty Eighth waged its longest sustained bombing effort in an all-out effort to destroy German transportation. It was also the longest for the 490th Bomb Group. We flew eleven missions in the last two weeks. Our missions to Ansbach at Kitzingen on February 22nd and 23rd were especially successful. Third Division Commander, Major General Earle Partridge, inspected the base and was pleased with base personnel and the work we were doing (1). Private Dwight Parrish had become our newest crewmember after Robinson was wounded. He was a good waist-gunner and stayed with our crew for the remainder of the war. Dwight had lost his stripes through some disciplinary problems but earned them again on a later mission. Parrish was from the "deep south" of Alabama and fit right in with our crew. He once told about the old town character who would gather kids around and read the paper to them. But he sometimes held the paper upside down!

The "Big Week" of February 19-26 1945 was a period of intensive bombing missions against targets crucial to the German aircraft industry and the Luftwaffe. Allied Generals knew that German air power must be reduced before an allied victory could be successful. Berlin, Leipzig, Regensburg, Stuttgart, Augsburg, and Schweinfurt and Luftwaffe airfields were prime targets. The RAF and USAAF bombers had a very successful week. The Eighth put up more than 3,000 bombers, and the 15th Air Force from Italy sent 500. Our forces dropped more than 10,000 tons of bombs on their targets. Germany's aircraft industry was severely damaged and many German fighters were destroyed in the air and on the airfields bombed or strafed by U.S. fighters. However, we lost 226 bombers and a majority of their crews that week (9).

Combat Fatigue

The "Stars and Stripes" newspaper stated in its February 22, 1945 edition that "Chances of air combat crews completing their tours of duty in the European and Mediterranean theaters were now nearly double what they were in the winter of 1943". The Army Air Force credited the improvement of rates of survival to the establishment of air superiority over the Luftwaffe fighters and increasing fighter plane escorts to protect the heavy bombers. In late 1943, statistics showed that aircrews had only a 36 percent chance of completing all 25 assigned missions. By January 1944 the figure had jumped to 66 percent This took into consideration those who parachuted to safety, those taken prisoner, and those otherwise rejoining their units. So the Bomber Command raised the required number of missions to 35! It was not good news for replacement crews such as ours.

There was a constant mental strain on aircrew members. We worried most of the night before a bombing raid, and "sweated out" every mission. There was always the reality of flak over the target and the threat of a fighter attack before or after the target. A direct hit by an 88mm anti-aircraft shell meant disaster. Severe flak damage that disabled a plane meant dropping out of the protection of the formation and becoming a prime target for lurking Luftwaffe fighters. Bombers of the 490th suffered many types of losses during practice and/or combat missions. Examples include crashes on take-offs or landings, mid-air collisions in fog, forced landings, fires on hardstands, being rammed by enemy fighters, anti-aircraft or fighter attacks. Combat fatigue was not uncommon, as some of the guys "snapped" and had nervous breakdowns under the constant fear of death. The common term around the base was "flak happy", but we all sympathized and knew that it could happen to any of us. The Air Force had several R & R (rest and relaxation) centers for crewmen who needed time to get away from it all for a week or more. Combat crews also received frequent three-day passes to London or other recreational areas.

Every combat mission was a test of endurance and doing the best job possible at our positions. Each man depended on the ability of the rest of his plane's crew. There was no place for a crewmember who was not in good mental condition. We were keenly aware of planes and men lost from our group. Many of us had adopted the attitude expressed in a Bill Mauldin cartoon when Willie said to Joe, "I feel like a fugitive from the law of averages". The "Stars and Stripes" kept us informed of total losses on each raid. We were always faced with the brutal statistics of the air war. Andy Rooney, of "Sixty Minutes" fame, was a reporter for the "Stars and Stripes" as a young man and flew several bombing missions as an observer in May 1943. These were the days of extremely heavy losses of planes and men. He captured the situation perfectly in his book, *My War* when he wrote, "A great number of American boys had their last night's sleep in a Nissen hut in England" (11).

Allied ground forces were winning on all fronts and re-taking land that had been conquered by Germany. The Russian armies were moving rapidly and avenging the brutal treatment of their citizens. U.S. pilots and crews were provided with identification cards printed in Russian in case we had to bail out or were forced to land in conquered territory. Each man also received a 7 x 9 inch page with a picture of the American flag and a paragraph in Russian asking captors to notify the American Mission in Moscow before doing anything drastic! Six instructions for the downed airman included pinning the American flag to the pocket over his heart. Perhaps the most important advice was to raise your arms and yell, "Ya Amerikanets!" I still have my copy and I.D. card.

Mission 12   Ansbach   February 22, 1945

Diary Entry

This 12th mission was a doozy---lasting nine hours, but we were only on oxygen two hours. Our target was railroad yards again. We didn't hit the briefed target, we hit the "target of opportunity" or practically "last resort". We blew a little town all to hell (we think). It was PFF again, results unobserved.

We were briefed for a 12,000 foot bombing altitude, but bombed from 21,000 feet. We went all over Germany (it seemed) through clouds. We saw no flak at all, so it was a pretty good day. It was a maximum effort and we bombed marshalling yards and canals. We had 6,000 planes in this all-out effort.

I cleaned ten guns today. I did it the easy way---oil in the bore and on the recoil plate (face of the bolt to you). We took several pictures when we landed, or rather the Public Relations department took them. It was our Oak Leaf Cluster mission. We got a picture of our crew and also individual shots. Today I am a man. I downed my post-mission scotch in one gulp!

The 490th Bomb Group put up 38 aircraft. Major Cochran was mission commander and Major Lightner was mission leader. Our crew flew lead plane, leading the middle squadron. Today, the base photo group took our pictures after we landed, and the crew and individual photos taken are included in this book. This was the greatest mass air assault on Germany since the D-Day invasion. Six thousand planes from seven different Air Commands participated in this coordinated raid. The Eighth Air Force put up 1,400 heavy bombers escorted by 800 Mustangs and Thunderbolts. The B-17 and B-24 bombers blasted more than twenty-four marshalling yards, bridges and highway. The "Stars and Stripes" headlines read, "Second Biggest Air Blitz Hits Nazis". Germany's transportation system was greatly damaged. The Nazis were beginning to feel the full wrath of the "bomber war" as tons of bombs rained down on cities and industries.

The tide turned in the spring of 1945 with extremely large Allied bombing raids on Berlin. In early March 1945, a ninety-mile stream of heavy bombers hit and destroyed critical targets in Hitler's capitol. The raid demoralized the civilian population of Berlin. Early in the war, German leaders had boasted that the city could not be bombed. Now, the city was in ruins and the food supply was critical. A "Stars and Stripes" photo depicts civilians butchering a dead horse in the streets of Berlin (9).

Our 490th Bomb Group flew fifteen missions this month (eight in a row). We flew twice as lead crew and made several equipment test flights. Eleven of the group's missions were against railroads and bridges.

James Lee Hutchinson, EdS

Mission 12-B Ulm March 1, 1945

Diary Entry

I was superstitious---so this is mission 12-B, not thirteen! We flew lead crew and I received one "Y'. I sent only strike reports with no control points. Major Wesson was our command pilot. The mission lasted seven and a half hours, and we were on oxygen for three hours. We hit a railroad yard—good job. I had trouble with my ears. I had a package from home when I got back to the barracks after debriefing and putting away equipment. Mom sent a pipe and some candy bars. Keen Umbehr, my old buddy from radio school in Sioux Falls, South Dakota, was waiting for me. I had visited his base at the 486th Bomb Group near Sudbury, and he was returning the favor.

[Briefing Order: Templeton lead crew – Command pilot, Major Blum – Command navigator, Captain Sullivan – Mission commander, Major W.C. Cochran – Stations, 0610 – Take-off 0710 – Formation assembly (rendezvous) at 15,000 feet with red and yellow flares.]

Keen Umbehr and I had a good time reliving the "good old days'. We shared what we knew about former radio school classmates. Those guys were scattered all over the globe. A few were serving in the Eighth, others were sent to fight the Japanese in the Pacific theater, and one guy was a "ground pounder" at a remote radio station in Alaska. We each had heard of a few who had perished. We had climbed the ladder of success and were now Technical Sergeants. A Tech Sergeant's salary was the grand total of $204 per month. This included extra for overseas and flight pay.

Our group sent 37 bombers on this raid as the Eighth Air Force continued the record effort they began in the last half of February. "Stars and Stripes" reported that more than 1200 B-17 Fortresses and B-24 Liberators took part in the Eighth Air Force's eighth consecutive day's raid of German communications system. The bombers had an escort of 450 Mustang fighters as they hit eight targets around Stuttgart and Munich.

A second article carried a report from prisoners of war who had been freed by American and British armies as they over-ran German concentration camps. The men reported that allied bombings had been so effective that German rail and communications systems were "shot to hell", and there was a terrible food shortage. They had spent four to five days on a train to Switzerland and safety, for what was once an eight hour trip.

Based in Italy, the Fifteenth Air Force concentrated on strategic targets in Austria and southern Germany while the Eighth and the RAF (Royal Air Force) Lancaster and Halifax bombers from England continued their "around the clock" raids on transportation and industry. The Allies were blitzing Germany by air in an all out effort to bring an end to this war (9).

Mission 14   Plauen   March 21, 1945

Diary Entry

Awakened at 0200, breakfast and briefing by 3:30. Take off, 0600. We were on oxygen five hours of this seven and a half hour mission. Our target was the marshalling yards at Plauen. We led the squadron. There were 38 aircraft and we flew at 21,000 feet. Major Cochran was mission leader. This was a tough mission, lots of flak and we were hit by fifteen ME 262 twin engine jet fighters. There were tracer bullets and flak puffs everywhere. Our group shot down two of the jets and we lost two bombers. We were commended by the two majors (command pilot and bombardier) riding with us. They said we were a real crew (ahem). Parrish got his Buck sergeant stripes back for being such a good waist gunner. We agreed with the Majors; we had always thought we were a "smart" crew. We four enlisted men were flying with all that "brass". We knew our officers were good and we did our best to stay alive!

[Briefing Order: Templeton lead crew – Major Cochran, command pilot – Major O'Dell, command navigator – Stations 0525 – Take-off, 0612 – Assembly at 8,000 feet on red and yellow flares – Chaff, twelve minutes on bomb run – note assigned radio channels, code words and flare colors – base altitude, 22,000 feet.]

Our 490th Group had its first encounter with the new German jet-propelled fighters on this mission, March 21st. Our target was the Plauen railroad yards but twelve to fourteen ME 262s hit the low squadron about twenty minutes before we reached the target. Two 490th Fortresses were shot down and a third was lost when an ME-262 crashed into it after being damaged by our Bomb Group's gunners. The air battle lasted nearly ten minutes. The Group was officially credited with one ME-262 destroyed and one damaged. Recently, Bert and Roddy told me that during that attack an ME-262 came in on our bomber at three o'clock high. He had us in his sights but peeled off without firing! Perhaps he was out of fuel or ammunition, or was chased off by our P-51 fighter escorts. Either way, we were again spared the possibity of serious damage. We went on to hit the target, but the flak seemed thick enough to walk on out there. The new jet fighter ME-262 carried a limited fuel supply and could only fly for short periods. They came up, fought and returned to their base. Our fighters were soon hunting out and strafing German fighter airfields. Today, an ME-262 fighter is on display in the WW II section of the US Air Force Museum in Dayton, Ohio. However, it doesn't look nearly as fierce as when it was attacking our formation with all guns blazing on March 21, 1945!

"Stars and Stripes" reported a savage blow by the Eighth Air Force to bomb and destroy Luftwaffe airfields and planes. The Eighth had some 2,200 bombers and fighters in the air, with nearly 2,000 concentrated on hammering eleven airfields, many of them bases for German jet propelled fighters and fighter-bombers (9).

The Eighth Air Force B-17 Flying Fortresses and B-24 Liberators made their bomb runs through heavy anti-aircraft fire (flak). Their prime targets were railroad marshalling yards and an armament plant at Plauen. The Royal Air Force (RAF) Lancaster bombers hit oil refineries at Bremen and an important railroad bridge at Weser. Our P-51 Mustang and P-47 Thunderbolt fighters dropped fragmentation bombs on German airbases and machine-gunned (strafed) building and planes on the runways (9).

A Freakish Mid-Air Collision

Our crew was especially nervous on this mission because two bombers in our group had gone down in a mid-air collision over Germany on the March 17th raid to Bitterfeld. One of the planes involved the Lt. Robert Tennenberg bomber of squadron 849, a pilot and crew we knew very well. We had buddied with them on the base and taken several trips to Diss and London together. Their radio operator, Ed Miller, and I were classmates in radio school at Sioux Falls. We later learned they had landed safely in Belgium when the "Stars and Stripes" carried a story about the B-17 that went on a mission with ten men and landed with eleven!

Pilot Robert Tennenberg later discussed the accident in an article for the Historical Record of the 490 th Bomb Group. The following is a condensed version of his report:

The group had tightened the formation for protection against fighters and headed for England. There was very poor visibility and they were only a short distance from friendly territory when they collided with a bomber that lost its position in the formation and pulled up in front of the Tennenberg plane. That plane broke in half from the mid-air collision and went down with no known survivors. Tennenberg's bomber was severely damaged with two large holes in the fuselage, a crushed plexiglass nose, two engines lost and a bent wing tip. The navigator and bombardier managed to crawl out of the crushed nose cone and back to the radio room. Lt.Tennenberg had lost engines two and three but still had control of the plane and advised his crew to delay bailing out because he thought they could make it to friendly territory. The sub-zero temperature forced him to leave the formation and descend below the clouds to a lower altitude where they picked up a P-47 escort fighter who led them to his airbase in Belgium. Upon landing they discovered the limbless and decapitated torso of the radio operator from the other plane in the damaged nose cone of their plane. The body had been caught in their bomber's "prop wash" and sucked into their nose when the other plane broke in half. A few days later our buddies were picked up and returned to the Brome Dome at Eye. Lt Tennenberg said, "When we got back to our barracks, we found that all our bags had been packed as though we had also been lost on that raid; apparently nobody had been informed that we had, in fact, survived". Men in the armed forces had a term for this type of mix-up, it was "SNAFU" (situation normal-- all fouled up). The Tennenberg crew was ready for a combat mission again on April 8th and flew at least four more missions before the end of the war. I met and visited with Bob Tennenberg and his ball gunner, Johnnie Mann at the 490th Bomb Group reunion in September, 2002 in Branson, Missouri.

Mission 15   Hanover   March 28, 1945

Diary Entry

Flak pretty accurate—not a bad mission though, six hours. We hit a tank factory in the middle of town. The flak was right on us or rather under us. We could hear the stuff exploding right beneath us. Jack (Mickey Operator) and I had a regular sweat session. I also saw a V-bomb (buzz bomb) starting on its way to England.

The 490th Bomb Group sent up 38 aircraft led by Major Blum. Our crew flew lead plane of the lead squadron at 18,000 feet. Our target was a tank factory and/or the central railroad station in the center of town. There was exceptionally heavy flak and we had some anxious moments while on our bomb run.

The Eighth sent out 900 bombers to destroy German industrial targets and railroad marshalling yards. Berlin was hit by 400 Fortresses, and more than 500 hit Hanover where the targets included railroads and plants making armored vehicles. Planes reported heavy flak from the German ack-ack (anti-aircraft) fire. Some 350 P-51 Mustangs flew escort and reported very few enemy fighters. Oil supply depots were hit by twin-engine bombers from the Ninth Air Force (9).

In the spring of 1945, the Luftwaffe had lost superiority in the air over Germany. They were now the "hunted" instead of the "hunters"and were mostly being used to protect important targets from the increasing allied bombing raids. The Fifteenth Air Force and RAF from their bases in Italy were increasing their raids and hitting targets in Austria, Romania and southern Germany. Allied armies were rapidly regaining territory and Germany was drawing back to a purely defensive position.

The Fifteenth Air Force

The Ploesti oil fields in Romania were the source for approximately 60% of Germany's oil and gas for their war machines.

They were heavily protected and one of the most dangerous targets aircrews could pull, second only to the Schweinfurt ballbearing plant or Regensburg aircraft factories in Germany. Once the allies conquered southern Italy, the airfields at Foggia became available for allied bomber bases. By April 1944, the Fifteenth Air Force became a large and efficient force, composed of twenty-one bomb groups which were supported by seven fighter groups. It was second only to the Eighth Air Force in England (28). Hitler's Third Reich was now caught between two powerful forces. The Eighth pounded from the north while the Fifteenth flew over the Alps and blasted them from the south. The Commander of Air Corps in Europe, General Carl Spaatz, declared after D-Day that one of the primary tasks of heavy bomb groups was the destruction of Germany's oil supply. The Ploesti, Romania oilfields supplied the bulk of Hitler's oil and became a prime target of the Fifteenth Air Corps. Airmen referred to Ploesti as the "graveyard of the Fifteenth" because it was such a heavily defended target. One of the most costly raids was carried out on August 1, 1943 when 177 bombers went in on a low-level raid (300 feet). The loss was 54 planes and 532 airmen. The B-24 Liberators of the 15th carried out twenty-four raids on the oil fields in the spring and summer of 1944. Over 300 bombers and 3,000 men were lost before Hitler's oil supplies were put out of business.

A parody of the popular song, "As Time Goes By" was composed by an anonymous crewman in the Fifteenth Air Force:

You must remember this

The flak can't always miss

Somebody's gotta die.

The odds are always too damned high

As flak goes by.

It's still the same old story,

The Eighth gets all the glory.

While we're the ones who die.

The odds are always too damned high

As flak goes by. (22)

Our crew could relate to the Fifteenth Air Force because Bert Allinder's older brother had served as a B-24 ball turret gunner and was shot down by a Luftwaffe fighter over the Ploesti oil fields on D-Day, June 6, 1944. He spent four months in a POW camp before being freed by advancing Russian troops. He had returned to the USA before our crew went overseas. He told Bert that the food shortage was a big problem in the stalag and the POW diet was very limited. He said starvation was a hard fact in concentration camps, and he didn't realize there were so many ways to cook cabbage.

Lt. George McGovern, later a senator, 1972 presidential candidate and an ambassador to the United Nations flew 35 combat missions as a B-24 pilot with the 455th Bomb Group in the Fifteenth Air Force. He was awarded the Distinguished Flying Cross for landing his flak-damaged B-24 safely on mountain-side airstrip and saving the plane and crew.

Targets that the Eighth Air Force had difficulty reaching from England were now caught in this aerial pincer movement by the allies. The Ploesti oil fields and Schweinfurt ballbearing factories were still dreaded targets but much closer for Fifteenth bombers coming in over the Alps. Another golfing buddy, Sgt. Bob Henry, was a B-24 gunner with seven missions. Light bombers and fighters from Italy also destroyed river transportation, railroad marshalling yards, trains and bridges and oil supplies. Germany's transportation and supply lines were grinding to a halt.

The Tuskegee Airmen

Escort fighter protection was necessary for the B-24 Liberators. One group of escorts was the Tuskegee Airmen, a squadron of P-51 African American pilots. The 99th Fighter Squadron, known as the Black Eagles, broke the race barrier and proved their heroism and skills as fighter pilots. Their Commander, Lt. Colonel Benjamin Davis Jr., was a West Point graduate who rose to the rank of Lt. General before his death in July, 2002.

The black fighter pilots in Lt. Colonel Davis' unit compiled an outstanding combat record against the German Luftwaffe. Squadron hero, Major Robert Diez, was featured on a war bond poster. They shot down 111 enemy planes and destroyed 273 on the ground. Lt. Charles B. Hall was the first Black Eagle pilot to shoot down a German plane. He was awarded the Distinguished Flying Cross (26). The Fifteenth Air Force bomber crews were very happy to have the

99th fly as bomber escorts on the missions. The 99th was later joined by other black American fighter squadrons and became Fighter Group 332. There was mutual respect between the aircrews and the talented Tuskegee pilots who protected them from German fighters. Before long, bomber groups were requesting the fighter group with their red-tailed P-51 fighters. They never lost a bomber from groups they escorted. The Tuskegee airmen lost more than 70 pilots in World War II while serving in North Africa, Italy and France (22).

Mission 16   Parchim   April 7, 1945

Diary Entry

Take-off 9030   Oxygen 5 hours

Mission 8 hours

We were up at 0400 o-clock and got delayed (Chicago-twelved). We were inside the ship (plane) 13 hours besides the time we spent getting ready. It was a raid over Northern Germany for jet bases. We were fighter bait. The whole Eighth Air Force went up today.

We got hit by two ME-109's. They hit one Fort, it caught fire, peeled out of formation and the crew bailed out. I didn't envy those boys I saw swinging down in those silken chutes. They all got out okay, or so we thought. The other fighter crossed over us and Rod (our top turret gunner) cut loose at him and he burst into flames. He pulled out about 250 yards and Rod hit him again with a burst. He (the ME-109) peeled off, put out his fire, and came in on a pursuit curve at us. Then Parrish (our waist gunner) and Lieutenant Rector (tail gunner) cut loose at him and he exploded behind us. The German

Through These Eyes

pilot tried to crash into us, missed and hit another B-17. Then the ME-109 exploded and went down. The B-17 did not go down. That German sure was trying for us, the lead ship.

We were leading the high formation today ---36 planes led by Major Adams. The flak was meager but accurate. We got about 25 holes in the plane. They were really coming close too. The Germans were using their flak trains. In briefing, the target wasn't charted for flak. All in all we lost two planes and our crew shot down an ME-109. The German pilot did not get out either. He was trying to get us. He wanted that Iron Cross (medal) with the diamond in it, I guess.

[Interrogation Report: Two planes from the 850 squadron went down on this raid. The Lt. Richard Drouht crew was lost in action and Lt. Carrol Cagles's bomber was rammed and severely damaged but managed to land in Belgium. These planes were rammed by ME-109 fighters from the Schulungslehrgang Elbe, a special "rammer squadron" formed in the last months of the war. Their suicidal tactics were a last ditch effort to prolong a lost cause.]

Take-off was delayed for an hour due to poor visibility. Sitting on the runway was boring, but today's target was an ME-262 jet airfield and we really wanted to hit it as a matter of preservation. Destroying planes and their fuel supply beats meeting them in aerial combat, but this turned out to be the Templeton crew's most dangerous mission. The bomber formations were tempting targets for the Luftwaffe pilots making last-ditch efforts to defend their country. We had a heavy P-51 fighter escort and we needed it! The

490th was hit by fighters just before we reached the IP (the start of our bombing run.)

The alarm came over the inter-com---"Bandits at two o'clock high"! This was the first time our crew had met fighters. Looking out my window, I could see two ME-109 fighters swooping down on our formation. The machine guns in their wings were blazing as they dived. Our B-17 gunners were sending a hail of .50 caliber slugs and tracers at the attackers. I stood to get a better view through the plexiglass roof of the radio room. Roddy's twin turret guns and Bert's waist gun jarred the plane as they blazed away. It was "fire at will" and we all knew which one was Will! This was the time for a lot of praying! Our tail gunner, Lt. Rector, and Parrish, the right waist gunner cut loose as the bandits swept over the formation. Lt. Druhot"s bomber went down, and we saw several parachutes as the plane peeled off to the left. One ME-109 was shot to pieces and flames were peeling the skin off his fuselage as he dived through the formation trying to ram a Fortress. He crashed into Lt. Cagle's bomber behind the left wing and caused severe damage before he bounced off and exploded. We had met the rammer squadron! Cagle's bomber managed to continue flying, drop out of the formation and land safely in northern France. The second fighter circled and came back for another pass at our formation

Bert swore he had us in his sights but failed to fire. Perhaps he was low on fuel, out of ammo, his guns jammed or he decided to get out of that flak He suddenly dived away, we were spared a direct hit and went on to bomb our target.

Through These Eyes

The airfield at Parchim was a hornet's nest and enemy fighters swarmed the skies. They continued attacking bombers and our escort fighters. Our group leader decided that we would bomb in formation in order to concentrate our fire power on the fighters. The Luftwaffe fighters had actually followed us during the bomb run. They were flying into their own flak! In spite of the fighter attack, the bombing results were excellent and our "formation" bombing destroyed the target.

The German Luftwaffe had organized a "rammer" squadron late in the war. It was reported that they had 300 ME-109 pilots volunteer for this duty. The plan was for the pilot to fly straight at his target while firing. At the last minute he was to clip the tail of the bomber with his wing then bail out if he could. If this wasn't a suicide group, it was awfully close! The Japanese had used suicide pilots since late 1944. The mission of the Kamikase (Divine Wind) group of young fliers was to crash their bomb loaded plane into allied warships. They were successful in sinking more than 50 ships and damaging many others. However, by 1945, Luftwaffe pilots were generally not that fanatic.

One of the planes hit was to the left of our position and I watched from my window as it peeled out of the formation. It was eerie to watch one of our bombers go down; everything seemed to be in slow motion. First, the B-17 fell out of formation, drifted lazily away and into the open sky as the crew began "bailing out". I counted the white chutes popping open and drifting downward and thought most crewmembers bailed safely out of the doomed plane before it went into a spin. Both downed bombers were from squadron 850.

Mission 17   Roudnice   April 17, 1945
Mission 8 hours, 20 minutes   Oxygen 3 hours

We went on a long one today as lead crew. I was busy as hell--- sent six control point (location) reports. I sent the strike report about four times before I got a receipt. We went to Roudnice, Czechoslovakia after an underground oil refinery and storage depot. We blew it up O.K. We led to bomb wing and went practically to Prague. We had 30 aircraft led by Col. L.S. Lightner.

This was one of our longest missions. Our group led the Third Division, and Col. Lightner was commander on this mission to destroy vital oil supplies. We were very alert because the Luftwaffe fighters had been very protective of their dwindling fuel supplies.

The "Stars and Stripes" reported that more than 850 Eighth Air Force fighters covered 1,000 liberators and Fortresses on raids deep into Germany and Czechoslovakia. The U.S. fighters downed 200 Luftwaffe fighters and destroyed another 240 on the ground. This brought the U.S. total to over 941 German fighters destroyed in two days. The bomber force hit four targets near Prague deep into Nazi territory (9).

We were flying under a new Commander-in-Chief. President Franklin D. Roosevelt died April 12th, and Harry S. Truman, who had been Vice President only three months, was sworn in as President. We were on pass in London at that time. It seemed unfair that President Roosevelt died shortly before the end of the War in Europe. He had led our country to the point of victory. Perhaps his June 1941 speech to Congress illustrates the type of "pep talks" he used to urge Americans to rally and fight:

> "We too, born to freedom, and believing in freedom, are willing to fight to maintain freedom. We, and all others who believe as deeply as we do, would rather die on our feet than live on our knees".

Germany surrendered May 8, 1945. It was Truman's birthday! (19)

Our Crew's Black Thursday

Our plane did not fly on the April 19th mission to Aussig, Czechoslovakia, but it was a black day for the guys in our crew. Thirty Fortresses from our group went back to Czechoslovakia on the 19th and were hit by eight to twelve German ME-262 jet fighters eight minutes from the target as they were making their turns to start the bomb run. An ME-262 made a frontal pass and shot down a B-17 in the lead squadron. Two more fighters came out of the clouds to attack the high and low squadrons. Three more bombers went down. These planes were some of the last heavy bombers shot down by the Luftwaffe (18). The four planes were piloted by: Lt. William Mc Allister, Lt. Paul A. Snyder, Lt. Burford E. Stovall and Lt. Robert A. Norvell (1). Two of the German jet fighters were destroyed. Wilbur Lesh, our former ball turret gunner, was lost on one of those Fortresses. He was flying as an ECM Jammer (equipment to foul up enemy electrical signals) on the Paul A. Snyder plane. It was tough to lose a friend who had been with us at Sioux City, Iowa, all through crew training. Wilbur flew the first four missions with us as ball turret gunner. He was assigned to the group "gunnery pool" after we made lead crew. He flew on our plane a couple of times when we needed extra help with chaff. Later, he and Ralph Moore often visited our hut in the evenings. This loss of a comrade was further compounded a few days later when we realized he had died on the next to last mission of the 490th Bomb Group before Germany surrendered. He was a smart man and the world lost a fine citizen with great potential. I recently learned that Wilbur had three brothers, and two of those also perished in World War II. Our armorer-gunner, Bert Allinder, served as a dentist in Wilbur's hometown of Independence, Missouri after the war. Thanks to Eric Swain of London, our 490 Bomb Group's historian/archivist, I have learned the fate of Sergeant Wilbur Lesh. Eric mailed me a letter on April 18, 2005, exactly sixty years and one day past that fateful mission to Aussig, Czechoslovakia on April 17, 1945.

Today, in Benesov, Czechoslovakia there is a memorial commemorating the nine U.S. bomber crew members who were captured by German SS troops after they parachuted from their doomed planes. Two days after they were captured, the SS squad murdered their prisoners in reprisal for the bombing. The stone monument is inscribed with the 490th emblem above an American flag. The following message in the Czech language is followed by the English version:

"We honor the sacrifice of these nine American airmen who were murdered while prisoners of war on April 19th, 1945"

849th Bsq
B-17G #43-38078

Lorenzo G. Smith, Jr.	1st Lt.
Lee L. Borden	2nd Lt.
Gordon P. Lake	2nd Lt.
Carl B. Johnson, Jr.	Sgt.
Robert A. Johnson	Sgt.
Peter Malires	Sgt.

850th BSq
B-17G #43-38701

Joseph A. Trojanowski	2nd Lt.
Wilbur L. Lesh	Sgt.
Lyle E. Dole	Sgt.

******** FREEDOM*******

The senseless murder of these helpless prisoners of war was a classic example of the cruelty of the fanatical thugs in Hitler's SS troops. This act represents Germany's treatment of people in the countries

James Lee Hutchinson, EdS

they had conquered during the Nazi reign of terror. The fact that the war was practically over did not deter this squad from ignoring the Geneva Convention rules of war and murdering their prisoners. The war ended eleven days later when Germany agreed to a truce prior to a complete surrender!

There were many stories of SS atrocities against airmen who bailed out over enemy territory and fell into the hands of the dreaded SS troops. Although it was sixty years ago, it is shocking news to learn the fate of those nine men of the 490th Bomb Group. Wilbur Lesh was a buddy and Templeton crewmember. These men should have been spared! I'm so pleased that the Czech people have honored them with a memorial marker.

Mission 18   Nauen   April 20, 1945

Wake up 0100   *Landed 1315*
Briefing 0230   *Mission 7 and ½ hours*
Take-off 0600   *Oxygen 3 hours*
(Target: Railyards)

A little town on the outskirts of Berlin. Didn't get any flak in our group. We hit railroads in support of our ground troops, since earlier we had been named a Tactical Air Force. We flew lead squadron (middle). I only had to send a strike report. (Wilbur mayday yesterday). It was our second Oak Leaf cluster mission. We took a couple of group pictures with our Mickey operator's camera when we landed.

We flew as group leader of the lead squadron. Our formation of thirty bombers was loaded with ten 500 pounders. Major Cochran was mission leader. We bombed the railroad yards from 22,000 feet. Some planes in other formations carried the new rocket-propelled bombs that fell at 1,100 feet per second, and penetrated deeply underground before exploding (1). Nauen was on the outskirts of Berlin but we encountered no flak or fighters. We dropped to 5,000 feet on our way home and saw some of the destruction of Germany. This proved to be the last combat mission for the 490th Bomb Group! However, April was a costly month. We lost ten planes and many men as we flew 15 missions in 18 days. It was a coincidence that our crew's first and last combat missions were to the outskirts of Berlin!

About this time, I received a clipping from my hometown newspaper announcing my Air Medal decoration and promotion from Staff to Tech Sergeant which occurred some time ago. The same article also listed the Air Medal for Charlie Haskett, a boyhood chum. Years later, I learned that he was a tail gunner with the nearby 487th bomb group at Lavenham.

490th bombers in action – note the red tipped tail

Я американец

" Ya Amerikánets " *(Pronounced as spelt)*

Пожалуйста сообщите сведения обо мне в Американскую Военную Миссию в Москве

Please communicate my particulars to American Military Mission Moscow

Identification papers in case we had to bail-out over Russian territory. We also had a pocket-size plastic card

Bert, Rod and Hutch in May of '44
We made contact again 49 years later.
There have been many phone conversations.

The clouds cleared over the target!

```
WOKE UP  0200              OXYGEON    5 hrs.
BRIEFING 0330              LANDED     1330
TAKE OFS. 0630             MISSION    7½ hrs
```

Led wing – had to change targets and bomb PLAUEN had lots of flak and were hit by fighters – ME 262's. Lots of shooting – tracers and flak every where. They got 2 fighters and we lost 2 planes. Our P-51 escorts – were off on a sortie some where. We were commended by the 2 Majors who were riding with us – they were our a feet crew (when) Paris. Got Buck Sergeant, 'cause the Majors – said he did a real of job

Original Diary Page

Luftwaffe's Airfields

In a savage blow aimed at crippling the Luftwaffe, which had appeared to be forming for a comeback in the past few weeks, U.S. heavy bombers and fighters yesterday thundered out to hammer 11 airfields, many of them bases for jet-propelled fighters and fighter-bombers, in northwest Germany, the Ruhr and southern Germany.

The 8th and 15th Air Forces combined to deliver this trip-hammer punch. The 8th had some 2,200 planes out, nearly 2,000 of which figured in the drive on airdromes, while the 15th dispatched a separate force of Liberators to lash at the Neuburg drome, jet base 50 miles north of Munich.

The bombers and fighters carried out their assault under excellent conditions —ceiling visibility was unlimited. In the greatest blow of the whole operation, approximately 1,100 bombers of the 8th

RAF Sees—and Hits— Through Camouflage

Typhoon pilots of the 2nd Tactical Air Force yesterday reported that the Nazis, in a desperate effort to preserve their battered supply lines, have taken to painting rails, ties and even bolts along the top of idle rail cars to make them blend with the real tracks.

The pilots came low enough to see through the slick camouflage job, however, and decorate it with a bit of cannon and rocket fire.

and most of its 800 fighters zoomed in over nine fields in northwest Germany to wield a three-ply blow.

First the bombers came in for their run, followed by fighters which laid fragmentation bombs on runways and other vital spots on the fields. Fighters carried out the third phase of the attack by sweeping in to strafe the dromes.

In a later operation, approximately 100 Liberators, covered by 100 Mustangs, struck an additional blow, pounding the Mulheim airfield between Duisburg and Essen. The remainder of the 8th's bomber force soared deep into eastern Germany to hit once more a tank and armament plant at Plauen, south of

(Continued on back page)

Nazi Airfields

(Continued from page 1)

Leipzig, which had been attacked Monday in poor weather.

The bombers at Plauen were tackled by some 15 jet-propelled Me262s, but escorting Mustangs drove them off and shot down two. In the whole operation yesterday, nine enemy fighters were shot down and 43 more were destroyed on the ground.

RAF bombers also hit the Reich with a tremendous salvo yesterday. In the morning, while Lancasters were on their way back from blasting oil refineries in eastern and northwest Germany, more Lancs took off to bomb another oil target, the refinery at Bremen.

Later, Lancasters carrying 11-ton bombs, dropped their crushing loads on a railway bridge across the Weser near Bremen while other heavies struck at the railway yards at Munster, a blow aimed at communications running from the Ruhr to Osnabruck.

Mosquitos took just three minutes to wipe out Gestapo headquarters in Copenhagen yesterday, the United Press reported from 21st Army Group Hq. The fast bombers shot through heavy flak to blast the five-story building to the ground.

Mid-Air Collision Adds Dead Man To Fort Crew

490TH BOMB GROUP.—A Fortress which took off from here on a mission with a nine-man crew miraculously crash-landed in Belgium with a tenth man aboard—a dead crewman from another bomber.

A mid-air collision in the clouds above Germany killed the radio operator in one plane and forced his body through the shattered plexi-glass nose of the other. The dead man's Fort was cut in two.

With a smashed engine, another partly disabled, a wing tip bent, the front of its nose knocked off, and the pilot's front-view window broken, the Fort piloted by 1/Lt. Robert H. Tannenberg, of Riverhead, N.Y., struggled onward out of enemy territory.

The plane was forced to land on the Continent where the crewmen stepped out, unhurt, and examined the wreckage. They found the mutilated torso of a man later identified as the radio operator on the plane with which they had collided.

After bombs away, the formation encountered heavy clouds closing in rapidly on the return trip. The Forts moved into tighter formation. A lower Fort suddenly veered upward and struck Tannenberg's plane.

The forward part of the lower bomber's fuselage, at the radio room, crashed into the nose of the plane above. 2/Lt. Chester A. Deptula, navigator from Chicago, dragged the stunned nose-gunner, S/Sgt. John W. Cann, of Little Rock, Ark., from the shattered nose to the radio operator's compartment.

Other crewmen on the surviving bomber were:

2/Lt. Joel R. Johnson, co-pilot from Alleman, Tex.; T/Sgts. Joseph J. Pour, engineer and top turret gunner from Rome, N.Y., and Edward J. Miller, radio operator from Tulsa, Okla.; S/Sgts. Joseph D. Kennedy, waist gunner from Lawrence, Kan.; George R. Janisse, ball turret gunner from Detroit, and Alvin Wilhelm, tail gunner from Wheatland, Wyo.

Chapter Nine
A Truce and Peace

Mercy Missions

The war was winding down and the allies were eager to send food to the starving people in Holland. Germany occupied the country in 1940, and destroyed dikes which flooded rich farmlands. Food had been rationed for four years, and toward the end the war many people existed on a diet of sugar beets and tulip bulbs. It was reported that more than 16,000 Dutch died of malnutrition during the harsh winter of 1944-45 (12). The Allied High Command was waiting for a German truce or surrender because they had worked out the "Chowhound Missions" as a means of getting food to the Dutch quickly. On April 30th the German High Command, with Hitler dead, agreed to a truce prior to surrendering. That night, the men of the 490th went to work loading 40 planes with boxes of ten concentrated meals. Special flooring had been installed in the B-17 bomb bays to handle the food cartons. The Third Division bombers were assigned the task of carrying out these food drops because our transport planes were in other peace operations. A total of 5,626 RAF and Third Division bombers participated in the five "chowhound missions". Only one plane was lost in the operation. Pasted in my diary is a copy of an article from YANK magazine by a reporter who rode a 95th Bomb Group plane on the first food drop flight by Third Division bombers. The following excerpts are from that story:

"The planes dropped to 300 feet when they made landfall in Holland. The drop area was a mile square field, marked by a large white cross. The field was surrounded by hundreds of people waving flags and bedsheets. Crewmembers were close enough to make out faces in the crowd as they dropped the food cartons. The Fort turned back for another look. The field was alive with people scrambling to gather the food. Many turned their faces upward and waved wildly in appreciation. Crowds of people were waving from streets and rooftops all the way back to the North Sea. Third Division bombers flew five "Mercy Missions" that week and dropped more than five million concentrated meals of 10 in 1 Army rations. British Lancaster bombers later delivered even more food. The starving Dutch received a total of over eleven million meals to ease their suffering".

The 490th Bomb Group newsletter "Bombs Away" recently printed a copy of a thank you letter from a Dutch lady who was a child in that crowd.

James Lee Hutchinson, EdS

Mission 19   Rotterdam Food Drop   May 1, 1945

Diary Entry

We dropped 10 x 1 rations to starving Dutch people. We flew at a very low altitude to drop the rations and saw them wave flags, sheets, and table cloths at us in gratitude. The whole country was flooded—water everywhere, lots of windmills and cute little houses. The towns had canals instead of streets. We gave them a "buzz job" and got a good look at the country ourselves. It was the first time I had seen German soldiers in uniform. After all this, I at last saw the Germans!!

Germany designated specific flight corridors, altitudes and drop areas. Planes were to fly in at low-level. The drop areas were square-mile areas, marked by a large white cross. The first "mercy" or "chowhound" mission was flown May 1, 1945. Approximately 400 Flying Fortresses flew in over enemy territory at only 300 feet and dropped over 20,000 waterproof food cartons (700 tons) to the cheering Dutch. Five food drop missions were flown; our crew flew on the first and second. We dropped food at Rotterdam on our first flight, and later dropped food at the Schipol Airfield at Alkmar. It was strange flying in at low-level over the airport where Luftwaffe fighters used to come up to attack our group. We saw armed German soldiers on guard at various checkpoints in the countryside below. We were a bit worried that they might be tempted to fire at us.

But they were probably as hungry as the Dutch. Thousands of men, women and children below were waving towels and sheets.

Through These Eyes

They were in the streets, in the fields and on rooftops. They were cheering for the bomber crews as we dropped the food they needed so desperately. Our 490th Bomb Group flew five "chowhound" missions, and on our second mission the people at one location spelled out on the ground in huge white letters, "Thank you boys". It was a pleasure to see the celebration of all the people who had suffered for years under German occupation.

Mission 20 Schipol Food Drop May 2, 1945

The "Stars and Stripes" carried many pictures of the grateful Hollanders cheering in streets and fields and many on rooftops. We dropped large waterproof food cartons approximately 18x12x24, which could float in the flooded fields and canals until they could be retrieved. This was the second of five food drop missions flown by our bomb group. We loaded 40 aircraft again and took off to drop food at Schiphol Airfield at Alkmar, Holland. For a time we wondered if the Germans would continue to honor the truce. The hundreds of Flying Fortresses flying at such a low altitude must have been a terrible temptation for the flak gunners to resist. However, the occupying troops realized the war was over and stood by and watched as we dropped our food cartons. The townspeople stood on the rooftops and in the streets and fields waving and cheering. It was a great sight, and it felt good to be dropping food instead of bombs.

I recently visited with Eugene Forrester in Memphis, Tennessee and we compared notes on those food drop missions. Eugene was a radio operator on the Edwin Allison crew in squadron 851. We recalled those tree-level flights and the cheering crowds of starving Hollanders. Eugene's crew flew a mission that our squadron missed, and witnessed the crash of a B-17 that flew too low. It was the only plane lost in the five "Mercy Missions".

Bombers were also used in "revival flights" to pick up and return prisoners of war to their homelands. On May 15th, the 490th Bomb Group sent fifteen planes to Linz, Austria, to return French soldiers home. The group flew a second "revival mission" to Linz on June 3rd. Eugene Forrester's crew made both of these trips. Those men had been POWs and "slave laborers" since 1940. The 490th Bomb Group gave some 450 Frenchmen a ride to freedom (1). Linz, Austria was an important railroad center and Hitler's hometown. Hitler was actually an Austrian, not a German, and he was not pure Aryan, so he was actually living a lie as he preached destroying the Jews and purifying the Third Reich (19). Linz had been heavily protected by anti-aircraft batteries and fighters, and it was often bombed by the Fifteenth Air Force. The German prisons for captured soldiers were horrible, and the released POWs told terrible stories of their suffering as slave laborers. However, these camps were not the same as those constructed for the specific purpose of exterminating the Jews.

Three of my granddaughters have flown into Schiphol Airport in the past three years while on European tours. It's truly a small world!

The Axis Reign of Terror

Most of the countries Germany had conquered were freed by allied troops advancing on all fronts by November 1944. Hitler's decimated armies were being attacked by U.S. and British forces from the west, the Russian army on the east and around-the-clock aerial attacks. The territory Hitler controlled was shrinking, German citizens were suffering greatly by April 1945. There was general agreement that Germany was defeated. The allied armies were approaching Berlin and Germany's new government had agreed to a truce on April 30th. Hitler and a few close friends retreated to his nineteen-room underground hideaway bunker in the garden of the Reich Chancellry. He married his longtime mistress, Eva Braun. A few hours later, Hitler, his new wife and a few other high-ranking Nazis committed suicide with cyanide capsules. It was one of the shortest marriages on record. Hitler also shot himself before the poison took effect to be doubly sure he wasn't captured alive. Perhaps he feared the same fate as that of his Axis partner, Italian dictator Mussolini, who fell from power after Allied Forces defeated Italian armies in North Africa and freed Italy. Mussolini and his mistress were captured April 28th while trying to escape to Germany. They were slain by Italian civilians and their bodies were hanged by the heels in the town square of Milan (21).

The Third Reich was in ruins. Germany was completely defeated. Numerous cities had been destroyed along with all utilities. The country had also lost millions of its citizens and soldiers. Hitler's refusal to surrender and admit defeat led to the terrible destruction of German cities and industries. Heavy bombing brought about the elimination of his transportation system and fuel supplies. Airpower was our major weapon before D-Day but after the invasion allied armies made gigantic gains. The soldiers fought to avenge the German destruction and atrocities carried out in Blitzkrieg attacks on the European and Russian areas they had conquered.

Hitler's Terrible Legacy

Hitler rose to power in 1933 and began a program to restore Germany which had suffered much since their defeat in World War I. His political speeches blamed the country's problems on the Bolsheviks and Jews. Germany's military forces were restored through compulsory military training. Pageantry, uniforms, and huge staged public rallies helped restore German pride. He preached the "big lie" in his many rallies and the German people bought his Nazi philosophy. He stated in his book Mein Kampf (My Struggle):

> "The great masses of the people……will more easily fall victim to the big lie rather than a small one".

The city of Nuremberg was the site of Zeppeliniviese, the 124,000 seat stadium and parade grounds used for giant Nazi political rallies. Prior to 1940, world newspapers, magazines and newsreels depicted the gigantic pageants and Hitler's maniacal speeches to convince Germans they were a "Master Race" destined to rule Europe. These

Through These Eyes

events lasted several days and featured thousands of goose-stepping storm troopers, military equipment, and patriotic events in a city decorated with thousands of blood-red Nazi banners with a black swastika in a white circle. The swastika was an ancient symbol of good luck. These rallies were very effective and the stiff right arm salutes and shouts of "Heil Hitler" by the crowds left no doubt of the Nazi threat to world peace. Hitler was appeased by the other European powers that ignored his growing military forces and murderous treatment of the Jews. They excused him when he annexed Austria and Czechoslovakia and then promised peace!

Hitler promoted anti-semitism in an attempt to create a pure German (Aryan) race. He convinced German citizens that the Jews had caused many of their problems. He had risen to power through the use of his Gestapo (secret police) and his elite bodyguard, the SS Storm Troopers. These henchmen were granted immunity to rob, beat and murder Jews. This persecution began in 1933, and by 1941 mass killings began in the concentration camps. The Nazi regime eliminated all suspected of being against the policies of the Third Reich.

Benito Mussolini, (Il Duce), and Adolph Hitler, (Der Fuehrer) had agreed on which countries to attack and signed a mutual alliance in 1939 called "The Pact of Steel". Italy invaded North Africa and Germany invaded Austria and Czechoslovakia by 1938. France and England declared war on the Axis when Hitler's armies invaded Poland in 1939. In September, 1940, Japan, Germany and Italy signed a mutual protection treaty, the "Axis Pact". Japan, Germany and Italy earned the hatred of the free world with the brutal treatment of prisoners and Jews in countries they conquered. Those countries were devastated by spring of 1945 and millions of their citizens were killed in the bombing and battles. Hitler's armies included boys thirteen and fourteen of age and senior citizens by the end of the war (21).

The concentration camps of Auschwitz, Treblinka, Belsen, Buchenwald, and Dachau were infamous. The horror stories of camp survivors and eyewitness accounts of the soldiers who liberated the camps more than overcame any regrets the allies might have had about the destruction of Hitler's Third Reich.

Hitler's armies perfected the "blitzkrieg" (lightning war). In the beginning of the war, tanks and armored vehicles overran the opposing armies and roared into new territory. Following behind were special "killer units" who were organized and authorized to follow the Blitzkieg forces as they advanced. Their task was to occupy the conquered countries, terrorize civilians and eliminate the Jews. These troops killed more than a million victims in two years. The greatest atrocity was the murder of thousands of Jewish men, women and children at BabiYar outside Kiev, Russia. Photographs taken by captured German soldiers revealed a line of naked Jewish women, some with babies in their arms, on the edge of the burial pit just before they were machine-gunned by Nazi troopers. Hundreds of these mass graves were discovered in Poland and Russia after the war (19). The

Nazi party had been persecuting Germany's Jewish citizens since they came into power in the mid 1930s. There were more than ten million Jewish citizens in the European countries Germany had conquered by 1941. Nazi officials needed a faster method of exterminating these prisoners. A January 1942 meeting resulted in the systematic plan of "gas showers" and crematoriums to speed up the process. Adolph Eichmann, Nazi party secretary, was the architect of the "final solution" for this crime against humanity. Victims of the Holocaust (destruction by fire) included Jews, homosexuals, gypsies and Jehovah Witnesses. The Aryan race was to become "pure" by committing genocide.

More than 100 special "concentration camps" were constructed to carry out this "Final Solution." Jews were rounded up and shipped in unheated cattle trucks and boxcars to the camps. Able-bodied men were assigned to slave labor and received an identification number tattoo on his/her left arm. The weak and infirm, including men, women, children and the elderly were ordered to strip for the "shower baths" which were actually gas chambers. Some German guards later said the unsuspecting victims welcomed the "showers" after riding many days in cattle trucks or boxcars.

These victims were slain because they were too weak, too old or too young to work in the slave labor gangs. Again, photographs taken by German officials, depict the long lines of naked Jews entering the "showers". German scientists had even invented "Zyklon B", a new deadly gas, which quickly suffocated the unsuspecting victims

Bodies of those slain were cremated in huge gas furnaces. It is estimated that more than six million Jews were exterminated in this systematic plan for genocide (28). German photographs of these atrocities were published in the "Stars and Stripes" after our troops "liberated" these camps. It was fitting that after the surrender, allied commanders forced German officers and local citizens to take tours of the "death camps." They were forced to view the "poison gas showers" and the stacks of human corpses that had not yet been incinerated in the gas furnaces. Many Germans living near concentration camps had denied knowledge of the gas chambers and furnaces, while others admitted to the constant stench of burning flesh. Our soldiers saw to it that the captured German soldiers and prison guards were made to bury those bodies. Most citizens of towns around the camps had witnessed the starved and dying slave labor gangs working in the community. Now they needed to witness the horrible atrocities inside the barbed wire. The freed surviving prisoners were walking skeletons with terrible stories to tell. German citizens needed to understand why the bombs, artillery shells and the wrath of the free world had destroyed their government and reduced cities to rubble.

Noted WWII radio newscaster Edward R. Murrow made the following statement in his broadcast from London, April 1945:

> "I pray you believe what I have said about Buchenwald. I have reported what I saw and heard, but only part of it. For the most of it I have no words".

The holocaust covered a twelve-year period from 1933-1945. Adolph Hitler's Nazi (National Socialist Party) regime rose to power by blaming Jews for Germany's economic problems. The leaders of the Nazi party targeted Jews for annihilation and confiscated their monies and properties in order to develop a pure Aryan race. A recent movie, "Schindler's List", gave the present generation an idea of the horrors of Hitler's death camps. One source reported that between November 1938 to May 1945 the Nazis murdered an estimated six million European Jews.

Estimates by Country

Poland	2.9 million
Soviet Union	1 million
Romania	400 thousand
Czechoslovakia	300 thousand
Germany	200 thousand
Lithuania and Latvia	200 thousand
Other countries	800 thousand

Japan was the most fanatical member of the Axis powers. The Japanese believed themselves to be a superior race with the divine right to expand their territory. Their emperor, Hirohito, was a holy person and the "wind gods" had blessed their island. Civilians and armed forces members were indoctrinated with a suicidal philosophy of never surrender. It was better to die fighting than to lose and bring dishonor to themselves. Those who felt dishonored would often disembowel themselves in the "Hari Kari" ritual. Japan had invaded

China and other Asian lands long before 1941. Their armies ravaged these areas with great cruelty and atrocities and never honored the rules of war in the Geneva Convention. This was made quite clear to the United States on December 7, 1941 when they launched the sneak attack on Pearl Harbor while their delegates were negotiating a peace treaty in Washington!

The Bataan Death March and numerous battle reports revealed the inhumane treatment of prisoners by Japanese forces. These atrocities included starvation, torture, bayonetting and beheadings. Japanese soldiers and civilians were fanatic in their willingness to fight and die with no chance of winning. Allied naval, air and ground forces were forced to recapture islands occupied by the Japanese. Thousands of our men were lost in the bloody land, sea and air battles to defeat the fanatic "spirit warriors" and "kamikaze pilots" who would sacrifice their lives rather than suffer defeat.

Our 20th Air Force B-29 bombers had made many raids on Japanese cities in 1945 but they refused to surrender and mobilized their island to fight invaders to the death. This mind-set of the enemy led President Truman to approve atomic bombs for Hiroshima and Nagasaki. He chose to force a surrender rather than lose thousands of American lives in an invasion. Once, again, fanatical leadership brought ruin to their own country. It has been estimated that a total of 43 million servicemen and civilians were killed in World War II, a terrible price to pay because free world leaders sat idly by and allowed Germany, Italy and Japan to rise to full military power.

The armies of Germany, Italy and Japan had ruled by fear and terror. They treated conquered people inhumanely through enslavement, torture and death. This policy unified the allied countries and strengthened the intent to preserve their freedom. General Dwight Eisenhower summed it up in a speech at Frankfurt, Germany on June 10, 1945 (25).

> "More than any other war in history, this war has been an array of the forces of evil against those of righteousness. It had to have its leaders and it had to be won---but no matter the sacrifice, no matter what the suffering of populations, no matter what the cost, the war had to be won".

International War Crimes Trials

The Allies selected Nuremberg for the trials of Germany's leaders for their crimes against humanity. This was the same city Hitler had used to stage his numerous Nazi rallies and pageants during his rise to power. The red, white and black swastika banners and most of the city buildings were gone. Justice had arrived in the form of judges and prosecutors form France, Great Britain, Russia and the United States.

The trials continued from 1945 through 1949. The guilty received sentences of death, life imprisonment, shorter sentences, or were acquitted. Five committed suicide before the trials were over. This included Luftwafff General Hermann Goering, who was found guilty but like Hitler, took the coward's way out. The Nuremberg trials were important because the evidence produced a full and public account of the horrors of the Nazi persecution of the Jews and their crimes against humanity.

War crimes trials were also held for Japanese leaders responsible for unspeakable atrocities that violated the Geneva Convention rules of war. A fellow church member, Merrill Lasley, reported serving as a Military Police guard in the Tokyo prison holding these criminals while they awaited trial. He owned a "Rising Sun" flag autographed by several of the most infamous Japanese officers.

Target for Amsterdam "food drop" mission

Direct hit on a railway station

Bombed out anti-aircraft gun

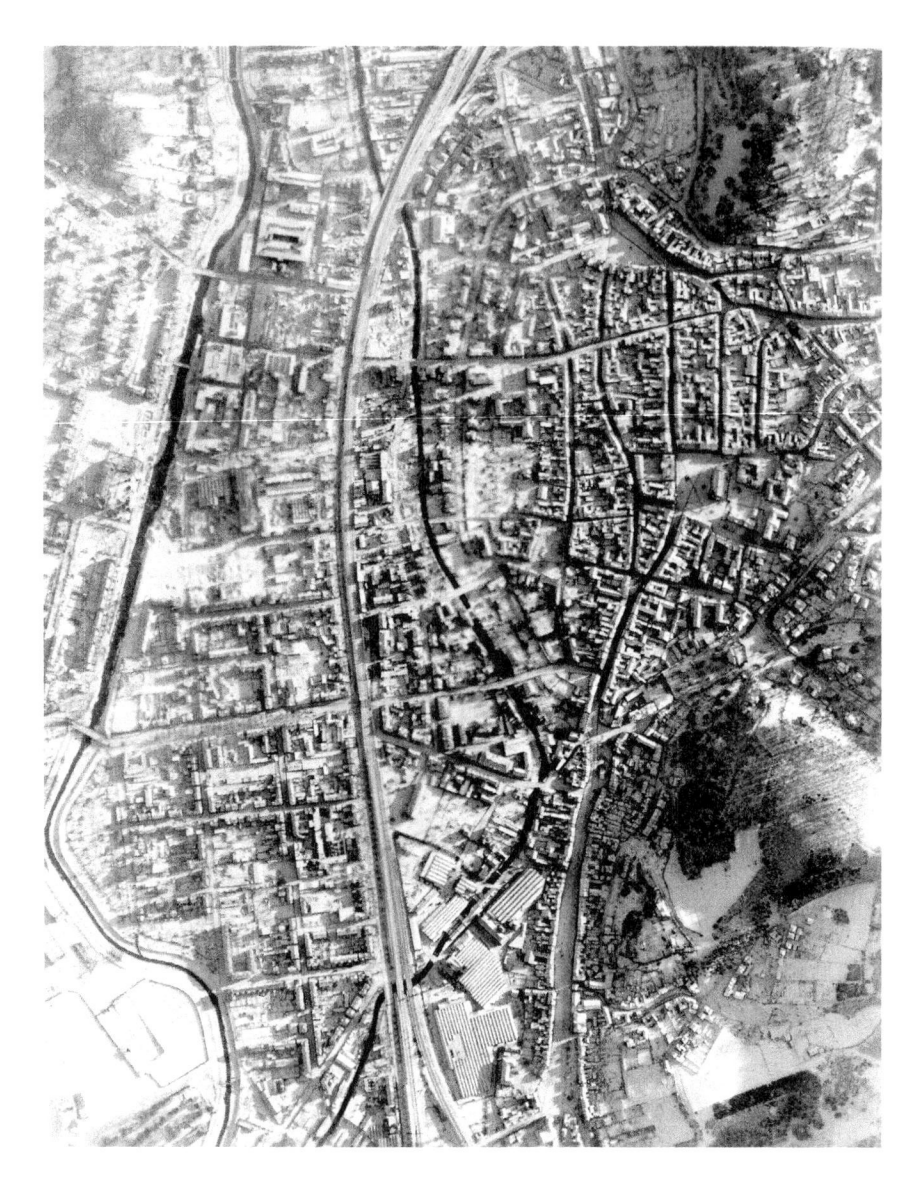

Bomb results

Welcome to Hut 29
Ready for a London pass

Chapter Ten
Operation Home Run

End of the War in Europe – VE Day   May 8, 1945

The Germans had agreed to a truce on April 30th and our Third Division bombers flew five "mercy" missions to get food to the starving Dutch. Our crew participated in two of these "chowhound" flights on May 1st and 3rd. After our second mission, we went into Diss for supper and as we were walking back to the base, the sky was lit up with flares of all colors. The announcement came on May 3rd---the Third Reich had surrendered! Everyone back at the base was firing Vary pistol magnesium signal flares that bombers used in flight. It was like the Fourth of July as all four squadrons engaged in mock combat. Airbases all over East Anglia joined the celebration and the dark sky was filled with red, green and yellow streaks of fire. They said our base commander joined the battle! We hurried back to hut

29 to get in on the fun. The official German surrender was signed on May 8th, and that became VE Day (Victory in Europe). Black-out curtains were no longer needed and the lights came on again over England!

It was difficult to realize that the war was over, we had survived, and there would be no more bombing missions! We would have a break before they transferred our group to the Pacific theater. I have often thanked God that I was spared in that gigantic air war. Sometimes in my reverie, I offer a toast to the 490th Bomb Group, the Bill Templeton crew (one of the best) and the B-17 Flying Fortress that brought us safely back from every mission. The world will never see another air armada of fighters and bombers like the "Mighty Eighth".

The Grand Tour

Our bomb group later took ground crewmembers on "Cook's Tours" of France and Germany. All 490th personnel from the mechanics to the cooks were loaded onto B-17s and flown low level over former target cities so they could get a first-hand look at what they had helped the aircrews accomplish in the bombing missions. It was an informative tour for the aircrew as well, because we had never been this close to the destruction we had inflicted on the German cities. We also circled Paris and got close-ups of Notre Dame and the Eiffel Tower, two landmarks that both sides had been careful to preserve. Those guys of the ground crews and airfield support groups were really impressed with what they saw on those flights. I really got a kick out of the low-level flights rather than the usual 25,000 feet on oxygen.

Those flights over Germany revealed the terrible destruction our thousands of bombing raids had delivered. Hitler had brought this upon his country. The allies had responded with all the power they could muster to protect their freedom. One cook on our plane summed it up for all of us, "Man, you guys really bombed the hell out of them"!

I was approved to graduate from Bedford High School in late May 1945. My mother wrote that she had been invited to come up on the platform and receive my diploma. That was one of her happiest days in that crazy war! I had only needed six credits to graduate when I was drafted, so after two years and eighteen combat missions, the school decided I had learned enough to earn a diploma. I was in gunnery school in Yuma on my nineteenth birthday. My twentieth birthday occurred in a peaceful England on June 12, 1945 and was much more enjoyable. I had survived the air war and our Group was preparing to fly the Atlantic to the USA. We needed to get our planes home for reassignment to the Pacific. I didn't feel any smarter, but Germany had surrendered and I was a high school graduate!

No Foxholes in the Sky

The Eighth Air Force was created to destroy Germany's factories, oil supplies and transportation systems. Daytime precision bombing by U.S. heavy bombers and RAF night missions were to blast the Third Reich war machine. Germany faced the possibility of around-the-clock bombing raids. Through the years people have debated the morality of precision bombing which destroyed cities and populations. Civil War general William Sherman was right when he said, "War is hell"! The allies had to fight to win, war is not a gentleman's sport.

My veteran friends who served in the ground forces have often teased me about airmen having warm huts and good food while they had K-rations, foxholes and tents or bombed-out buildings for shelter. I always point out that there were no foxholes in the sky. Then I emphasize the terrific percentage of casualties and loss of planes we suffered as we bombed the Germans and made victory easier for the ground forces! The air war was very impersonal because we never saw the enemy. The Germans never saw us---only our bombers. We fought the invisible enemy by destroying their factories, transportation systems and cities. We were dropping bombs and braving enemy fighters and flak while they filled the air with flak and sent up their Luftwaffe fighters to shoot us down. The crew of bombers that went down was listed as missing in action (MIA). The wounded on planes returning to base were treated in hospitals, and those who survived were later sent back to the United States. The dead were buried in the American Cemetery at Cambridge, England.

Crewmembers understood the importance of high altitude precision bombing, and that it played a vital part in the allies' plans to defeat Germany. We understood we were fighting for our country's freedom and existence as a democracy. The future of the free world was on the line in World War II. General Omar Bradley, rated as the best Allied General in World War II, brought Shermans' idea up to date, "In war there is no second prize for the runner-up".

My tour of duty included 128 hours of combat flying over Germany. Crew training flights in Sioux City, Iowa, and chowhound missions boosted the total to 160 hours in a Flying Fortress. The Army Air Corps eventually had a total strength of 2,411,294 men and women, and by war's end had taken delivery of 230,000 aircraft. The Eighth became the world's greatest air armada in the spring of 1945.

The 490th Bomb Group was notified in late May that we would be the second group from the 3rd Division to return to America. Meanwhile, we made many practice flights to check out the planes and equipment for the long flight home. Flying the North Atlantic air route in our war-weary bombers would require planes and crews and B-17s in good condition. There were also ground training sessions and lectures on "War in the Pacific", "Psychology of the Japanese" and many other topics that made us sure we would eventually be assigned to B-29 bombers in the Pacific.

Each B-17 was to carry twenty passengers, including the regular crew and others authorized to make the the flight home.We spent time loading everyone's duffel bags and planning seating arrangements for the passengers. Our crew members rode in their regular positions, the waist area served as the lounge area for the passengers on each leg of the long flight across the Atlantic. The crew of Templeton, Rector, Roddy, Hutchinson, Allinder, and Parrish were joined by Navigator, Chester Deptula, and Bombardier, James Cambell both of whom had flown bombing missions with us at various times. Others were Richard Fleck, Foster Wisdom, William King, Martin Orsan, John Piwkiewicz, Stanton Raimey, John Robinson, Daniel Quattrocchi, Claude Dowling, John Collins, John Sedor, and William Buchanan. Many years, later I learned that Ralph Moore flew home with the Oscar Kenyon crew. My buddy, Phil Placentino, was radio operator on that crew.

"Operation Home Run" was our long-awaited exodus from Eye. Many of the local citizens came down to wish us well. On July 6, 1945, the first 30 planes left for Prestwick, Scotland, on to Iceland, Goose Bay Labrador and home. The remaining numbers, including my 848th squadron flew out on Sunday, July 8th. The first leg of our journey was to Valley, Wales, our new "Happy Valley" where we spent one night. No one could understand the Welsh language, so there wasn't much conversation with the locals. The next day we were flying over icebergs in the North Atlantic to Reykjavik, Iceland. A two day layover because one plane's mechanical problems gave us time to check equipment and walk into the small seaside fishing village. The landscape was barren and full of rounded rocks. The highlight of our stay at Iceland was a treat. The mess hall served our first hamburgers and fresh milk since leaving Camp Kilmer, New Jersey in November. On July 12th we flew on across the North Atlantic over the southern tip of Greenland to Gander, Newfoundland, spent one night and headed for the USA! Our destination was Bradley Field, Connecticut, but first we flew to Hartford, Connecticut and "buzzed" our pilot, Lt. Bill Templeton's parents' house. It was great, his family was out in the yard waving gleefully as we circled the house a few times before heading on to Bradley Field. There we turned in our plane and all our equipment, including the wristwatch I had worn on all my missions. That was my last B-17 flight.

Later, we were sent to Camp Miles Standish, Massachusetts. We were all scheduled for 30-day furloughs before reassignment. Our crew was separated and we were sent to various bases close to our home so we could enjoy our 30-day furloughs. It was the last time I saw any of the men I had served with on those terrible eighteen bombing missions.

The ground personnel left Eye August 24th for Southampton, where they sailed on the Queen Elizabeth for the USA. The Eye airfield was closed after the war and the land was reclaimed for farming and an industrial park. Veterans of the 490th who have returned to visit say there are memorial plaques to honor the boys who gave their all in the great aerial war for freedom. They report that all but a few of the buildings are gone. The control tower was razed in the 1970's. The main runway is still used occasionally by light aircraft (1). I recently contacted a young English girl who lives next to that runway. She had a photo of WWII bombers flying by the family home at the Eye airfield. She and her father are fliers and are interested in the history of the 490th Bomb Group.

My furlough over, I returned to Camp Atterbury, Indiana, and was shipped to Drew Field, Tampa, Florida. Later I was assigned to Kessler Field, a B-29 airbase in Gulfport, Mississippi. I never got to board a B-29, but was classified as a radioman on air-sea rescue boats to patrol the Gulf of Mexico. Finally, I was assigned to a rescue boat unit in Lake Charles, Louisiana. Actually we were stationed fifty miles south near Cameron on an island in the Gulf of Mexico. We were housed in box tents, a box with a tent roof. A herd of horses ran free on the island and at night would run through our camp. They often kicked the sides of our box tents and tore up our boardwalks. Our main duties were repairing broken boards, fishing for sea snails and waving to the steamers sailing up the channel to Lake Charles. Our boats were these propeller swamp buggies that skimmed the water through the marches. We also had rescue boats large enough to be used in the Gulf.

On August 6, 1945, Colonel Paul Tibbets in his B-29 "Enola Gay" dropped the atomic bomb on Hiroshima. Later, the second bomb was dropped on Nagasaki, and the handwriting was on the wall. I was home on furlough on August 14, 1945 when Japan surrendered. V-J day had arrived, and it was great to be in my hometown of Bedford, Indiana to take part in the celebration around the town square. The circle was complete. I had started the war in my hometown and now it ended there! I packed the next day and reported back to the Gulfport, Mississippi airbase. The barracks were empty. Everyone else had been shipped out to a separation center. I packed a few clothes and mailed them home before reporting to headquarters.

Home from the War

A week later, I was transferred to the Air Force Separation Center at Baer Field in Ft. Wayne, Indiana. The Army's discharge plan rewarded combat veterans with early release, based on a point system. I had flown in a B-17 for more than 160 hours, more than two-thirds of which were in a combat zone. With twenty bombing missions, my service record gave me a quick Honorable Discharge (that piece of paper I had wanted for over two years) on November 16, 1945.

I was an example of the typical WWII draftee. I had gone directly to basic training, combat and discharge. I was one of the last of my high school classmates to be drafted, and one of the first to be discharged. Promotions, flight pay and combat pay had all proceeded as scheduled. I was a Tech Sergeant with enough points to be discharged ahead of many veterans who had not seen combat..I returned to Bedford with the promise of a $300 bonus and membership in the "52-20 Club". Veterans were entitled to $20 per week unemployment pay for fifty-two weeks, or until they could find a job. So, there I was, at the age of twenty, a discharged combat veteran with two years and two months service, looking for a job and a future. I soon returned to my job at Bill's Auto Store, but after two months, decided to take advantage of the G.I. Bill of Rights. I was going to be a college man.

Through These Eyes

My Eighth Air Force aerial combat experience was the biggest event in my young life. I considered myself very lucky to have survived Word War II in one piece. The war claimed 405,399 lives. The Eighth Air Force had over 34,000 casualties. Many of my classmates perished, were wounded or had been imprisoned in POW camps. The war claimed the lives of 126 servicemen from Lawrence county. Thirteen of the dead were close friends I had known for years. However, I put the war behind me and reorganized to prepare for the future.

Now, sixty years later, my old diary reminds me of my teenage experiences in a time when our country was fighting for its freedom in a world wide conflict. My generation lived through personal hardships and conditions which "baby boomers" and their children can only imagine.World War II called on every American to sacrifice to achieve victory and a maximum effort was required. The majority of able-bodied men enlisted or were drafted into the armed forces. Many women also enlisted to serve their country.

Combat veterans of all wars remember the hardships and terrors of facing the enemy in a kill or be killed situation. You rely upon your leaders, your training and equipment and your God to protect you.

My written accounts of missions, the articles from "Stars and Stripes" and research in other books on WW II have helped me recall those days when I was five miles high, my life was on the line and I was soaring with the eagles!

The Oscar Kenyon crew
note the flight gear
Radio Operator—Phil Placentino

Home at last!

Chapter Eleven

Victory's Price

Realities of War

History reveals the horrible cost of life. The Eighth Air Force alone lost over 8,000 planes of which more than 5,500 were B-17 Flying Fortresses and B-24 Liberators with nine to ten crewmembers on each plane. More than 34,000 members of the Mighty Eighth gave their lives for their country. The 15th Air Force flying out of Italy lost more than 3,000 planes in combat. The British Air Force (RAF) lost more than 10,000 planes and 45,000 airmen were killed in combat. The German anti-aircraft and fighters took their toll but the around-the clock bombing raids on German targets stopped Hitler's ability to wage war. The combined heavy bombers of the RAF and the USAAF 8th and 15th Bomb Groups delivered more than a million tons of bombs on Axis war industries and oil supplies between 1939 and 1945.

Through These Eyes

The 490th Bomb Group flew 158 bombing missions, 40 in B-24 Liberators, in the eleven months of its service beginning May 31, 1944 to April 20,1945. These missions included everything from recalls, "milk runs" (easy missions), and the toughest targets. Records show that our group dropped a total of 13,600 tons of bombs, nine tons of chaff, and gunners fired over 450,000 rounds of .50 caliber ammunition. The 490th lost a total of 47 bombers in this period of training and combat. Twenty-one planes went down in combat and twenty-six were lost in mid-air collisions and crash landings. The 490th Bomb Group's claim to fame was that it had the lowest casualty rate of any Eighth Air Force unit in combat—180 lives lost.

The war destroyed cities, industries, homes and lives. The economy of Europe was ruined. The death of millions of civilians and servicemen was the greatest in history. A majority of the victims were young men. It has been estimated that Germany lost thousands to allied bombing raids seeking to destroy Hitler's ability to carry on the war. He brought ruin to the country he professed to love. Berlin and all large industrial areas were the prime target of the Allied bombers. In turn, the Luftwaffe dropped thousands of tons of bombs on their foes in the attempt to conquer Europe.

Today, I have a friend, Hein Tlusek, who was on the receiving end of those "around the clock" bombing raids near the end of the war. The Tlustek family lived in the outskirts of Berlin, and Hein vividly remembers those days as a nine year-old in the bomb shelters. He said they ran for shelter each time they heard the air-raid sirens. He admits that sometimes he would race to the rooftop of his house to see the raid. He said the British RAF night raids were unbelievably bright with the bursting bombs and fires, searchlights probing the darkness and the flashes from the anti-aircraft guns. There was also the "Chirstmas Tree". That was what the children called the red and green flares reflecting on the aluminum chaff floating down over the target. The flares were dropped to illuminate the target area when planes dropped bombs in a "saturation pattern" to cover the entire area. The people feared the "pencils", the long, thin incendiary phosphorus bombs most because they could create fire-storms and destroy large areas of the city. Hein and the neighborhood children also collected and played with the aluminum chaff sheets the daylight bombers dropped to foul up the radar on the Berman anti-aircraft guns.

We are friends today, and I am amazed that we can sit in Bedford, Indiana, sixty years later and recall those terrible days when the war made pawns of those on both sides. I have assured Hein that my Eighth Air Corps crew only made two trips over Berlin, and that while we were up there running the gauntlet of flak and fighters, we obviously missed his house (thank God)! He said he got even with me years later by sending his six children to the elementary school where I was principal! The joke is on him because they were fine pupils, and three became teachers. After the war, Hein migrated to Canada at the age of twenty-three and later served as a Morman Missionary in Switzerland. He graduated from Brigham Young University and taught school for several years before moving to Bedford. He is married to the daughter of another old golfing buddy. She later served as President of my school's Parent-Teacher Association. It's a small world after all!

Medals and Honors for the Mighty Eighth

The Eighth Air Force with its high casualty rate and intensive service was one of the highest decorated units in World War II. An oak leaf meant the medal was awarded again.

Medal	Number	Oak Leaf
Medal of Honor	17	
Distinguished Service Cross	220	6
Silver Star	817	47
Distinguished Flying Cross	41,497	4,480
Soldier's Medal	487	2
Air Medal	122,705	319,595
Purple Heart	6,845	188
Bronze Star	2,972	12
Distinguished Service	11	1
Legion of Merit	207	2

The top three medals were for heroism. The Distinguished Flying Cross and Air Medal were for high achievement in combat, and the Distinguished Service and Legion of Merit awards were for meritorious service. Of the seventeen Medal of Honor winners, ten were posthumous. The Purple Heart was awarded for combat wounds, many of which were awarded posthumously.

Britain Says "Thanks Yanks"

The British people never forgot the young airmen who served there and the sacrifices of those 28,000 young American airmen who gave their lives to bring peace. Monuments, historical markers and stained-glass windows in churches are plentiful in the English countryside today. Great Britain deeded land for the Cambridge American Military Cemetery at Cambridge to the United States. Thus, Americans killed in action could be buried on American soil. There are 5,123 names on the Wall of Honor at the cemetery. One of those names is Spencer Flinn, a former classmate of mine at Bedford High.

The Royal Air Force and the U.S. Army Air Force received much credit for turning the tide of the war. Many English citizens have compiled pictures and records and authored books on the men, planes and missions of the U.S. Eighth Air Force which helped them save England and destroy the Third Reich. The Mighty Eighth was in England from 1942 to 1945 but left a lasting impression. There are many excellent books complete with data on the planes, combat photos and information on the heavy bombers and fighters available in bookstores today. Some British authors have made the history of World War II their life's work. We were a long way from home and the English welcomed us into their country. Their friendship was evident in the pubs and shops of Eye and Diss as well as London.

Through These Eyes

It is estimated that 210,000 airmen flew out of England to carry the war to Germany. Twenty-eight thousand American airmen lost their lives. The "Brits" recognized the sacrifices made by the Yanks, and the government and citizens of Great Britain wished to honor their memory. A nationwide fund drive was initiated shortly after the end of the war. King George VI gave his blessing to the project. The "Jesus Chapel" in the east section of St. Paul's Cathedral in the center of London was destroyed in the 1941 German Blitz. It was decided to construct an American Memorial Chapel in this damaged area. The project would take several years but the people were determined to demonstrate their appreciation to the United States and those who perished in the victory over Germany.

The reconstruction proceeded, and a commemoration ceremony was held July 4, 1951. General Dwight Eisenhower formally presented the book entitled the "Roll of Honour" for display in the Memorial Chapel. The large red leather-bound book contains 473 pages that list the names of the 28,000 Americans who lost their lives while stationed in the British Isles. The project was completed in 1952. The chapel features stained glass windows with insignias from the forty-eight states, and a glass enclosed marble pedestal which holds the "Book of Honour". One page is turned each day. Copies of the book are available for visitors wishing to find names of relatives or friends.

English school children, grateful citizens and the government were generous in their contributions to the American Memorial Chapel. There were additional funds to further express gratitude to the "Yanks" who had perished in defense of freedom. It was decided to publish a hardback book to mail to the next-of-kin of the 28,000 U.S. dead. The informative book contains sixty-nine pages of information on the Memorial Chapel and photographs and stories about life in the British Isles during World War II. The book was a goodwill gesture to American families who had lost loved ones in the battle for Europe. I found it to be very important to those seeking to learn more about those stationed in Great Britain during World War II. The copy I reviewed carried the name of Staff Sergeant Spencer E. Flynn, USAAF. His sister, Kathryn Hencheon, allowed me to use the book received by her family. Spencer was a year ahead of me in school but we shared the same duties in high school. We guarded the bicycle racks during lunchtime for 25 cents an hour. Spencer was an engineer gunner on an Eighth Air Force B-17 and had flown several combat missions. He died in a mid-air collision over England November, 1943. He is buried in the American Cemetery in Cambridge. The cover of the 8"x10" sky blue book is embossed in gold with a drawing of St. Paul's Cathedral, and the title *"Britain's Homage To 28,000 American Dead".* The deceased airman's name is embossed at the bottom of the cover.

The Mighty Eighth Museum

The museum is located at Pooler, Georgia on Interstate 95 near Savannah. It is a "must visit" destination for anyone interested in the history of the Eighth Air Force. Hundreds of items and pieces of equipment are on display to provide a feel for the equipment used by crewmembers on WW II bombing missions. Visitors can take part in a simulated bombing mission over Germany. The raid is complete from the briefing room to the target and back. It is a very realistic experience to aid in understanding the Mighty Eighth.

U.S. World War II Memorial

The $170 million World War II Memorial was completed May 2004. A spokesman for the American Battle Monuments Commission estimated before the dedication that of the sixteen million who served in uniform in World War II, fewer than four million are alive today and they are dying at a rate of about one thousand a day.

World War II, our nation's largest war, required the total effort of all Americans. Civilians sacrificed for the war effort as well as the men and women who served in the Armed Forces .The war was fought in the air, on the sea and battlegrounds around world. The National World War II Memorial is located in Washington, D.C. on the mall between the Washington and Lincoln Memorials. National chairman, Senator Bob Dole, stated, "The Memorial will ensure that this nation, indeed the entire world, can never forget the men and women who won the largest war of all time".

United States Air Force Museum, Dayton, Ohio

My recent visit to the largest and oldest aircraft museum in Dayton, Ohio was a great experience. This facility is free to the public and hosts over a million visitors a year. There are ten acres

James Lee Hutchinson, EdS

of indoor air-conditioned displays of the development of flight from the Wright brothers to our space program. The Air Power Gallery contains planes, photos, uniforms and memorabilia of World War II, the jet age, Korea and Vietnam. The World War II gallery contains planes and materials from the Luftwaffe and Japan. A nine-acre Memorial Park adjacent to the museum displays statuary memorials and plaques dedicated to various individuals and combat units. An ME-109 and an ME-262 were on display. They didn't look nearly as dangerous on the ground as they did attacking us in 1945!

The Mighty Eighth

The Dayton memorial to the Eighth Air Force men and combat units was a ten-foot, three sided stone monument with a three-bladed propeller of a B-17 Flying Fortress imbedded on top. One side carried a large bronze replica of an Eighth Air Force shoulder patch. The next featured a bronze map of England's East Anglia area with the location of every Eighth Air Force bomb group. Beneath the map was a list of every air base with the planes and number of bombing missions.

A bronze plaque on the third side listed statistics on casualties and medals awarded. Combat data recorded the heavy losses of aircrews and planes. North of the museum on an outdoor runway was a display of twenty or more historical planes. There was also a replica of a World War II Eighth Air Force control tower and a Quonset hut used on English airbases. Data showed the heavy loss of aircrewmen of the Eighth Air Force. The Eighth listed 34,362 crewmen killed, 13,708 wounded and 43,035 missing in action. Of the aircrafts, 27,694 were lost--- 8,314 heavy bombers, 10,899 medium and light bombers, and 8,481 fighters.

> "Our debt to the heroic men and valiant women in the service of our country can never be repaid. They have earned our undying gratitude. America will never forget their sacrifices."
> ------ President Harry S. Truman

Taps

(Bugle played at the funeral of servicemen or veterans)

Day is done
Gone the sun,
From the lakes, from the hills, from the sky.
All is well,
Safely rest,
God is nigh.

(First played in 1862 at a Civil War battle in Harrison's Landing, Virginia.)

Hutch and Bert meet after 57 years at the 2002
Reunion of the 490th Bomb Group

490th Branson Reunion 2002
Eric Swain group historian/archivist, Hutch, Stu Swain

I still have my jacket – but it doesn't fit!

Two 1953 "Baby-boomers"----my daughters

June and Lee Hutchinson celebrate fifty-eighth anniversary

THE UNITED STATES OF AMERICA

TO ALL WHO SHALL SEE THESE PRESENTS, GREETING:

THIS IS TO CERTIFY THAT
THE PRESIDENT OF THE UNITED STATES OF AMERICA
AUTHORIZED BY EXECUTIVE ORDER, MAY 11, 1942
HAS AWARDED

THE AIR MEDAL

and Two Oak-Leaf Clusters

TO

Technical Sergeant James E. Hutchinson, A.S.N 35707192

FOR
MERITORIOUS ACHIEVEMENT
WHILE PARTICIPATING IN AERIAL FLIGHT
European Theater of Operations
GIVEN UNDER MY HAND IN THE CITY OF WASHINGTON
THIS 24th DAY OF May 1949

SECRETARY OF THE AIR FORCE

OFFICIAL:

Colonel, USAF
Acting Air Adjutant General

490th control tower at Eye airbase

The G.I. Bill

The American Legion originated and sponsored the G.I. Bill of Rights for WWII veterans. Congress passed the landmark legislation in June, 1944 while the war was still raging. This was a great morale builder for the troops. It was the government's assurance that returning veterans would have financial aid to escape the economic depression of their childhood. Among the G.I. Bill provisions were:

1. A monthly unemployment check for one year, if needed
2. Tuition and monthly stipend for college or job training
3. Low interest loan for home purchase

College tuition at that time was $7.00 per hour. Most veterans could never have afforded college without the G.I. Bill. The number of college graduates doubled between 1940 and 1950. Careers of the Templeton crew included: dentist, architect, career military, doctor, buisnessman and school administrator.

The estimated cost of the G.I. Bill was 14.5 billion dollars, but that amount was returned to the U.S. Treasury at least seven times in the form of increased taxes (5). The September 2001 issue of the American Legion magazine reported the following statistics on the G.I. Bill education:

450,000 engineers	240,000 accountants
230,000 teachers	97,000 scientists
67,000 doctors	122,000 dentists

B-17G Specifications

Wing Span	103 ft. 9 in.
Tail Span	43 ft.
Length	74 ft. 8.9 in.
Height	19 ft. 2.4 in.
Power Plant	four 1,200 HP radial engines
Gross Weight	54,000 lbs.
Top Speed	325 mph at 25,000 ft.
Cruising Speed	170 mph at 5,000 ft.
Landing Speed	75 mph
Service Ceiling	37,500 ft.
Range	4,420 mi.
Fuel	2,789 gallons
Oil	148 gallons
Crew	10
Armament	thirteen .50 caliber machine guns
Bomb Load	2,600 to 17,600 lbs.
Rate of Fire	400-450 rounds per minute
Rate of Climb	1,200 ft. per minute

Eighth Air Force Bomb Groups in England

Group	Station	Aircraft	Missions	Combat Losses
34th	Mendelsham 156	B-17	170	34
44th	Shipham 115	B-24	343	153
91st	Bassingbourn 121	B-17	340	197
92nd	Padington 109	B-17	308	154
93rd	Hardwick 104	B-24	396	100
94th	Bury St. Edmonds 468	B-17	324	153
95th	Horham 119	B-17	320	157
96th	Snetterton Heath 138	B-17	321	189
100th	Thorpe Abbots 139	B-17	306	177
303rd	Molesworth 107	B-17	364	165
305th	Cheveston 105	B-17	337	154
306th	Thurleigh 111	B-17	342	171
351st	Polebrook 110	B-17	311	124
379th	Kimbolton 117	B-17	330	141
381st	Ridgewell 167	B-17	296	131
384th	Grafton Underwood 106	B-17	314	159
385th	Great Ashfield 155	B-17	296	129
388th	Knettishall 136	B-17	306	142
389th	Hethel 114	B-24	321	116
390th	Framingham 153	B-17	300	144
392nd	Wendling 118	B-24	285	127
398th	Nuthampstead 131	B-17	195	58
401st	Deenethorpe 128	B-17	256	95
445th	Tibenham 124	B-24	382	95
446th	Bungay 125	B-24	273	58
447th	Rattlesden 126	B-17	257	97

Group	Station	Aircraft	Missions	Combat Losses
448th	Seething 146	B-24	262	101
452nd	Deopham Green 142	B-17	250	110
453rd	Old Buckenham 144	B-24	259	58
457th	Glatton 130	B-17	237	83
458th	Horsham St. Faith 123	B-24	240	47
466th	Attlebridge 120	B-24	232	47
467th	Rackheath 145	B-24	212	29
486th	Sudbury 174	B-17	188	33
487th	Lavenham 137	B-17	185	48
489th	Halesworth 365	B-24	106	29
490th	Eye 134	B-17	158	40
491st	Metfield 366	B-24	187	47
492nd	North Pickenham 143	B-24	64	12
493rd	Debach 152	B-17	158	41

Total Planes Lost

B-17s – 4,754   B-24s – 2,112

(Fighters Lost)

P-47s –1.043   P-38s – 451   P-51s – 2,201

Summary of "Hutch's" Missions

1. December 5, 1944   Berlin   Technical Buildings
2. December 15, 1944   Hanover   Railyards
3. December 16, 1944   Stuttgart   Railyards
4. December 24, 1944   Frankfurt   Airfield
5. January 2, 1945   Bad Kreuznach   Rail Junction
6. January 3, 1945   Aschaffenburg   Railyards
7. January 14, 1945   Derben   Oil Storage Depot
8. January 15, 1945   Augsburg   Railyards
9. January 20, 1945   Sterkade-Rheine   Railyards
10. January 28, 1945   Hoenbudburg   Railyards
11. February 17, 1945   Frankfurt   Railyards
12. February 22, 1945   Ausbach   Railyards
13. March 1, 1945   Ulm   Railyards
14. March 21, 1945   Plauen   Railyards
15. March 28, 1945   Hanover   Railyards
16. April 7, 1945   Parchim   Airfield
17. April 17, 1945   Roudnice, Czech.   Oil Depot
18. April 20, 1945   Nauen   Railyards
19. May 1, 1945   Schipol Airfield, Holland   Food Drop
20. May 5, 1945   Schipol Airfield, Holland   Food Drop

Missions completed during Air Force service from August 4, 1943 through November 16, 1945. My overseas time was from November 10, 1944 until July 14, 1945.

Bibliography

1. Lightner & Holland (Oct. 1943 – Oct. 1945). *Historical Record of the 490th Bombardment Group (H).*

2. Boyle, D. (2001). *World War II in Photographs.* The Netherlands: Rebo Productions.

3. Morgan, R. (2001). *The Man Who Flew the Memphis Belle*, New York, NY: Penguin-Putnam.

4. Currie, J. (1987). *The Augsburg Raid.* London: Goodall Publications, Ltd.

5. Shields, M. (2001). American Legion Magazine.

6. Kaplan, P. (2000). *Bombers.* New York, NY: Barnes & Noble.

7. Gunston, B. (1997). *Fighters.* New York, NY: Barnes & Noble.

8. Donald, D. (1995). American Warplanes of WWII. New York, NY: Barnes & Noble.

9. Stars and Stripes (news article, 1944-45).

10. Jackson, R. (2001). *The B-17 Flying Fortress.* St. Paul, MN: MBI Publishing Company.

11. Rooney, A. (1995) *My War.* New York, NY: Random House.

12. Hawkins, I. (1990). *B-17s Over Berlin: Personal Stories from the 95th Bomb Group.* Phoenix, AZ: Hunter Publishing Company.

13. Ethell, J. & Sand, R.T. (2001). *Fighters of World War II*. Ann Arbor, MI: Lowe and Hould Publishers.

14. Apple, N.P. & Gurney, G. (1978). *The Air Force Museum*. New York: NY: Crown Publishers, Inc.

15. Jablonski, E. (1971). *Air War*. New York, NY: Doubleday & Co.

16. Freeman, R.A. (1981). *Mighty Eighth War Diary*. London: Jane's Publishing Co., Ltd.

17. Hutton, O.C. & Rooney, A. (1944). *Air Gunner*. New York, NY: Farrar & Rinehart, Inc.

18. Freeman, R. A. (1976). *The Mighty Eighth*. New York, NY: Doubleday & Co.

19. McCombs, D. & Worth, F. (1994). *World War II Facts*. New York, NY: Wings Books.

20. Neillands, R. (2001). *The Bomber War*. New York, NY: Overlook Press.

21. Time-Life Books, Eds. (1995). *Time Life History of World War II*. New York, NY: Barnes & Noble.

22. Ambrose, S.E. (2002). *The Wild Blue*, New York, NY: Simon and Schuster.

23. St. Paul's Cathedral. (1952). *Britain's Homage to 28,000 American Dead*. London Times.

24. Dibbs, J.M. (1998). *Flying Legends.* Ann Arbor, MI: Lowe and Hould Publishers.

25. Bartlett, J. (2002). *Bartlett's Familiar Quotations.* Boston, MA: Little, Brown and Company.

Films and Videos

1. Warbirds of WWII (2002). Entertainment Distributors, Box 22738, Eugene, OR 97402 (www.timeless-video.com)

2. World War II Documentary (1997). Madacy Group, P.O. Box 1445 Quebec, Canada.

3. Twelve O'Clock High (1949). Twentieth Century Fox.

4. The Memphis Belle (1998). Warner Bros.

5. Hart's War (2002). MGM/United Artists.

6. The Memphis Belle (1943). William Wyler, P.O. Box 1992, Memphis, TN 38101.

NOTE

Xerox copies of the complete WW II diary, photos and scrapbook are available. The legal size, 78 pages of material contains the handwritten diary entries, cartoons and Stars and Stripes news clippings concerning U.S. bombing raids and war news of the era. Material could prove interesting to WW II historians and researchers. <jlhutch5@localnet.com>

Printed in Great Britain
by Amazon